ELEVATE
YOUR HR STRATEGY

RAMESH SOUNDARARAJAN
SOMNATH BAISHYA

PUBLISHERS & DISTRIBUTORS (P) LTD

7/22, Ansari Road, Darya Ganj, New Delhi
Tel.: +91-11-4077 5252, 2327 3880
E-mail: orders@atlanticbooks.com
Web: www.atlanticbooks.com

This edition published in 2024 by Atlantic Publishers & Distributors (P) Ltd.

Printed & bound in India by Atlantic Print Services

Advance Praise

The biggest challenge for the field of human resources is to figure out how to support businesses in competitive environments. Can there be such a thing as "best practice" when organizations have different goals and strategies? 'Thriving On Talent' takes this challenge head on. It offers a clear answer that turns on the ubiquitous need to transform organizations and understanding how to make that happen. This is a wise and sensible story rooted in the realities of contemporary business.

—Peter Cappelli, George W. Taylor Professor of Management, The Wharton School, University of Pennsylvania

One of the most compelling reads of strategic and operational HR in action, something unique that has not been attempted in the last twenty years. It is written by HR leaders for HR practitioners who would like to step back to reassess their contributions. Sans jargon, the journey of transformation from owed to shifts and shocks to envision and engage is truly unique. The authors Ramesh and Somnath have set out their experiences as nuggets of wisdom. A must read for any HR professional.

—Nathan S V, Partner and Chief Talent Officer, Deloitte India & National President, National Human Resources Development Network, India

Strategy is a difficult concept/ subject in the best of times and when applied to HR it's even more difficult because it deals with the context and the emotions that people bring to work. Somnath and Ramesh have done a great job of linking the two in a manner that's easily understood without jargon.

—Shiv Shivakumar, Operating Partner, Advent International. Ex-Chairman, PepsiCo - South Asia

Human Resource is a business function, as practitioners of HR, it's vital to have a business lens on everything we do. Every business has a long-term strategy / vision that in turn drives the product / business strategy and the financial planning. However, this strategic planning exercise is incomplete without an organization and talent plan that will enable us to achieve the vision. This book offers great insights into how some of the most successful organizations do this, and practical approach to how HR professionals and leaders can adopt this in their organizations. As we all set out to define the Future of work, this is a very timely read for all leaders.

—Suman Gopalan, Former Chief HR Officer, Freshworks

I had the privilege of HR Leaders Somnath and Ramesh to build a resilient talent backbone for my business unit, which was instrumental in scripting a global success story of an enterprise software product. Great to see this awesome twosome come together again to share their wisdom and talent strategies for new age businesses. Through this book they add the sixth P i.e. People to Henry Mintzberg's definitive treatise on Five Ps for Strategy - Plan, Ploy, Pattern, Position and Perspective. A must read for HR and Business Leaders.

—Haragopal Mangipudi, Founder, guNaka;
Board Member, ISPMA;
Adjunct Faculty of IIM Bangalore and former
Member of Executive Council, Infosys & Global Head, Finacle

To the many bright minds and kind hearts
who walked with us on our
learning journeys.

Contents

Foreword

For many years—if not decades—I have had conversations where the key question was, "Does HR have a seat at the table?" In this book, Ramesh Soundararajan and Somnath Baishya blow past the question to reveal that not only does HR have a seat at the table, but quite often, it is HR that gets the top team talking.

The value-addition of the HR function in Indian organisations is no longer in question. Two cases underscore this point. In the longer term, acclaimed global software giants such as Google, Microsoft and Adobe, as well as global consumer goods companies such as Pepsi and Mondelez, have continued to add to their workforce in India. This sort of addition could not have been possible without a capable HR organisation at the helm of their Indian operations. In the shorter term, Indian companies managed to retain, or in some instances, even increase productivity during the Covid-19 pandemic. Once again, this feat points to a diligent HR function quietly doing what is necessary.

This timely volume can well serve as the 'go-to' book for ambitious HR professionals. Four aspects make this book exceptional. First, I like the way in which the authors underscore the primacy of organisational strategy. In my work with board members and executive teams, I find that it all starts with the strategy, and so should be the case for the HR function. The authors provide a comprehensive overview of the popular strategy frameworks that are in use today. The authors provide a case study for key frameworks such as the People Capability Maturity, McKinsey 7S and SWOT to help the reader understand how to deploy such concepts from the strategy literature. Familiarity with the usage of these strategy frameworks speeds up the HR professional's path towards the top table. The outlook on strategy is nicely complemented by a comprehensive survey of HR professionals from a wide variety of organisational forms and industry sectors, delving into the practices that translate strategic priorities into operational results. Taking in the survey results can help the HR professional benchmark where their organisation stands in terms of the alignment between strategy and people-related operations.

The second aspect that I like is the way the authors dive comprehensively into the key themes required to elevate HR's ability to align with strategic goals. In their exposition of how organisational capacity can be enhanced through workforce planning and capability creation, the authors also discuss the design and deployment of multipliers such as talent assembly and employee-owned learning and development. The authors then go on to show how capabilities can be orchestrated into high performance through organisational design, leadership alignment, performance management, reward systems, employee engagement and transparency. Once again, to earn a seat at the table, it is important for HR professionals to understand the nitty gritty of how talent can be transformed into organisational performance. I have seen this first-hand in my interactions with HR professionals in European multinational corporations—the best of them are thoroughly skilled in the techniques of capacity building described in this book. The level of detail provided by the authors can serve as the roadmap for mastering the required skills.

The third outstanding aspect of this book is the focus on transformation and execution. The authors provide comprehensive coverage of transformational scenarios, from growth to decline; they also emphasise the need to use a robust set of metrics to ensure the constant alignment of the HR strategy to the business strategy. Towards the end of the book, interviews with experts on specific topics under the label of "Viewpoint" are a compelling feature of this book. The authors harness expert voices on scaling start-ups, future trends and HR's role in strategic points.

Collectively, these viewpoints provide a glimpse into the cutting-edge practices in use today.

Fourthly, one clear strength of the book is the breadth of industries and contexts covered by way of examples. Ramesh Soundararajan and Somnath Baishya are clearly seasoned executives and, from an HR management perspective, seem to have seen it all in terms of different contexts of organisational life, from start-up and rapid growth to stagnation and decline. To have had a hand at the wheel, for example, when Infosys went from 3,000 employees to over 100,000, when Adobe went from selling shrink-wrapped software to cloud-based services and when Nokia pivoted from the mobile phones industry to telecom infrastructure are clearly experiences that generate plenty of insights for a reflective practitioner. The authors have been generous in sharing those insights, which are no doubt of great value to an emerging generation of HR leaders.

This book should be on the shelf of every astute HR practitioner, both as a ready reckoner for aligning best practices today and as a guide for things to come.

Anand Narasimhan

Shell Professor of Global Leadership,
IMD Lausanne

Acknowledgements

Our journey to write this book began when both of us were freelancing and had the opportunity to look at the corporate world from a different lens. We realised how privileged we had been to have the opportunity to work with various organisations, leadership teams and talent at large and to solve big business challenges involving scaling, transformations, culture and capability building, among many others.

When we commenced our careers, Human Resources in India was akin to Personnel Management and Industrial Relations. The expectations, challenges and respect for the profession were very different. Beyond a few visionary organisations and leaders, 'labour' was still not valued as a competitive differentiator. India has changed since then, and so has the HR profession.

Our working careers have provided us with great perspectives from larger organisations. As we engaged with MSMEs and startups while consulting, we could see the spread of maturity around HR both among business and HR professionals. It is true that the worlds of large and small organisations are different, as are realities across industry sectors. Yet we found that the core—understanding, ambition and value—of HR and its alignment with business has significant opportunities to progress.

As practitioners of HR, we decided to sketch our thoughts by building on pedantic content, our career learnings and experiences and that of others in the ecosystem such as academicians, leadership coaches and consultants, as well as an array of practitioners across geographies. Through these enriching discussions, our writing journey turned into a learning experience for us, too.

We both graduated from XLRI Jamshedpur and would like to acknowledge the headstart it provided and the network of friends from there whose insights helped shape this book. Both of us also spent more than a decade with Infosys, which helped create a basic framework for this book.

Our experiences with several other leading companies helped this become more holistic. Likewise, we are also thankful to the business and HR leaders from our various consulting engagements. We have drawn upon our experiences from all these associations to elucidate real-life scenarios in the context of the concepts and discussions at various points in this book.

We leveraged the power of social platforms as we pursued our survey online. We appreciate the known and unknown respondents who took out time to share their valuable inputs that provided us a starting point to evolve our conversations. We acknowledge the support of the 100+ executives who contributed to the survey and nearly 50 professionals who spent time talking to us.

We are also thankful to Anand Narasimhan (Shell Professor of Global Leadership IMD Lausanne) for composing the wonderful foreword. We acknowledge the deep perspectives of Pavan Bhatia (Founder GenWE, former SVP & CHRO, Asia & MENA, PepsiCo), Prof. Vasanthi Srinivasan (IIM Bangalore) and Anurag Shrivastava (CEO HRNEXT), which have helped construct the last chapter. We also thank Mr. Akash Agrawal (Co-founder and CEO Sahaj.ai) for his candid thoughts, which have been represented as a case in this book.

The wonderful team led by Manisha Mathews at Atlantic Publishers & Distributors (P) Ltd have our respect for reading, reviewing and making very thoughtful suggestions on the manuscript. Their strong motivation kept us honest as we progressed through this two-year journey on the book.

Every success has a ray of sunshine and for us, it was the valued support of our family and friends, who provided us with the encouragement and understanding to find the needed time and joy in achieving our goal and to make this small contribution by sharing our career learnings. Our hope is that by writing this book, we can inspire and accelerate the journeys of success for many other professionals who are and will be shaping the future of HR in organisations.

Preface

> "Give me six hours to chop down a tree and I will spend the first four sharpening the axe."
>
> —Abraham Lincoln

Strategy is not something that is easily observed. However, the absence of strategic thinking can impact us daily.

Let us start with a simple illustration of the city where we live, Bengaluru. Twenty years ago, after many delays, the Outer Ring Road (ORR) was finally commissioned. This was supposed to help heavy vehicles bypass the city and carry on to their destination.

However, the opening of the ORR coincided with the establishment of Global Development Centres. There was an Intel and then an Accenture. Soon enough, companies, from software to financial services to retail, set up their GDCs on ORR and traffic burgeoned.

Flyovers were constructed at multiple places to accommodate the increased traffic, enabling the vehicles to cross over busy intersections. At the same time, Software Export Zones that could employ tens of thousands of employees were being built.

Even as the flyovers were completed, the SEZs were launched, putting more cars, SUVs, vans and buses on the road. In some cases, the peak traffic came from the left side of the road, while the SEZs were on the right side, resulting in time-consuming U-turns and the like.

People endured the situation for a period. However, the roads flooded in heavy rains and the top surface was reduced to rubble, slowing down the traffic and leading to accidents. From 2013–2017, the next major program called “white topping” was launched, which involved breaking up the asphalt tarmac and paving it over with concrete.

After that came the next idea, which had been tried in different cities, creating a separate lane for buses. Bollards were kept on the road to mark lanes where only the buses could ply. As this was being negotiated, the pandemic struck, and there were more pressing issues for the Government and corporates than traffic.

Finally, the decision was made to lay down the metro on the Outer Ring Road, connecting the city to the airport. A ride on the ORR today will show us some metro work, some bus lanes and some tarmac in concrete.

Every single change stressed the commuters in terms of increased time spent in traffic. While most employees were willing to return to the office regularly post-pandemic, it was the long commute that scares everyone.

At the outset, this looked like a problem that kept growing, and the responses attempted to address every eruption. That was one way of looking at it.

Another perspective would be that in 2007, there were enough ongoing plans for growth on the ORR by land acquisition. Many new companies had set up or were in the process of setting up GDCs, either stand-alone or in SEZs.

Bangalore metro constructions started in 2007. However, the first few phases of the metro were laid in places with steady traffic flow. Was it possible to foresee the growth in commuting on ORR and initiate the construction of a metro there when it was easier? It could have caused inconvenience to commuters, but only a smaller number and once completed, it could have saved millions of person-hours.

This is not to criticise anyone; traffic problems are not unique to Bengaluru alone. The idea is to highlight the importance of identifying trends and making decisions ahead of time. Otherwise, we may still arrive at the same decision after trying time-consuming alternatives.

Now, does strategic planning only apply to a long twenty-year horizon? I have heard people say that those days are over. Their businesses are run from quarter to quarter, and alert responses are more critical than detailed strategy.

They may have a point. However, let us look at another domain that is more entertaining than traffic, cricket.

Cricket evolved from a traditional five-day and then one-day format to the T20 format, a match that would conclude in an evening. It was introduced to evolve with people's shortening attention span.

Initially, people thought it was a joke. What could be done in twenty overs? However, with the advent of the high-stakes Indian Premier League, modern techniques were incorporated and teams extensively started using analytics for player auctions as well as selections. Coaching gained prominence and teams hired specialist coaches for batting, bowling, fielding and fitness. Traditional cricket had batsmen, bowlers, keepers and all-rounders, while T20 cricket brought in super specialisation in the form of death bowlers, death batsmen, pace hitters, spin hitters and so on. Today, T20 has spawned its own lexicon in terms of matchups, par scores and even retirements. The planning happens almost on an over-to-over basis.

In this book, we briefly explain the concepts of gig employment and dynamic capabilities. One day, we came across an announcement that Albie Morkel, a famed big hitter, now retired, had joined Bangladesh as a power-hitting coach for their limited-overs tour of South Africa. We found this to be a perfect example that explained both concepts! A very specific capability that needs improvement can be developed by an expert coach for a particular assignment.

One expected T20 cricket and IPL to be a bit of harmless fun. However, in some ways, they have now become the most important event in the annual cricket calendar. The high stakes demand a degree of strategising to ensure the best allocation and deployment of resources. A shorter timeframe and rapid change have led to greater strategising, not less.

Again, analytics and strategising are not unique to cricket. Football games with a 90-minute span also use analytics and technology extensively. Even a small advantage in one game can multiply in leverage across a league with multiple games.

Strategising applies as much to a few hours as it does to a few years. How does it apply to your work in HR management?

The long-term HR roadmap in many organisations resembles the ORR. Go with one trend first, and when the external trends change, go with another. Change management techniques do not compensate for a lack of strategic clarity or first principles.

Much like ORR, big transformations are deferred in favour of what seems more doable, eventually adding to the stress on the system.

Unlike IPL teams, there is a mindset that a strategic approach is too slow to respond to quickly emerging and fast-changing market scenarios.

It is easier to write a book on a well-defined subject like HR analytics, as one of us had done. Strategy, on the other hand, is such a vast subject that you can write an entire book and still cover only 5% of all available literature.

We have followed an emergent approach to this book. While there was a clear plan, we tried to:

- Share our perspectives, gleaned from 50+ years of cumulative work experience in more than ten organisations.
- Go where our research has taken us by including inputs from practitioners and academicians through discussions and surveys.
- Take an approach driven by first principles (organisation capacity), not trends (hybrid model, AI-based hiring and so on).
- Leverage both management literature and stories.

John Milton wrote *Paradise Lost* in the middle of a pandemic, and pandemics remained a threat throughout William Shakespeare's career.

We are not in the league of John Milton or Shakespeare. However, we hope this book will help you ask relevant questions and guide you in making choices wherever you work, regardless of your function and role. Our book also acts as a reference to which you can periodically return.

Many sections in this book were written during the pandemic and lockdowns. It did sometimes feel odd to be writing about workforce planning when people you knew were suffering. At times, it felt like the future was uncertain. Yet here we are and the worst is hopefully behind us as we are aided by vaccines created rapidly, relying on off-the-shelf technologies developed for this exact scenario.

It pays to be prepared and allocate time to think about the future.

Introduction

I* was a decade into my career and a part of a very successful HR team that usually achieved what the business expected and employees wanted. We had gone for an off-site with the intention of creating a strategic plan. We discussed with enthusiasm and debated together as well as in breakout groups. The facilitator kept asking us to come up with something that could tie some of our many ideas together, but the task eluded us, despite our efforts. We were left wondering what exactly the facilitator was looking for.

Fortunately, within the next few years, we participated in assessments under frameworks like the CII-EXIM Bank Award for Business Excellence, PCMM and so on. These applications do not provide us with infinite space to capture all our exuberance. Instead, one needs to look at the criteria outlined and convert one's efforts and results to fit the criteria. This helped us recognise ways by which our work fits with business requirements.

A little later, the organisation created a balanced scorecard to articulate its long-term strategy and specify the themes as well as the measures to track progress. I was part of the team that put together a more detailed HR scorecard. In this process, it became clear that:

- There were specific outcomes that the business was looking for.

* We have used I/ we interchangeably throughout the book. 'I' refers to an individual experience of either author, while 'we' refers to something we experienced together.

- Out of many approaches, the organisation opted for a few specific ones.
- Each of these approaches needed to become successful before its target date.
- Success would be assessed by a mutually agreed upon measure. The measure may not be readily available, and it could occasionally need to be coaxed from multiple sources.
- Achieving the strategic goals was possible only by assigning ownership for each approach and measure. This, in turn, made the strategy a living document.

Even earlier, the HR team used to present in the strategic planning meets. Our presentations were creative and full of interesting content, but the work ended once the annual meet was over. We did attend follow-up meetings, but the movement lost steam. However, once the scorecard was in place, the presentations were not creative, but the process ensured that we were aware of the challenges, what we were doing to address them and our action plans to make sure all goals were met. Subsequently, I gained a greater perspective by developing a dashboard for one of the organisation's international clients, along with a consulting colleague. Objectives, strategies, initiatives and measures all become clearer.

In the next decade, I moved on from being a member of the HR leadership team to leading the team in a different organisation. Unlike the earlier role, here, the business faced more urgent challenges almost daily. Our employee attrition was nearly three times that of the market, and it was hurting the business. Just retaining the people we wanted and being able to backfill the other losses ended up grabbing most of our attention. The HR strategy with some core themes was in place, but we all knew that we had to overcome turnover for HR to be successful. We had mixed success at best.

One of the advantages of working in a senior role, of course, is that you have access to the board composed of experts. We had an annual review of HR strategy with the board. This was the conversation I had with the strategy expert on the board:

> "So, why is our attrition so different from what the industry has? Do we not pay enough?"
>
> "Most other services organisations lose talent to their competitors. On the other hand, we lose to product companies as well. In fact, the disparity of our turnover rate is primarily because of losing people to product companies."
>
> "What can you do to prevent such losses? What would be the cost if we were to provide parity with such companies?"
>
> "People jump when they get two to three times the pay for doing the same work. It won't be possible for us to structurally pay such salaries without deeply compromising on the profitability of the organisation."
>
> "If so, is it a battle that you can win? If you cannot, why don't you take a reasonable target for attrition and focus on making the business less individually dependent instead? In the short term, it would mean creating capabilities for a larger pool and, in the medium term, shifting the dialogue from individuals to capabilities that can be used for reassuring the customers?"

Of course, I am compressing a few discussions here. However, I realised that it may not be sufficient to understand business and isolate focus areas. It is also important to know whether you have chosen the right approach to the problem. To paraphrase Stephen Covey, going fast on a ladder that is kept against the wrong wall is not progress! Mitigating an attrition problem needs strategies not just for employee engagement but also for capability building. The conversation helped us steer in a direction which helped better mitigate the talent risk.

Let us fast forward to the present. I conduct training programs and workshops on analytics in HR for working professionals. As part of these sessions, we explore the cost structures and critical metrics of the business in which they are working. When asked about business measures like revenue productivity, very few employees from HR can answer with conviction. It is not just with rank and file. When asked about whether they have a documented HR strategy, the answer is never a straight "Yes, we do". It more often is "Yes, but it is not documented / We have it in many presentations / We may need to relook", and so on.

This takes me back in time to my initial experience. Why are smart, hard-working professionals unable to take a disciplined approach to work? The following may be the reasons:

The "Strategic Work" Trap

Often, strategy is seen as an abstract word and not as part of a cascade, such as:

> Business Objectives -> Business Strategies -> HR Strategy -> HR Programs -> HR Scorecard.

In the absence of appreciation of this flow, organisations often follow:

> Business Objectives -> Business Strategies -> HR programs -> HR metrics.

The success of programs is seen as HR success, supplemented by progress largely on transactional internal SLAs and employee turnover. Due to this, there are senior executives who say that strategic HR work is something that is not operational.

Recruitment is perceived to be operational, while developing KPIs or competency models is not. A person developing performance indicators is seen as doing strategic work.

Unfortunately, in reality, branding for talent, talent pool classification and efficacy of operations all help deliver business goals. However, since the perception is that recruitment is more operational, "conceptual" work is seen as strategic. Conceptual HR becomes strategic, whereas, in practice, any HR program that impacts business goals meets a strategy.

The "Busy" Trap

The PDCA cycle, as everyone knows, is comprised of:

- Plan
- Do

- Check
- Act

Many people subconsciously think “Doing” is the most important step. However, “Planning” is as important as “Doing” as is “Checking” after “Doing” to course correct. Planning, as well as checking, needs reflection. It is said that after every mission, the Air Force conducts a debriefing, where they go through what the plan was, what happened and what needs to be improved upon. Air Force missions are a matter of life and death. However, not every organisation is able to assign time and resources to make people realise that while taking action is important, all actions need to be reviewed within the PDCA frame.

The “Latest Fad” Trap

HR has significant ownership in areas like employee motivation, performance excellence and so forth. Applying PDCA takes a lot of effort in these areas, as it is challenging to establish systemic causality. What appeals to one set of employees may be irrelevant to others. Even within the same cohort, what appeals to one employee may not appeal to another. There are underlying differences due to age, gender, location, expertise and so on. Technology has enabled us to capture individual aspirations and degrees of motivation to some extent, but a lot remains.

Given this, it is no wonder that HR functions are attracted to external awards and prizes that validate their doing. “Great Places to Work”, for instance, has seen significant traction. There is a model, there is an assessment, and it gives a surge to the entire team when an organisation is selected as the top employer in the country. It is becoming acceptable for even mature organisations to say that their objective is to become the Best Employer.

However, at best, the connection between being rated the best employer and achieving business success is indirect. There are articles that argue that it is excellent business performance that causes high employee motivation and not vice versa. So, becoming a great place to work can contribute to success in some strategies, but cannot transplant a strategy wholesale.

Workplace diversity is another interesting example. It is a movement whose time has come, and in India, it is gender diversity is at the forefront of change. However, it is not clear what the strategic objective is in most organisations. Diversity is not about just having women in greater proportion in individual contributor roles but eventually having a truly diverse organisation right from the top. A study of top Indian IT companies reveals that women comprise less than 5% of their leadership teams, and the proportion could even be worse in some companies than what it was a decade ago.

So, while diversity is a buzzword, strategies to systematically increase diversity and debias compensation are much less spoken about. One needs a five to ten-year roadmap for gender diversity alone. Hopefully, it does better than the high-performance culture and "Employer of choice" that every organisation wants to be!

Strategy as a Document Trap

Mature organisations realise the importance of strategy. They identify a few bright individuals and assign them the task of developing an HR strategy. Directed by the CHRO, the task gets done before they move on to other assignments.

In this process, a documented strategy is created. However, the depth of the team and consultation decide whether the strategy is owned by function heads and used as a living document or whether it is a statement of intent alone.

Many organisations, even with the right intent, are distracted by one or more of these traps. However, it is not entirely a hopeless situation. During my learning, I came across a strategy document created by one of India's leading companies. This document, created in the 1990s, was in free format, unencumbered by any framework other than the traditional SWOT. However, it showed a rare depth of understanding of the business issues and meticulously detailed the strategic responses from HR to the same. To that extent, HR strategy is not a newly fangled buzzword but a mature practice.

So, where does this book come in? As co-authors, we have more than 50 years of cumulative experience in the HR function, from being individual contributors to leading the function in

Indian and multinational corporations. We have distilled those perspectives and supplemented them with conceptual frameworks and perspectives from people from academics as well as the industry. The objective is that the book would help any reader to reflect upon what is happening in their industry and organisation and enhance their strategic perspective. This, in turn, should lead to better-aligned and crafted workforce strategies.

We seek to achieve this in three parts. The first part is about perspectives from the authors, strategic frameworks and industry. The chapters revolve around:

- Context setting using our own reflections.
- Conceptual frameworks and how they can be leveraged. HR frameworks like PCMM, CII Model for HR Excellence as well as the HR scorecard; some classic frameworks like SWOT, 7S, Design Thinking and so forth; and those with roots in strategy literature like Resource Based View (RBV) and Dynamic Capabilities that help in framing strategy.
- Highlights from the survey we conducted on people strategy in which more than 100 HR and business leaders took part.

This leads us to the second part about specific domains and strategic questions that are relevant to each one. The classification of domains is different from regular HR processes. The chapters encompass:

- Workforce capacity, which was traditionally a linear, localised function of manpower planning and recruitment. It captures the complexities of capacity, including globalisation, automation and hybrid modes of organising and delivering work.
- Workforce capability, which is about the approaches to uplifting the competency levels. Traditionally, this was centralised and needs-based. With increasing focus on workforce skills, workforce capability has evolved

into internal talent markets and employee-owned competency development. Both are covered in separate chapters.

- Workforce performance, which is about achieving organisational outcomes leveraging culture, collaboration and recognition. A traditional approach would give pride of place to culture and engagement as standalone themes. However, unless culture and engagement lead to superior performance, they are not producing the optimal outcome for the organization. An effective strategy includes them in scope and is not limited to the obvious performance management process.
- Highly successful or not, all organisations are transforming from what they are to what they would want to be—sometimes due to market demands and other times due to growing organisational maturity. Here, we focus on the context and appropriate response for transformation. We illustrate the journey with a deep dive into digital transformation.

In our view, using these themes enables HR executives to align their deliverables to business strategy better. This elevates the strategic discussion from just tinkering with specific practices.

In the third part, we explore how we can integrate these threads into an organisational strategy by:

- Focusing on a set of organisations from across the spectrum and assessing their strategic choices for business success. While every organisation would like to increase profitability, sales growth, productivity and so forth, the priorities vary based on the industry as well as the competitive situation of the specific organisation. Using market information, we explore different strategic approaches.
- Outlining the strategic challenges that the future of work will bring about, especially in a time of rapid change and the competencies that an HR professional needs to thrive in these times.

The survey with consolidated responses forms the annexure. The book is peppered with examples, case studies and where the subject deserves, in-depth discussions with thought leaders. We also have schematics that summarise the overall landscape for talent strategy.

After completing the book, we expect the reader to use the Capacity-Capability-Performance-Transformation framework to analyse their challenges and arrive at solutions that are unique to them.

On completing, we realised two commonalities:

- We have primarily worked in the Information Technology and Communications industry. This has led to the IT industry being used as the primary frame of reference and more than one reference to our shared experience with Infosys. This, however, should not prevent a reader from extending the frameworks to their specific industry.
- We wrote this from 2020 to 2022. This was a time of great change, where organisations managed through a pandemic, the unicorn boom and now what looks like a slowdown. In this decade, it appears that every year brings forth not just a new challenge but also a path-breaking opportunity. In 2024, hybrid working does not seem as inevitable as it did in 2022. In this book, we have dedicated some perspective on start-ups based on our perspective then. They have cooled off since then. You may not find many references to ChatGPT either. However, it is difficult to capture every trend in a book. We feel that it is a matter of time before start-ups become hot again, and the chapter on Digital Transformation is deep enough to provide for the possibilities of Generative AI. In our view, the recency effect does not hinder the reader from making their own inferences.

So, let's get started.

1
Strategy: A Conversation

In the course of our work, we had several conversations with CXOs and academicians in the area of HR and strategy. These conversations were about sharing ideas and following through on what we had been reading and observing. They also helped us build a narrative.

We envisaged a chapter that reflects the spirit of conversation and enquiry using a question-and-answer format.

How would you look at strategy?

Let us start with the business. There are two important dimensions on which an organisation must make strategic choices.

1. The market, customer and competition:

   The business needs to be clear on who they are serving, the needs of the customers that they are fulfilling and what the competition is.

2. Internal organisation:

   The organisation's strategy should be organised to best serve the client, manage capabilities needed for competing effectively and ensure its profitability.

This classification is not limited to the business alone. Like other functions, HR also lays down policies and processes that define the internal organisation. However, unlike other functions, HR also competes in the market for talent. Often, companies that compete for the same customer also compete for the same employee.

At the same time, HR and leadership are also custodians of organisation culture. Culture is arguably derived from how people in an organisation do their work. However, this also influences how the customer is treated, what value is generated for them and so forth. So, you need to use these internal levers to create a competitive advantage.

Michael Porter has said that strategy is about making choices. This is where the challenge for HR comes in:

- How do I create an organisational structure that maximises external orientation without devaluing internal responsibilities?
- Is my culture as client-focused as it should be? If not, what levers do I pull to transform it?
- How does my employer brand compare against that of my closest competitors? What market victories do I need to play up to improve my internal advocacy?

These are simple illustrations, but the complexity behind the choices is not to be scoffed at. For instance, culture is influenced as much by structured compensation and performance management mechanisms as by intangibles like quality of management, leadership credibility and so forth.

An organisation I had worked with was losing a lot of employees to multinationals who were easily out paying us. Given this was a technology services organisation, our ability to retain people was critical. The business leaders (as it often happens) were strongly pushing for higher salaries.

The CEO was invested in the many conversations on this topic. He directed us to do an analysis for the following proposition—what if we could increase the salaries to what multinationals were paying? HR ran the calculations and came back with a finding that to avoid the fear of losing employees to such multinationals, we needed to increase the salaries by roughly 40%. The CFO joined the discussions and said that we would go from profitability to making losses if we tried to match the pay. So, the cost of retention would directly impact business profitability, at least in the short term. Hence, that was not a choice open to us.

While not increasing the salary was not a choice, increasing dramatically also was not possible. So, the only workable choice was to increase the compensation progressively using the increasing revenues while staying profitable. Almost always, the strategy involves balancing conflicting demands for finite resources.

The same holds true for talent acquisition, too. In many organisations, employees get a merit increase of 10% to 15%. This is adequate to retain employees but not sufficient premium to switch jobs. Let's say the premium must be at least 10%. Then, we end up with an organisation where a large set of employees have had a 10% to 15% increase and a small group who have a 25% increase and have joined newly. Both new joins and older employees often perform the same role. The business is protected, but the engagement could be impacted in the medium term. Here, the paradigm for performance recognition and retention runs counter to the paradigm for talent attraction. Again, the challenge is to strike the right balance between the two, not wishing away inherent contradictions.

How do you know what are the right choices?

This is a fascinating question. In my view, it stems from asking the right questions. In one of my earlier jobs, I was on a shop floor where they had an autoclave machine used to thread the wires. The production people claimed that the expensive autoclave was used for only three hours a day due to labour productivity. They voiced that in the upcoming agreement, the position should be to insist on eight hours of production. Given the Trade Union's opposition, it seemed difficult to achieve. The General Manager of the plant took stock of the situation and asked a question, "Do we have the ability to run it for eight hours?" He initiated an analysis which revealed that the biggest culprit was management productivity. The autoclave ran for three hours a day because of limitations in resource planning, timely purchasing and scheduling. The management processes need to be strengthened to achieve even six hours per day. So, the agreement was concluded at six hours with an onus on the management to ensure a timely supply of materials needed for threading the wires. In the absence of this question, we might have continued to be frustrated with labour and they, in turn, with the management.

Let me share another illustration to reinforce the thought. In the early 90s, IT was scaling up fast in Bangalore. This created an increasing demand for experienced IT talent, which led to rampant attrition. It was a gold rush. I remember attending an NHRD session where the CEO of an organisation bemoaned the prevailing talent challenge and sounded almost helpless.

However, one organisation that did not complain as much was Infosys. A strategic choice they made then was to invest in hiring from campus. This was 30 years ago, and campus hiring was not as mainstream. Not only could Infosys choose which campuses to hire from, but they could also hire in large numbers from the campus talent pool. They built a strong training infrastructure that converted raw campus talent into ready-to-depute software engineers. But, after all the investments, what if these trained employees quit? Infosys then made the second choice—to invest in an emotional value-add, which today is termed "employee experience". A brand-new campus was built that augmented a great work environment. On top of it, the organisation rolled out its now famous ESOP program. Other organisations could also have arrived at the same decisions. However, they mostly did not. They looked at the existing attrition challenge not as a strategic business problem but as an HR problem, which in turn oversimplified into a compensation problem. On the other hand, Infosys looked at it holistically, which took it into an orbit of great growth.

Thus, what choices you make depends on how you frame the problem and what questions you ask.

Right questions, right choices and right strategy. Seems quite straightforward?

Leonardo Da Vinci is supposed to have said, "Simplicity is the greatest sophistication". So, what sounds simple ends up being quite challenging.

An organisation I worked with had a great program to teach coding to campus recruits from engineering colleges. They felt that increasing business domain knowledge would sharpen the value added to clients. To address this, the organisation decided to hire MBA graduates and Chartered Accountants. The advertisements drew applications from a great number of qualified candidates. Since these applicants had cleared the CAT or the CA exam, it was believed that they possessed good analytical skills and would adapt easily.

However, the program ended up being a big failure. The MBA graduates thought they would play a business analyst role with some exposure to coding and had not signed up for a coding-first role. On the other hand, the business, with mostly people with an engineering background, valued the ability to code above the MBA credentials. In the absence of a clear role definition and shared understanding of the value of the MBA and CA hires, the organisation failed to benefit from their capabilities. Most of the recruits ended up leaving within a short time. While the intentions were right, the management had failed to build a case for business domain knowledge with the managers. As a result, managers to whom the MBAs reported ended up treating them with the same yardstick, leading to suboptimal outcomes for the organisation as well as for the eager hires. Right logic by itself, without the right communication, can prevent a strategy from becoming successful.

Sometimes, companies can also implement strategies that are antagonistic to each other, even progressing them parallelly. I have heard of a story where an organisation was running "Participative Management" workshops in the morning and layoffs in the evening! Both had a clear outcome, but the layoffs cancelled whatever goodwill the workshops tried to generate. So, the strategies can be oriented to the future, but the implementation and alignment need to be frequently validated.

Is strategic alignment cast in stone?

For an early-stage start-up, talent strategy starts the moment an entrepreneur wants to expand their team. I have had calls with such friends who were planning to hire a couple of people and were faced with some never-before questions—who should we hire, how much should we pay and so forth are all big decisions for a small organisation. Often these are driven by affordability, and this sets a certain limitation on the quality of the workforce. The entrepreneurs themselves have to fill in for the gaps in talent quality. However, if such start-ups reach the next orbit of growth and must hire in the tens, they are forced to think more strategically about talent.

Thus, being strategic about talent is one of the big demands of an entrepreneur's time. Often, one of the co-founders holds that responsibility. The decision to bring in a full-time HR person itself is a move towards formalising the organisation. In a fast-growth organisation, there is a need to keep redefining the talent strategy.

Does strategy evolve with an organisation's growth?

While consulting with a start-up, it was very interesting to see their journey through the various collaterals used in sharing who they were during their client pitches. The founders had rich experiences, having worked in large corporate environments. Thus, it was not a surprise to see well refined vision and values and an honest effort to articulate the strategy.

Every potential pitch and deal in the early runs for start-ups is a big part of their progress, often an existential lifeline. Here, too, the founders had made huge efforts to customise every pitch to narrate their story in the hope of ensuring the best fit with the client each time. However, as the team grew, this flexibility became an obstacle due to the absence of a singularity of vision and a common understanding of direction. The same thought had multiple articulations and interpretations. The language was not consistent across channels either.

The Founder and CEO realised that this reality would only slow the team down when it needed to move even faster. Over the next few months, the team worked through these challenges. But what was revealing here was the need for being consistent with the core and the alignment of the reality with the rhetoric—a high 'Say-Do' ratio.

So, the challenge is the gap that evolves between what is perceived by different founders in an organisation itself when they are growing. Any thoughts about large companies? Could the problem could manifest differently?

Let me quote Mintzberg here. He espoused the concept of intended, realised and emergent strategy[1]. What the CEO articulates to the employees is the intended strategy. But when the rubber hits the road, that is, when strategy moves out of the boardrooms and PowerPoint decks and flows to the broader organisation, things often don't go as envisaged. According to him, an organisation realises only 10% to 30% of its strategy through implementation. Well, we can argue that with better technology-enabled communication and collaboration, the above number would surely trend up, but even then, a significant leakage would be a reality. Thus, it becomes all the more important to articulate the intended strategy and connect the organisation so that the communication flow is much better.

This is truer for larger organisations, considering the scale of people involved. A large organisation I was consulting with had identified a set of Strategic Capabilities that it believed, if invested well, would strengthen its competitive advantage and reinforce its leadership in the market. In the first few conversations, it was evident that good intent and passionate efforts had been made to identify the capabilities.

As I further examined the workstream investments on each of the capabilities and conversed with people in the organisation, it was very clear that the intended and realised strategies were quite separate. It also brought in the third dimension of what Mintzberg had articulated—Emergent Strategy, the primary determinant of the realised strategy, where individuals interpret the intended strategy and adapt to changing circumstances. This resulted in each of the identified Strategic Capabilities taking different directions, losing the strong alignment with the core intent of building competitive advantage through bottom-line impact and enhanced customer value.

1. Henry Mintzberg and James A. Waters. "Of Strategies, Deliberate and Emergent." *Strategic Management Journal* 6, no. 3, (July 1, 1885): 257–272

While the organisation had great strategic intent here, the execution of the same was missing harmony and alignment. In such scenarios, the focus shifts from falling in love with the problem to falling in love with the solution. The need to show results pushes people to fabricate outcomes that may not be best aligned, and the gap keeps widening over time. Developing a strategy takes precious management bandwidth. Financial and other resources are invested. Over time, the enthusiasm dwindles, and something new takes over. The organisation moves over to its next strategy wave, leaving some disillusioned and many disconnected people behind. Every such wave is met with more resistance and cynicism.

Falling in love with the solution is an interesting metaphor. I suppose isn't that what happens when we hear and read about some brand-new trend and want to implement it right away?

Before the onset of information technology, most work was in manufacturing and services that needed physical presence at the workplace. You cannot work on machinery from home. This paradigm got carried forward into even newer IT jobs where the capability to work from anywhere existed. Yet, working from home was seen as a perk or an exception and not a preferred mode of work.

Some people were supportive of it, and there were many who felt it led to lower productivity. Now, Covid has led to the biggest experiment with working from home. People have realised that working from home is about low productivity, and organisations can work with many employees without even visiting the office. This happened by being forced into the hybrid mode by a pandemic.

Fortunately, a pandemic is a once-in-a-century event. It might be useful for organisations to re-examine their core assumptions about work and people without being forced by an externality or a new buzzword but as a regular process.

When I started working, MBO (Management By Objectives) was the catchphrase. Set objectives, review against them and allocate rewards. Some organisations improved significantly in the process. Then, there was a drift towards using performance reviews for only development. I had taken over the leadership of a function during that phase. With our pen and paper forms, data took a long time to process. At the end of it, we found that only 50% of employees had an appraisal, and of them, 84% were rated Very Good or Excellent. This was not a development, surely.

Then, we swayed to normalisation, which ended up being a layer on top of MBO and Development. You set and assess goals, give feedback and then rank people on whatever distribution. This had a decade's run before organisations pulled the plug and moved towards conversation. Technology has evolved to facilitate all: MBO, normalisation and now check-ins. Many organisations have written wonderfully about their new approach.

Yet, when hit with a slowdown, organisations lay off a certain percentage of their headcount and say this is an annual process of exiting poor performers. Now, unless you normalise, how will you be able to identify the people for layoffs?

So, approaches change with time and the state of business. Staying true to a process with its strategic objectives and revising based on its continued evolution would be much better than going with trends. Imagine we tried to implement a bottom 5% rule in an organisation that was growing at 30% and always looking for people.

But I suppose it is up to the leadership to reduce the gap between intended and realised strategy?

Absolutely. I suppose it starts with the process and communication.

Some of the leaders we conversed with shared the rigour that goes into the strategy planning exercise each year. There is a huge amount of collective leadership time that gets invested, multiple reviews are refined and negotiated to reach the best possible alignment.

We also heard that strategies achieved success when the leaders who framed them made efforts to connect them to the workforce in a planned and sustained manner. These connections also created a greater sense of belonging to the organisation.

I was very surprised to see the CEO of one of the MNCs I had worked with spend a day each year visiting the larger employee locations across the globe to articulate the organisation's strategy and build a deeper understanding. When this organisation had a CEO transition, the new leader continued with this practice. Employees were excited when he revealed his six-year, long-term goals to take the organisation to a new level of market leadership.

I remember speaking to a few employees, mostly young engineers, in the days after this visit to gauge how they connected with the CEO's strategy narration. Apart from the positive emotions, what I learnt was that the engineers loved the way that the CEO not only shared the lofty ambitions but also delved into the 'how' and did a great job of quantifying it. A pattern soon emerged in what I heard—"He spoke strategy in the language of the engineers". I could see good recall as they shared their own reflections.

In another organisation I had worked with, we had a town hall meeting every quarter, where the CEO used to address the employees. While people used to look forward to the session, one feedback we received was that he repeated the same theme every time, with new stories. Then, I realised that it is important to do it. The saying goes, "Repetition does not ruin the prayer". Leaders cannot go in front of their employees and talk about multiple things. They should articulate the strategy clearly and consistently to create a commitment to realising the outcomes desired. When the team has a fragmented understanding of the strategy, the outcomes tend to be sub-optimal. Thus, when the articulation is weak, individuals interpret the strategy differently and start executing it their own way. In larger, globally distributed organisations, such duplication leads to the passion being diverted or dissipated.

Leadership indeed plays a crucial role. A lot of what has been shared here is relevant when there is stability. What happens when there is change? What is the leader-dependency on strategy?

Change in leadership often drives shifts in strategy. Change in leadership also affects how an existing strategy is executed and thus influences success. It starts with the mindset and thinking itself, as I witnessed at an organisation where, over an extended period, the HR leadership transitioned across leaders from HR, Finance and Business domains.

The shift in strategy, at times, is driven by the motives of the new leader. In the extreme, an agenda of self-glorification would mean setting aside everything from the past—a new leader, a new strategy. At times, the new leader takes time to sense the organisation before making calls, but that could lead to a period of stagnation or drift. Often new leaders are hired with the mandate to accelerate some or most of the existing investments.

During one of our many conversations with CHROs while writing this book, it was clearly visible how, as an individual, one of the leaders had created a differential impact in both the direction and execution of the talent strategy. This leader clearly understood the need for alignment with business and the importance of prioritising and building accountability to achieve the desired outcomes. Add to that the focus on scaling, technology and employee experience. While the leader deserves the kudos for the elevation achieved, true success would be in institutionalising the practices so that they do not wither away with the leader moving on.

When multiple leaders are involved in the success of a strategy, it becomes very important to articulate the decision spaces. Some organisations often try the leadership concept of 'two-in-a-box'. While the core belief is that two leaders working together bring in better thinking, more ideas and the ability to manage stakeholders in a more robust way, it also demands greater clarity to the rest of the organisation on 'who to go for what' for smoother functioning.

John Chambers, former Executive Chairman and CEO of Cisco Systems, had stated, "Disrupt, or get disrupted"[2]. In an arena where the pace of change has been faster than

2. Frank Holmes, "Disrupt Or Get Disrupted," *Forbes*, March 7, 2017, accessed June 17, 2017, https://www.forbes.com/sites/greatspeculations/2017/03/07/disrupt-or-get-disrupted/?sh=44a890dc304c

ever before, how do organisations keep their strategy relevant?

Gone are the days when disruptions stemmed from immediate competition or within the same industry. Disruptions now stem more often from the periphery than the core.

It took Apple and Google to disrupt the mobile phone industry by providing customers the value of being part of an ecosystem, which was way more than just a product. Apple and Google were not even a blip on Nokia's radar when the strategy was winning against the known competition of Motorola and Ericsson. In 2010, while I was at Nokia, the outgoing head of Nokia's smartphone division even downplayed the threat from Android OS by comparing mobile phone makers who were adopting this new OS to Finnish boys who "pee in their pants" for warmth in the winter. What he meant was that many mobile phone makers were not thinking long-term but were being lured by these new OS providers. Once locked to the then-new Android OS, for example, he felt that many such organisations would be pained by low profitability and inability to differentiate their products from the competition. True. But what did the end user desire? What are the benefits of an ecosystem or the individuality of a great product? By the time I moved on from Nokia in 2013, the answer was for all to see. Nokia was soon after taken over by Microsoft.

More recently, Tesla drove in to disrupt the established auto industry by being more than a car organisation. Brands such as GM or Ford have had long celebrated histories. It is difficult to believe that they couldn't make better cars than Tesla. So, what was the Tesla magic? What did they pivot on to disrupt? Very simply put, Tesla changed the narrative through a singular focus on electric and their pace of innovation.

The same implications on disruption hold true on the talent side. In the 2000s, when the IT industry in India flourished and started hiring students from all disciplines of engineering to satiate their unending hunger for talent, traditional engineering organisations realised that the talent game had changed. The competition for talent was not for civil engineers between organisations in the construction industry or for mechanical engineers among automobile organisations but for engineers within the IT Services sector.

Similarly, established companies faced attacks from the emergence of start-ups in their ability to attract and retain talent. Start-ups could value talent even at the level of an individual, which larger companies could not. There was a significant portion of the workforce who were willing to play the high-risk, high-return career game, thus preferring the start-up environment. Bigger companies continued to scale but more aggressively started focusing on not losing the gift of small company culture. In one organisation I worked with, I was able to drive the 'floor-wise engagement' strategy, where employee cohorts on each floor were seen as a start-up of 100 rather than a monolith of 1000+ employees across two buildings. This, in a way, replicated some of the attractions that the start-ups were flaunting. The fact that this organisation went on to be recognised as one of the Best Places to Work demonstrated how the shift in engagement strategy triggered by the ecosystem was adopted with success.

So, staying true to first principles but being agile in reacting to market changes and what the employees desire helps companies stay relevant. Changes made on the basis of market realities have a better chance of success than flashy best practices.

Point taken on how even market leaders need to see the upcoming trends and adapt accordingly. However, is it only one-way traffic? Can organisations get proactive in influencing what is going to happen?

Strategy needs to be in harmony with the ecosystem that the organisation operates in. It is well accepted that these ecosystems influence the talent strategy an organisation pursues—attracting, skilling, rewarding, retaining and so forth. But then, this is not a unidirectional flow. There is a reverse influencing in play, too, where the organisation needs to lead desired changes in the ecosystem.

In the mid-2000s, the IT Services sector I was associated with was in a bullish growth phase—70% of talent supply was coming in through fresh engineering graduate hires. This

70% skew while hiring 20,000 graduates annually threw a new challenge. The supply of this talent was clustered around two to three months in the middle of the year, linked to the graduation of the students. However, for the business, the demand was distributed across the twelve months. Also, these new hires had to start with three to five months of initial training. While the organisation had huge investments in its training infrastructure, it was still not designed for these surge volumes. The supply had to be flattened out.

As part of its talent strategy, the organisation was able to influence the local colleges to turn the final semester for the students into one where those holding an offer to join could intern with the organisation. This then allowed the opportunity to provide the initial training to these students during their final semester. So, on graduation, they were business-ready. This significantly balanced out the inflow of talent. The post-training salaries were higher. These hires benefited by being shifted to the higher ranges early. The colleges were able to leverage this, too, by positioning their brand story as one where they built greater industry readiness in their students during the term of the course. Thus, a win-win for everyone in the ecosystem of organisations, students and academic institutions.

We hear that there are added complexities in talent strategy in multinational corporations. How do you bring in agility and flexibility there?

An HR leader in multi-national organisations is always faced with the reality of establishing alignment between global and local priorities. Regional nuances necessitate attention, but overall local efforts should be supplemental to the global talent strategy. In a Silicon Valley headquartered MNC, the new global leader for Talent Development decided to discontinue the long-running program for high-potentials. The intent was to reimagine the program. In regional locations like India, this program was strongly leveraged beyond just the learning objectives. Being nominated for this program was positioned as a reward to reinforce how the organisation was invested in that person. It also helped retain the best talent in a very dynamic talent economy.

When the global program was taken off without a supplement, it created distress.

The Country leadership team in India thereon took on the charter to create an offering for the high-potentials at the site and help boost the leadership pipeline. Four cohorts were successfully executed with high net promoter scores (NPS). However, when the new global program for high-potentials was reintroduced, the local program was withdrawn. The strategy was to stay deeply invested in the development of the high-potentials and not be stuck with the offering curated locally. The local program had served its purpose and now had to be retired. The ability to make these decisions and avoid parallel action on strategies makes the global and the regional setups execute seamlessly. The same paradigm could also be extended to multi-locational organisations in the same country.

Strategic Frameworks

There are many frameworks available. Companies use one of them or just have a homegrown process to develop their strategy. What are HR strategic frameworks? What are some of the all-purpose frameworks that can be useful? What does emerging literature say?

Let us explore these and more in the next chapter.

2
Strategic Frameworks

The word "strategy" is used in many contexts. Like most management paradigms, strategy has its roots in military theory. It comes from the Greek word *stratēgia*, "art of troop leader; office of general, command". It is a plan to achieve one or more long-term or overall goals under conditions of uncertainty.

Strategic planning, as a process and function, exists in organisations to look at trends and develop long-term plans. Literature on business strategy goes back at least to the 1950s. Peter Drucker recommended eight areas in which a business can set objectives.[1] These include worker performance and attitude, manager performance and development. Over the subsequent decades, many thought leaders focused their attention on strategy. They focused on answering one or more of the following questions:

- What is the purpose of the organisation?
- Should strategy be led by internal capability or customer needs?
- What are the forces to be considered when implementing a strategy?
- How to match the internal capabilities to market needs?
- What are the core competencies of the organisation?

---

1. Peter F. Drucker, *The Practice of Management* (1954; repr., New York: Harper Collins, 2010).

- How to differentiate from competition?
- Should strategy be fixed or dynamic?
- Should strategy be planned or emergent?
- What is the value chain of the organisation?
- How to choose markets in which to operate?
- How to build corporations that last a long time?

Noted academics and practitioners like Michael Porter, C. K. Prahlad, Henry Mintzberg, Tom Peters, Igor Ansoff, Jim Collins, Clayton Christensen and Chan Kim have written in depth about how an organisation handles these challenges.

If we consider a set of organisations in any industry or geography or cutting across these, it would be easy to analyse and articulate what they do well or not. But that would only be surface-level information—making an interesting read. But for a corporate executive to drive change, the diagnosis and understanding have to be more structured and deeper. It should be pivoted to a framework or a model that has a larger acceptability in the ecosystem. Why is this acceptability important? Most change initiatives have a financial impact and have to wade through resistance. Also, any change narrative that is based on larger social proof has easier acceptability.

Frameworks provide our brains with a pattern to connect with and understand. Frameworks are the underlying structure to build or assess the effectiveness of a thought or a plan. They bring in standardisation and a common understanding. Quite often, a framework comprises an overarching model and a set of diagnostic tools to assess where the companies are on the model and what they need to do. Frameworks provide a path to action.

CATEGORISING THE FRAMEWORKS

There are several frameworks in the realm of business and HR. Some of these have been in vogue for more than 50 years, while others have evolved with the changes in business trends, internationalisation, quality management, measurement and so forth. Two threads emerged on this journey around the idea of organisation and strategy. Firstly, around the 70s, it was felt that the Japanese organisations were winning by focusing on product quality and reliability. Manufacturing companies like Toyota had created a management system that ensured product quality by focusing on quality across the board or total quality. This led to the creation of models like Malcolm Baldrige, EFQM, LEAN and CII models for business excellence. These models are prescriptive and have sections dedicated to leadership, strategy and so forth.

The second thread was around execution. After a point, the quality of execution becomes more important than the quality of strategic planning. Well-executed strategies are more successful than well-crafted but badly executed strategies. Ram Charan is the pioneer in articulating the importance of execution. We need to have a measurement system to track the success of the strategic plan. This, in turn, needs us to capture not just financial measures but also measures of other internal processes. Balanced Scorecard is a methodology that aids strategy execution by identifying and mapping measures that relate to learning and growth, internal business processes and customers.

These frameworks refer to the importance of employee motivation, skills and capabilities to achieving goals. We can segment the frameworks into:

- **Organisational Excellence Frameworks**

  These frameworks take a comprehensive view of the organisation and help create a roadmap for continuous improvement. For example, EFQM and CII Model for HR Excellence, People CMM Model (PCMM), HR Scorecard and 7-S Framework. They emphasise process capability, measurement maturity and alignment with business goals.

- **HR Frameworks**

  These are specific to HR processes mapped to the employee life cycle. For example, the Great Place to Work (GPTW) Model. These frameworks highlight one specific people-related outcome like engagement or performance.

- **Problem Solving Tools and Techniques**

  These help in quick assessments in a specific area of interest. For example, SWOT analysis and design thinking. These are tools that come in handy when solving any business problem.

Let us explore these frameworks in some detail.

EFQM AND CII MODEL FOR HR EXCELLENCE

EFQM stands for European Foundation for Quality Management. Their globally recognised framework supports organisations in managing change and improving their performance. In its evolved 2020 version, the EFQM model goes beyond assessment and enables organisations through a structured methodology to deal with global shifts like the COVID-19 pandemic.

For Total Quality Management, EFQM created a model with eight fundamental concepts.[2] These concepts include people and leadership dimensions like:

- **Developing Organisational Capability**

  Excellent organisations enhance their capabilities by effectively managing change within and beyond the organisational boundaries.

- **Harnessing Creativity and Innovation**

  Excellent organisations generate increased value and levels of performance through continual improvement and systematic innovation by harnessing the creativity of their stakeholders.

- **Leading with Vision, Inspiration and Integrity**

  Excellent organisations have leaders who shape the future and make it happen, acting as role models for their values and ethics.

- **Succeeding Through the Talent of People**

2. European Foundation for Quality Management, "The EFQM Model", *EFQM*, Accessed on June 21, 2022, https://efqm.org/efqm-model.

> Excellent organisations value their people and create a culture of empowerment for the achievement of both organisational and personal goals.

The Confederation of Indian Industries (CII) adopted the EFQM Model to provide India with its own total quality framework through the Business Excellence Model. Based on the same, the CII HR Excellence Model has been created. The model[3] is as follows:

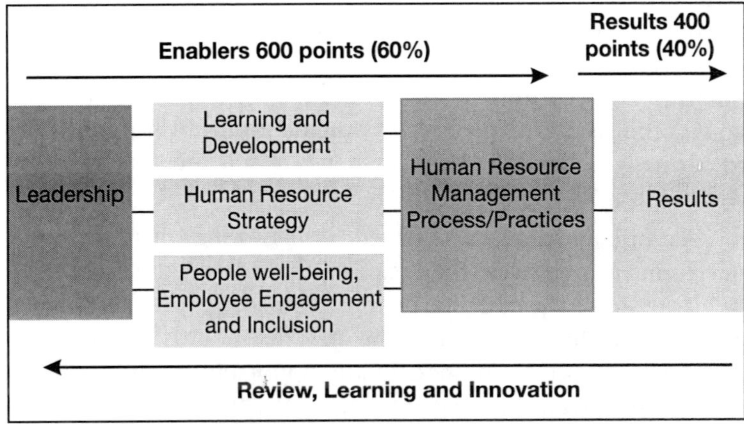

Figure 2.1: CII HR Excellence Model

This model explicitly mentions Human Resources Strategy, suggesting that an organisation should:

- Have practices for gathering trends in the external environment.
- Have practices for understanding internal performance levels, skill sets and competencies.
- Identify and manage strategic HR risks.
- Communicate HR strategy.
- Be dynamic with changes in business.

The organisation should also have a mechanism for developing long-term HR plans and reviewing them at regular

3. "CII National HR Excellence Award," *Confederation of Indian Industry*, accessed June 21, 2022, http://ciihrexcellenceaward.com.

intervals. This should be complemented by a measurement system.

The CII HR model is quite popular in India. Companies like NTPC, Saint-Gobain and TCS have adopted the framework, and many others undergo the assessment process.

PEOPLE CMM MODEL

Experts in the Software Engineering Institute created the Capability-Maturity Model for software development based on data collected from organisations that were working on contracts with the U.S. Department of Defence. The term "maturity", according to them, outlined the degree of formality and optimisation of processes, ranging from ad hoc practices to formally defined steps, to managed result metrics, to active optimisation of the processes.

As organisations progressed in assessing their software development practices, they realised that the biggest impact on software quality was from people. These organisations lacked proper workforce management practices, and symptomatic problems varied from inadequate opportunities for training and career advancement to inconsistent performance feedback and rewards. It was very clear that to be able to develop proper software, these organisations had to mature the way they managed their people. The CMM model focused on processes and technology and not people. This led to the evolution of the People CMM in 1995.

PCMM has progressively seen applicability in various industries like Software Development, Business Process Outsourcing, Energy and Utilities, Banking and Financial Services, Insurance, Consulting, Defence, Pharmaceuticals, Hospitality and so forth, along with different organisation sizes.

People CMM divides HR practices into four themes, which are:[4]

4. Bruce Curtis, William E. Hefley, and Sally A. Miller, "People Capability Maturity Model (P-CMM) Version 2.0," Carnegie Mellon University, June 1, 2001, https://apps.dtic.mil/sti/pdfs/ADA395316.pdf.

- Continuously improving individual competencies
- Developing effective teams
- Motivating improved performance
- Shaping the workforce.

According to PCMM, the maturity of an organisation on the above four themes lies at five different levels—Initial, Managed, Defined, Predictable and Optimising, as shown in Figure 2.2 below. Each level represents a progressively higher level of the capability of the organisation towards managing and developing its workforce.

Levels	Developing Competency	Building Workgroups & Culture	Motivating & Managing Performance	Shaping the Workforce
5 Optimising	Continuous Capability Improvement		Organisational Performance Alignment	Continuous Workforce Innovation
4 Predictable	Competency-Based Assets, Mentoring	Competency Integration, Empowered Workgroups	Quantitative Performance Management	Organisational Capability Management
3 Defined	Competency Development, Competency Analysis	Workgroup Development, Participatory Culture	Competency-Based Practices, Career Development	Workforce Planning
2 Managed	Training & Development	Communication & Coordination	Compensation, Performance Management, Work Environment	Staffing

Figure 2.2: PCMM Model

Within this matrix, there are 22 Key Process Areas. Each KPA consists of goals and measures. Taken together, these enable an organisation to develop, measure and continuously improve HR processes in alignment with organisation requirements.

For instance, if an organisation wants to improve customer satisfaction, then as per PCMM:

- Organisational performance objectives are set for customer satisfaction.

- The competencies of the workforce are modified to include behaviours that impact customer satisfaction.
- The effectiveness of development mechanisms in improving competencies is baselined.
- A current capability level of the impacted workforce in such competencies is baselined.
- The organisation arrives at the capability goals required to achieve the desired levels of customer satisfaction and implements the programs.
- Rewards and recognition, as well as performance management, are aligned to higher customer satisfaction.
- Based on the outcomes and their impact on customer satisfaction, the programs are evaluated and improved continuously.

Reimagining Workforce Processes at WQ Tech

WQ Tech was a mid-sized IT Services organisation which had missed out on being one of the tier 1 players in India. As the tier 1 companies scaled and leveraged technology to get smarter, the gap started growing wider for WQ Tech. During the last year, some of the biggest prospects had dried out after initial conversations. There had been leadership transitions due to falling morale. A new CHRO had been hired. Having joined from a very successful organisation, he soon realised that the workforce processes at WQ Tech were very scattered and low on maturity. No wonder the organisation had not been able to provide clients with the needed confidence in the quality of talent and the readiness to scale up with business. The CHRO had candid conversations with the executive leadership at WQ Tech and agreed to invest in an industry-wide accepted certification framework PCMM to reimagine the core workforce processes.

Post a rigorous assessment, WQ Tech was assessed as Level 3. This was not great, but it gave the organisation great clarity on the journey to move to Level 4 and then Level 5. Amongst the various work streams, one was formed to evolve the maturity of Performance Management.

To its credit, WQ Tech had a formal annual performance assessment process and had deployed it across its workforce. Managers and employees had been made aware of their responsibilities. Adoption and discipline in some parts of the organisation had been challenging but had seen positive traction during the last cycle. Two years ago, a focused effort had led to competencies being defined for most of the roles. The auditors had observed that the competencies were a great start but still not consistently understood amongst the newer employees. Also, there was a need to drive more consistency and skill among the people managers on how they leveraged these competencies.

At the next meet-up of the Performance Management work stream, the team deliberated in detail on the glide path to the next stage of maturity, Level 4. They could clearly identify the need for the right metrics that would help measure performance objectively. Once these measures were stated and monitored, employees would have a clear understanding of how they were trending over a period of time on their performance. They would also be able to assess where they stood viz-a-viz their peers. The organisation would also benefit as there would be a consistent view of the workforce quality, readiness for promotions, development and other investment opportunities.

"Our ambition is to mature to Level 5," stated the CHRO. "Does the workstream have a view of what would get us there?" he asked, looking earnestly at the others in the conference room. "Yes indeed," responded one of them, flipping the presentation slide to one titled 'Our Pathway to Maturity Level 5'. Listed, there was the need to build a strong alignment with business performance. The core strategy had to transcend into individual goals, which would help the organisation leverage talent in areas of strategic importance and also drive a sense of purpose among employees. They would be able to clearly gauge how they fit into the larger picture and how they were making an impact. The CHRO couldn't be happier to see this need being explicitly stated. It was agreed that the workstream over the next four weeks would evolve a clearer thinking on the ambition of maturing to Level 5.

Both the CII Model of HR Excellence and PCMM are rooted in the Total Quality Paradigm of continuous improvement. Organisations can use them as a reference or choose to undergo formal external appraisals to assess where they are and identify opportunities for continuous improvement.

HR SCORECARD

Balanced Scorecard ties up the measurement of an organisation's progress on strategic goals with financial and non-financial measures. HR Scorecard is derived from the same principles and connects HR strategic themes with measures. This is intended to operationalise HR strategy by facilitating reviews around the scorecard.

In *The HR Scorecard: Linking People, Strategy and Performance*[5], the authors posit that traditional HR measures follow a bottom-up process of aggregation, and they usually indicate the efficiency with which HR practices are performed. It is a challenge to use them to align with business outcomes.

To align with business, a top-down measurement system is created to articulate strategic goals. This system has four components:

- **High-Performance Work Systems**
  The measures are set against the best outcomes possible. For example, while a 10% attrition rate may be a good number, it will not be worth it if half of that 10% is of high performers. A high-performance engagement system would reduce high performer attrition to levels much lower than that of average performers.
- **HR system alignment**
  The HR system is composed of different HR practices. These need to be aligned to high-performance outcomes. The alignment happens by enlisting different measures used and classifying them into operational and strategic.
- **HR Deliverables**
  For strategic alignment, one needs to establish causal linkages. Let us say an organisation would like to

5. Brian E. Becker, Mark A. Huselid, and Dave Ulrich, *The HR Scorecard: Linking People, Strategy, and Performance* (Boston: Harvard Business Press, 2001), http://ci.nii.ac.jp/ncid/BA5142836X.

improve their ability to integrate acquisitions. What HR practices play into it? Onboarding of new employees, employee communications and employee sentiment tracking would be a few. The measures of these practices need to be reviewed and analysed to establish causality. An illustration is given below.

- **HR Efficiency**

  This captures the baseline efficiency of different processes to ensure that the strategic framework is built on a solid foundation.

These lead to business impact. An HR Scorecard is designed using a seven-step process.

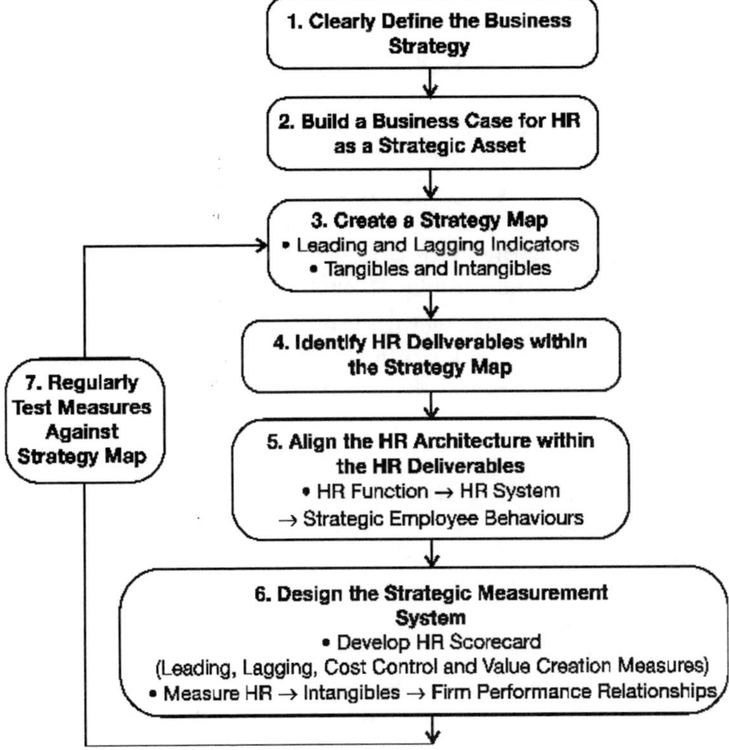

Figure 2.3: HR Scorecard

The HR Scorecard has been used by HR organisations to align their outputs with business outcomes. Valuing people is another framework to align HR outcomes to business leveraging measurement systems.

7-S FRAMEWORK

Getting JC Manufacturing to Hum Again:

JC Manufacturing, led by the Goel brothers, was, at best, a modest set-up in a tier 2 city in the northern part of India. However, three years ago, a chance opportunity opened the market for JC Manufacturing in an exponential way. The Goel brothers responded with agility and scaled up the organisation, bringing in professionals and opening two other manufacturing units in the south and west of the country. The sales teams were spread out. Everything picked up with a buzz.

However, three years later, something did not seem right. The different parts within JC Manufacturing were not operating in a rhythm, and fault lines started to appear. A culture of blaming emerged amongst the different functions. Communication channels and trust started breaking down. The core practices in the organisation took various forms in different regions. Critical talent was lost as they felt 'it was not the same old place anymore'.

The 7-S Model was leveraged to diagnose and very clearly demonstrated the lack of effectiveness arising from the shift in alignments between the seven elements.

The multi-locational growth had built complexity in the structure and governance. Over the years, the organisation was used to the leadership style of the Goel brothers. However, with many new leaders brought in to manage growth, different leadership styles and power equations emerged. As long as the revenues kept going north, the organisation had overlooked the reality that some leaders were running the show very independently, creating variants to hiring norms, vendor management and sales strategies. New hires had been pulled into the job even before they were onboarded properly with the right skills. They carried with them the culture and values from their previous jobs. Very soon, the one core culture and values of JC Manufacturing started receding.

Over the next six months, the Goel brothers and the collective leadership invested in driving alignment back amongst the seven elements.

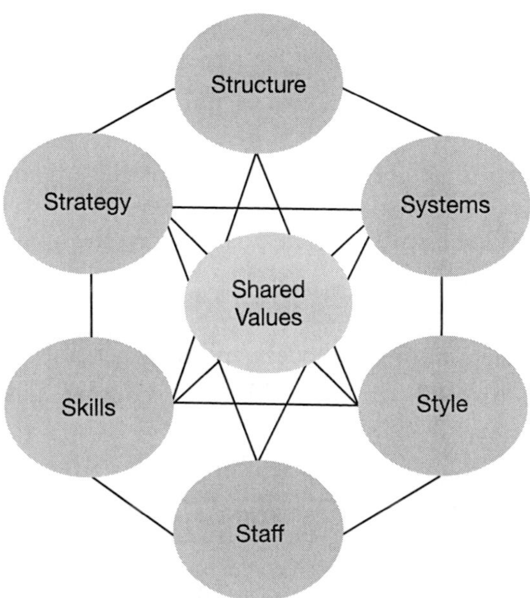

Figure 2.4: 7S Framework

The 7-S model was crafted by Tom Peters and Robert Waterman, former consultants at McKinsey & Company in the late 1970s. It was made popular through their book *In Search of Excellence*.

For an organisation to be successful as it scales, there are seven internal elements that need to stay in coordination. Strategy, Structure and Systems are termed as 'hard' elements. These are easy to identify and influence. The other four elements—Shared Values, Skills, Styles and Staff—are termed 'soft' elements. They are less tangible and directly influenced by the culture of the organisation. The central location of the Shared Values shows how they are core to the organisation and maintain balance with the other elements. The 7-S model works as follows:[6]

- Strategy is the organisation's plan for building and maintaining a competitive advantage over its competitors.
- The Structure shows how the entity is organised or how departments and teams are structured, including who reports to whom.
- Systems are the daily activities and procedures that staff use to get the job done.
- Shared values are the core values of the organisation, as shown in its corporate culture and general work ethic. They were called "superordinate goals" when the model was first developed.
- Style is the style of leadership adopted.
- Staff refers to the employees and their general capabilities.
- Skills are the actual skills and competencies of the organisation's employees.

The 7-S framework has stayed popular over an extended period of time due to its simplicity and holistic nature. By valuing the human side through the 'soft' elements, the framework demonstrated greater effectiveness and thus gained popularity with the HR organisation. Valuing the centrality of the shared values, this framework enables organisations to build sustainable strategies and stay true to who they are.

These frameworks are integrated and are helpful for a holistic assessment. They require strong commitment and sponsorship to achieve the right outcomes. What if you are interested in analysing a specific problem without having to think holistically? We can look at the following popular problem-solving framework.

SWOT ANALYSIS

SWOT is an acronym that stands for strengths, weaknesses, opportunities and threats. SWOT analysis is a strategic planning technique. Its popularity stems from its simplicity. It enables an

6. CFI Team, "McKinsey 7S Model," Corporate Finance Institute, October 15, 2023, accessed June 21, 2022, https://corporatefinanceinstitute.com/resources/management/mckinsey-7s-model/.

organisation to assess its strengths and weaknesses, as well as the external ecosystem reality through opportunities and threats.

The popular representation of the SWOT framework is through a 2x2 grid. The short descriptions below would help in providing a consistent understanding of each of the four key blocks:

Strengths (S): These are things that an organisation does well. These bring in a competitive advantage. The focus should be to value these and continue to retain them as strengths by building upon and augmenting them.

Weaknesses (W): These are things that an organisation does not do well. These are where competition gains an advantage. Once the weaknesses are articulated, the organisation can work through to mitigate them.

Opportunities (O): Every organisation is influenced by changes in the ecosystem in which it operates. Changes in factors like technology, regulations, political and social environment and so forth could catalyse opportunities for an organisation to invest, grow or take advantage of.

Threats (T): When changes in external factors impact an organisation negatively, they are considered threats. Organisations may not be able to control them but should be aware of them and do the best they can to mitigate possible impacts.

Most often in team settings, collective brainstorming is used to list out the strengths, weaknesses, opportunities and threats. The thoughts captured then should be listed in order of priority in each of the four quadrants. It is important to remember that opportunities and threats result from external factors. Acting on a weakness does not mean an opportunity. Similarly, acting on a threat does not result in forming a strength.

Completing the SWOT is a great start. What is most important, then, is to identify a set of goals and action items and list them below the 2x2 matrix. Each section is headed by some questions like how can the strengths help create success? What weaknesses should be prioritised to work through? What opportunities should be pursued? What threats should be focused on to mitigate possible risks?

SWOT analysis has found diverse usage in HR. In the recruitment function, SWOT has been used for workforce planning strategies involving the attractiveness of certain talent markets or capabilities. Business leaders and HR business partners have leveraged SWOT during Talent Reviews to provide a smart assessment of the readiness of talent in their business units to executive leadership and thereby triggered conversations on how to stay invested. SWOT has been leveraged to create smartness in Employee Engagement and a sense of belonging while operating in highly competitive talent markets. More recently, HR has been investing in technology to create agile and delightful employee experiences and capabilities to scale. SWOT has been leveraged to assess the maturity of such technology investments.

Hiring Data Science Talent at Zentra Technologies

A year ago, Zentra Technologies, under a new CEO, declared a long-term vision to transform itself into an AI-based platform organisation. To enable this strategic priority, the Chief Data Officer at Zentra Technologies led the workstream to infuse a three times growth in talent with Artificial Intelligence and Machine Language capabilities across the global technology hubs of the organisation.

In her visit to the Indian centre six months ago, she had crisply outlined her vision to build the Data Science team, drawing upon the smart talent available locally. This generated huge excitement both amongst the business leaders and the HR team. The Talent Acquisition (TA) leader invested huge energy to incubate the Data Science team thereafter. The Chief Data Officer would be in India again in two weeks' time.

The TA leader leveraged the SWOT analysis to construct an update and articulate the proposed action areas on Data Science Hiring in India.

STRENGTHS	WEAKNESSES
100% alignment to the staffing plan. More aggressive on rewards through Hot Skills Bonus & Additional equity grant plans. Data Science 12-month learning program launched to build an internal talent pipeline.	Time to hire increased to 80 days (33% off target). Offer acceptance at 70% (25% off target). Lost two critical hires. The internal assessors' pool is not broad enough. Delays impacting candidate experience
OPPORTUNITIES	**THREATS**
IIIETS and NeXUp Universities have great data science talent. Early conversations regarding hiring interns. Pilot of the new branding campaign has seen a two times increase in engagement. Launch the full campaign.	A competitor aggressively hires similar profiles for their research lab. Two data scientists lost to this organisation this month. The pool of senior-level women talent is not broad enough.

ACTION AREAS

1. Launch the internship program for Data Science talent at IITES and NeXUp Universities within 60 days. Ensure the highest sponsorship and participation from businesses.
2. Build a pool of 10 additional assessors in the next 30 days to engage better with candidates, lower hiring time and offer decline rates.
3. Partner with an external agency to map out data science talent in the market by the end of the quarter. Invest in passive talent engagement to improve diversity hiring.

The Chief Data Officer was very impressed with the clarity of thinking achieved using the SWOT Analysis. It built her confidence as the action areas were clearly identified. She knew exactly what to commit to and support the hiring efforts. The TA Leader walked out of the conversation with approval to progress on all three action areas. Later in the day, at the Town Hall, the Chief Data Officer shared her commitment to investing in the India centre and her belief that there was a clear plan to ramp up talent. She also remembered to share a note of appreciation to the TA Leader.

DESIGN THINKING

Reimagining Internal Mobility at Edwise Systems

Technology companies compete for talent in very dynamic talent economies. Edwise Systems has had success in attracting good talent but, in recent quarters, has seen employee retention challenges. Employees have also voiced a lack of career growth opportunities through the last engagement survey. While the leadership envisaged building a culture that encouraged employees to grow through mobility, the traction on applications had been minimal. Edwise Systems has been a firm believer in design thinking to drive innovation. This framework was leveraged to reimagine the internal mobility process.

Feedback collected from stakeholders on the different stages of the mobility process showed that the least engagement was with transparency on open positions and the support received from managers on mobility. The below problem definition was arrived at regarding the lack of transparency on open positions.

Edwise Systems, thus, knew exactly what to focus on to enable greater momentum in their internal mobility process. Results showed in terms of better retention of talent. This also helped them with a richer talent pipeline.

Customer Problem Statement

I am: an employee who has spent 5 years in my current role and now looking for a rotation. **I am trying to:** find out information on all open positions in the organisation so that I can apply. **But:** I am unable to source the right information. **Because** the career portal is not updated and open positions are shared primarily through informal network. **Which makes me feel:** frustrated and cluseless.	**In a perfect world:** I get visibility to open positions. **The biggest benefit to me is:** to have complete transparency to make right career choices. **Which makes me feel:** value and being provided with opportunities to grow my career in this organisation.

Figure 2.5: Design Thinking: Problem Statement

Design thinking is a creative approach to problem-solving. At its very core, it is customer-centric. It encourages a narrow and sharp focus on an unmet customer need and then drives an innovation process to solve that specific need and provide value to the customer.

With the Industrial Revolution and post-World War II, a convergence of minds was seen as engineers, industrial designers and cognitive scientists came together to creatively solve the so-called 'wicked problems' that would address big societal needs. Over the 1960s and 1970s, various academicians and researchers delved into combining left-brain and right-brain thinking to evolve a more holistic approach to problem-solving.

In 1987, in his book *Design Thinking*, Peter Rowe from Harvard demonstrated the power of inquiry in architectural design. Design thinking gained popularity as a framework through the work done by IDEO in the early 1990s and the Stanford Design School or the **D School** thereafter and now the Hasso-Plattner Institute of Design at Stanford.

The Institute has proposed a five-stage framework for Design Thinking.[7]

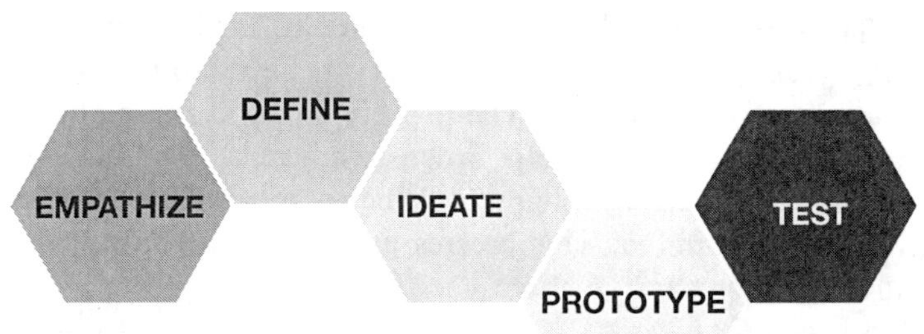

Figure 2.6: Design Thinking Framework

Empathise: It starts with learning the felt needs of the customer by deep observation in their own environment. This

7. Hasso Platner, "An Introduction to Design Thinking PROCESS GUIDE," Institute of Design at Stanford, n.d., https://web.stanford.edu/~mshanks/MichaelShanks/files/509554.pdf.

is a very human-centric approach and weeds out any personal assumptions carried into the problem-solving process.

Define: The deep observations recorded on the specific needs are then leveraged to construct and define a point of view or problem statement. The Define stage helps to 'go narrow' and focus on what is seen as the single biggest problem that needs to be solved for the customer.

Ideate: This stage relies on brainstorming to ideate creative possible solutions to the problem statement already defined. Generating as many ideas as possible, including 'out of the box' ones, is very helpful. The more diverse the group involved, the greater the propensity for varied ideas.

Prototype: At this stage, inexpensive working models are made on one or more of the ideas. The features of the prototypes would give a good understanding of what dimensions of the problem each one could solve.

Test: In the fifth and final stage, the prototypes are tested out by returning to the original customer group at the first stage. Feedback is continuously collected, and alterations are made to the prototypes to service the felt needs in the best possible way.

The framework allows the loop back to earlier stages in an iterative way to create a solution that is believed to best address the needs of the customer. The prototyping and testing help to 'fail early' and thus mitigate downstream risks. The beauty of the framework lies in solving for what is most needed and not what can be offered. This creates great customer engagement and delight.

While product companies and those high on innovation and customer-first mindset have valued Design Thinking, a key limitation of this framework remains in its orientation to the existing present needs and solving for them. It does not bring in foresight on future needs resulting from shifts in factors such as technology, laws and so forth.

The Design Thinking framework is very useful to HR when existing processes or offerings need to be reimagined to drive higher levels of employee adoption and satisfaction. This framework drives a sharp understanding of the employee need not being serviced, thus rendering the process ineffective. This clarity is then leveraged to trigger the needed redesign and accountability.

Of late, the focus has been moving from creating a "great workplace" to creating "great employee experiences". While a great workplace can follow an integrated framework, it is in co-creating experiences that design thinking has been especially helpful.

THE GREAT PLACE TO WORK MODEL

ZenX has been participating in the Great Place To Work assessments for the last seven years. It took two years to break into the rankings of the 100 Best Companies to Work For in the country. The last five years have seen ups and downs in the rankings, but ZenX now features amongst the top 30 companies.

While the progress on the rankings is cherished and helped build a stronger employer brand, the overall gains for ZenX have been much broader. By competing with the best companies from across sectors, ZenX has reimagined and evolved its people process with the adoption of best practices.

Access to data resulting from the survey reports has helped them set improvement goals and specific targets to aim for.

The budgets were allocated in a much more strategic way to programs and priorities that they believed would bring the greatest returns.

The organisation has also built greater transparency in sharing with its employees about the changes in practices and policies, including the context and why and how they would bring greater value to them.

This has generated greater trust and improved retention, and employees have turned into stronger advocates, rippling out the goodness on social media. This kind of genuine belonging has further helped ZenX attract high-quality talent in a very competitive market.

The Great Place to Work Institute narrates a fascinating story about the origin of this model. In 1981, a New York editor asked two business journalists—Robert Levering and Milton Moskowitz—to write a book called *The 100 Best Companies to Work for in America*. Though the pair was sceptical of finding 100 companies that would qualify, however, they agreed, starting a journey that would lead to more than 30 years of researching, recognising and building great workplaces. Today, the Great Place to Work Institute partners with more than 10,000 organisations every year around the world to help create and sustain a High-Trust, High-Performance Culture.

The Great Place to Work Institute evolved its core model to the present version called Great Place to Work For All.

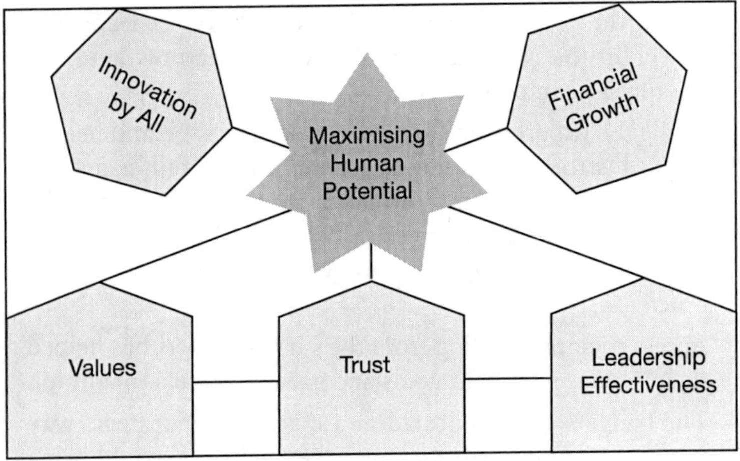

Figure 2.7: Great Place to Work Model

Great workplaces for all are able to maximise their human potential through effective leaders, meaningful values and a deep foundation of trust with all employees, regardless of who they are or what they do for the organisation. Companies that have succeeded in creating great workplaces for all benefit from improved innovation and sustained financial growth.

- Values: Company values are not just what's written on the walls or website but what employees actually experience in their day-to-day work lives, particularly in how they see their leaders.

- Leadership Effectiveness: An effective leadership team has an emotional connection with their organisation's culture and its people, as well as an ability to create a coherent and effective strategy at every level of the business.
- Maximising Human Potential: A great workplace for everyone regardless of who you are or what you do in your organisation.
- Innovation by All: A culture that enables an organisation to continuously improve, adapt quickly and generate pivotal opportunities by tapping into the intelligence, skills and passion of everyone in the organisation.
- Financial Growth: This is an outcome of great workplaces.

The versatility of the Great Place to Work model lies in its applicability to organisations across industry sectors. By focusing on the 'what', the model helps evolve the people's practices and policies that are progressive. With the rich data available, the model helps build science to the journey of improvement. The model also drives a huge focus on the 'how', which is the way the organisation connects with its employees to build trust and experiences that they value. Such an investment drives a high level of belonging and advocacy.

The Great Places to Work model has been wildly successful, even spawning imitators. However, it has also led to a situation wherein many companies look at it not as an input but as an output. Getting rated as a great place to work should, in turn, address specific business objectives like improving the ability to attract talent or retain high-potential employees. So, being a great place to work is a tool to attain organisation-specific goals, in addition to the branding value. Much like design thinking and SWOT, becoming a great employer is contextual and treated as such. In times of continuous change, even the best employer may be required to rationalise headcount and make policy moves that don't always deliver happiness to all employees. Becoming a great workplace is not just rational but emotional as well. Companies need to be conscious of the trade-offs required before committing to a plan of action.

STRATEGY LITERATURE & LINKS TO STRATEGIC HUMAN RESOURCE MANAGEMENT

HiLeap Solutions had a very successful run ever since it had set up its offices in Bengaluru in 2014. They had grown to over 3100 employees in this period. Their ambition was to cross the billion-dollar mark in 2025. The last 18 months have seen a slack in their growth momentum due to COVID. However, the last eight months have turned out to be the most challenging in hiring and retaining talent.

The much talked about Great Resignation was showing up in the Indian ecosystem, too. The talent dynamism in India was fuelled by growth—more jobs resulting in greater demand for talent. Attrition was already close to 35%, which was about two times the pre-pandemic levels and offer rejections had tripled to over 22%. Talent had turned into the most talked about topic in the leadership team during the last two months. Something needed to be done and done fast.

"We should avoid taking short-term populist measures. We cannot compete with what some of the start-ups are doing. Permanent work from home, giving 60-70% hikes to some of our talent they have made offers ... No, we can't be doing that," echoed one of the leaders in the leadership team meeting. "Did you read about this Delhi-based organisation offering all kinds of fancy gadgets to their new hires?" remarked another leader.

"Well, we got to do something. I can't run my business with attrition getting closer to 40%. Even I am not sure that the candidates waiting to join will actually do so," remarked the first leader. The CHRO stood up and made his point, "I had a two-hour conversation with my team. I had invited the best of our talent across levels. There were some good thoughts that came in—here are the top two."

"Hire 30% of our talent from colleges. Let us hire from the Tier 2 colleges, from where we have seen that talent has a higher level of stickiness. We should offer them the proposition that they can learn as they work. We can explore some learning courses with IIM Bangalore and IISC, which would have some certification on successful completion. They would be highly aspirational and can help us lock in talent for two to three years at a minimum."

"But we have never hired from colleges. There is so much investment to be made to train and manage them," commented the second leader. "Aren't we spending a lot more now in time and effort and also money trying to backfill for the 35% attrition, which keeps increasing? Imagine the amount of time being spent by our employees in interviewing. Also, the leakage is not helping us in knowledge management and confidence with our customers," asserted the CHRO. "These are unprecedented times, so if we have to win this, we have to do things we have not done before. If bringing in fresher talent is a gamble we should sign up for, then it is on us to transform internally and set up the right processes and investments that would help them succeed at HiLeap. Wouldn't you agree?" added the CEO.

The CFO nodded and said, "In fact, that helps us alter our cost structure on talent in the long run. We need the savings to fund our growth plans. Otherwise, it will not be easy to move at the pace we want to."

"What was the second idea you wanted to share?" reminded the CEO. The CHRO said, "Yes, of course. We felt that for some of our high-growth areas, we should look at outsourcing more aggressively. It would be a good way for us to de-risk ourselves. I tested this thought earlier today with Singhal (one of the leaders). You were quite positive to go for it. Weren't you, Singhal?"

HiLeap leadership hired 100 college graduates. It went on to partner with a training institute to provide the basic skills to these hires so that they were ready for the job. HiLeap had considered various operating models but decided to partner with the training institute instead of setting up an internal learning centre, which would require an initial investment. It also tied up with IIM Bangalore and IISC for courses in management and technology that saw huge sign-ups from its graduate hires.

In addition, HiLeap identified two of its growth areas and hedged its risks by signing up with an external partner who would run the work for 50 resources. Such talent investments were distinct shifts in HiLeap's talent strategy.

The human resource function has often been viewed to have stayed rooted in its functional focus rather than stepping up to address larger enterprise-level strategy. It has been more of a support function than an accelerator, except for progressive thinking organisations, which have been able to appreciate and unlock the potential of this function.

However, talent is now emerging as an enterprise-level agenda through shifts posed by the effects of the pandemic, leaps in digitalisation, the gig economy, evolving regulations and career choices as demonstrated by the Great Resignation. To effect strategic choices in the midst of such dynamism in the ecosystem requires going beyond functional and prescriptive frameworks and building a better appreciation of emerging strategy literature and its linkage to strategic human resource management.

We will consider two reputed perspectives from the strategy literature—resource-based view and dynamic capabilities.

RESOURCE-BASED VIEW

The resource-based view (RBV), popularised by scholars like Barney, is a managerial framework that focuses on the sustained competitive advantage of an organisation through the exploitation of its internal resources. This was in contrast to the 'positioning' view from the Porter school of thought, which considered external factors like industry structure that determined an organisation's performance. The RBV framework is represented through the following visual.[8]

Barney (1991) has defined firm resources as: "all assets, capabilities, organisational processes, firm attributes, information, knowledge, etc. controlled by a firm that enable the firm to conceive of and implement strategies that improve its efficiency and effectiveness". Firm resources are tangible or intangible. For example, in the retail industry, it could be the stores and distribution centres of individual organisations. These are visible and tangible. Organisations would also have intangible resources in the form of experience, intelligence, relationships, reporting

8. Jay B. Barney, "Firm Resources and Sustained Competitive Advantage," *Journal of Management* 17, no. 1 (March 1, 1991): 99–120.

structures and so forth. Anyone with the financial muscle can flow in the capital required to set up the tangible resources. The same is not easily possible with intangible resources.

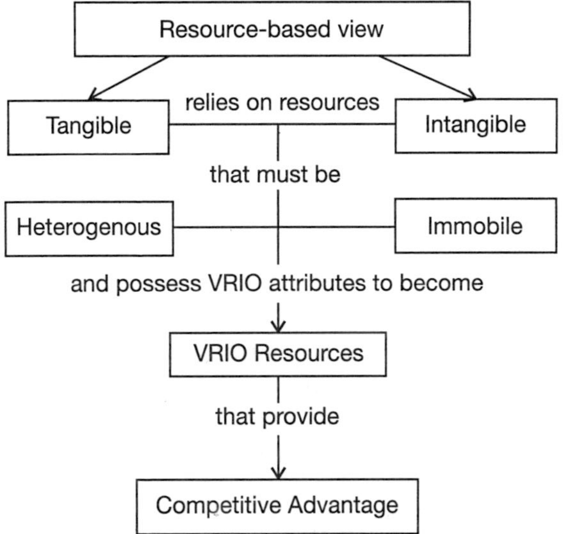

Figure 2.8: RBV Framework

RBV also states that resources should be heterogeneous and immobile. Let us consider Airtel and Jio. They compete in the market and operate in the same industry structure, yet their performance is different. This is due to the heterogeneity in the internal resources of these two organisations. I have been using an iPhone for the last many years. Apple has focussed on innovation as a primary driver towards its customer retention. Other phone manufacturers would love to duplicate Apple's innovation capabilities; however, that is not easily possible. It will take a lot of money and time. This can be understood through the concept of resources being immobile. Simply put, resources cannot easily move from one organisation to the other in the short term, and competitors cannot easily replicate the resources or strategies of their rivals quickly.

Four specific attributes have been stated for resources according to the RBV framework. They are referred to by the acronym VRIN and represented as below:

- Valuable: Resources are valuable if they exploit opportunities and neutralise threats
- Rare: Resources are rare if they are not easily available to competitors.
- Imperfectly Mobile: Organisations who don't have these resources can't easily get them. Thus, imitation is not easily possible. Also, competitors would not have the needed knowledge to implement them.
- Not Substitutable: Not able to be replaced by some other non-rare resource by competition. Both finding an alternate resource and switching is costly for a rival.

Organisations are able to focus on value-creating strategy leveraging internal resources when resources represent the above attributes. Competitors are not able to simultaneously implement such strategies, and this creates a competitive advantage. However, organisations aim to retain such an advantage over a longer period of time. Herein, the concept of Sustained Competitive Advantage became more relevant. This is possible when competition is not able to duplicate the benefits of the organisation's pursued strategy even over a longer period of time.

DYNAMIC CAPABILITIES

Organisations, in reality, do not operate in stable environments. Dynamism could be low, moderate or high based on the internal realities of the organisation, the industry factors and the maturity and the change in the ecosystem in which they operate. The last 50 years have seen multiple macro-level realities like the oil shocks of the 1970s; the dotcom bubble bursts at the turn of the century, the financial crisis of 2008 and the more recent COVID-19 pandemic that have had a significant impact on the survival of organisations on the one hand, while others have evolved and thrived on the other hand.

A *Financial Times* feature titled "Prospering in the Pandemic: The Top 100 Companies" listed Amazon at the top as it added over 400 billion USD in market cap as consumers were pushed towards online shopping.[9] Similarly, as travel came to a halt and remote working prospered, Microsoft's shift to the cloud saw its Teams communication offering usage grow nearly four times from end 2019 levels to 75 million on a single day in April 2020. Social distancing and the need to build consumer confidence led to PayPal introducing new features for contactless payments, while Nvidia prospered through its shift to online gaming as people spent hours playing games during lockdowns. Reliance Industries grew its market cap by over 7% during the pandemic. Even as its core energy business struggled, it added USD 15 billion as foreign investors were attracted to its digital business. Jio broadened its footprint from telecom to e-commerce.

However, there were losers too. From filing bankruptcy to shutdowns, a large number of organisations across the globe did not survive the pandemic. A NASSCOM study conducted in 2020 highlighting the impact of COVID-19 on start-ups found that 40% of start-ups were either temporarily shut down or were on the verge of closing. Many had to reimagine their focus to stay relevant in the future.

What had the organisations which had prospered done differently from the ones which were fighting for survival? Had they evolved themselves differently, making strategic choices that turned the pandemic from adversity to an advantage?

Let us try looking at it from an organisation that has been referenced in other places in this book. The Nokia of today is very different from the one I worked with in the early 2010s. To understand this, let us reference the Nokia Strategy segment on the organisation's website:[10]

> The world is facing enormous challenges with environmental issues, resource scarcity, inequality and stalling productivity. We believe that critical networks will be a crucial solution in responding to climate change through more efficient

9. "Prospering in the Pandemic: The Top 100 Companies," *Financial Times*, June 19, 2020, accessed on June 21, 2022, https://www.ft.com/content/844ed28c-8074-4856-bde0-20f3bf4cd8f0.
10. "Nokia's Strategy," Nokia, accessed June 21, 2022, https://www.nokia.com/about-us/company/nokias-strategy-2021/.

> use and re-use of the world's resources to provide more inclusive access globally to work, healthcare and education and to restoring productivity growth by bringing digital to physical industries.
>
> Our industry is undergoing profound changes. Industrial automation and digitalization are increasing customer demand for critical networks with a trend towards open interfaces, virtualization, and cloud native software. This will revolutionize how we design, develop, deploy, manage, and sell our products and solutions to an expanding market of Communications service providers, webscales and enterprises.

For an organisation that had lived through over 100 years and received a 'burning platform' wake-up call from its CEO, it is interesting to see how its future strategy is worded now with "enormous challenges, environmental issues, resource scarcity, profound changes, automation and digitalization, expanding market, service providers etc."

Understanding Dynamic Capabilities

The dynamic capabilities view has drawn significant attention over the years in the field of management since the work of Teece et al. (1997).[11] This perspective extended the then prevalent resource-based view (RBV) of the firm proposed by Barney. RBV was, however, static in its nature and inadequate to explain how firms could achieve competitive advantage in changing environments. The seminal work by Teece and his colleagues filled in this gap. They defined dynamic capabilities as the "firm/s ability to integrate, build and reconfigure internal and external competences to address rapidly changing environments."

Further research on dynamic capabilities has helped frame its definition as below:

---

11. David J. Teece, Gary P. Pisano, and Amy Shuen, "Dynamic Capabilities and Strategic Management," *Strategic Management Journal* 18, no. 7 (August 1, 1997): 509–33.

Zahra, Sapienza, & Davidsson (2006)[12]

The abilities to reconfigure a firm's resources and routines in the manner envisioned and deemed appropriate by its principal decision maker(s).

Helfat et al. (2009)[13]

The capacity of an organisation to purposefully create, extend or modify its resource base.

Teece (2007)[14]

Dynamic capabilities can be disaggregated into the capacity (a) to sense and shape opportunities and threats, (b) to seize opportunities and (c) to maintain competitiveness through enhancing, combining, protecting, and, when necessary, reconfiguring the business enterprise's intangible and tangible assets.

Teece (2018)[15] has proposed the simplified model below that connects dynamic capabilities, business model and strategy for an organisation:

The competitive advantage of any organisation, according to the Dynamic Capabilities concept, lies in its organisational and managerial processes, the resource or asset positions and the paths available to it. Every organisation has a way in which things are done, which refers to the processes, routines and practices that are followed. Organisations vary in their routines in how they capture and process information. Resources or assets

12. Shaker A. Zahra, Harry J. Sapienza, and Per Davidsson, "Entrepreneurship and Dynamic Capabilities: A Review, Model and Research Agenda," *Journal of Management Studies* 43, no. 4 (May 26, 2006): 917–55.
13. Constance E. Helfat et al., *Dynamic Capabilities: Understanding Strategic Change in Organizations* (Hoboken: John Wiley & Sons, 2007).
14. David J. Teece, "Explicating Dynamic Capabilities: The Nature and Microfoundations of (Sustainable) Enterprise Performance," *Strategic Management Journal* 28, no. 13 (January 1, 2007): 1319–1350.
15. David J. Teece, "Business Models and Dynamic Capabilities," *Long Range Planning* 51, no. 1 (February 1, 2018): 40–49.

range from technological, financial and reputational assets to also include knowledge and structural assets (such as hierarchy). These assets determine the competitive position of the organisation at any point in time. The current position and the paths available determine where the organisation can go. In fact, the current position is based on the path the organisation has travelled. While path dependence inherently points towards stability and rigidity, the dynamic capabilities view emphasises flexibility.

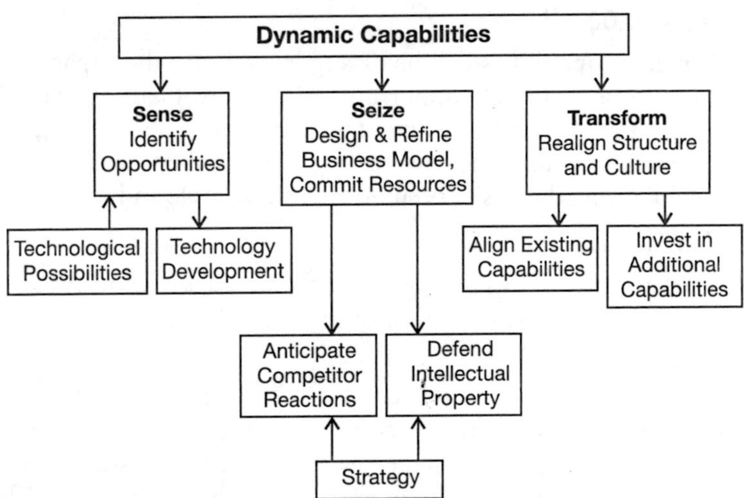

Figure 2.9: Dynamic Capabilities Model

Understanding Dynamic Managerial Capabilities

While dynamic capabilities focused on the organisational level, it was observed that differences in decision-making existed across managers in the same organisation. What made managers interpret and act differently? Were these differences related to individual managers' prior experience or expertise and their ability to leverage their networks to acquire additional information or resources? Was it related to their behavioural characteristics such as confidence, beliefs, emotions and so forth?

Heterogeneity in the performance of organisations based on the differences in the decision-making of managers was explained by Adner & Helfat (2003)[16] through the concept of dynamic managerial capabilities, which they defined as "the capabilities with which managers build, integrate and reconfigure organisational resources and competencies."

Subsequent research has focused on managerial cognition, managerial social capital and managerial human capital as the three underlying factors that influence dynamic managerial capabilities.

Managers deal with huge amounts of information on a daily basis. Even considering our immense mental capacity as humans, such information needs to be structured to help make complex decision-making faster. This is possible through cognitive processing and cognitive structures. As per Helfat and Peteraf (2015),[17] managerial cognitive capability has been defined as "the capacity of an individual manager to perform one or more of the mental activities that comprise cognition". Research has shown that experts are able to categorise information faster and deal with multiple cognitive frames simultaneously, compared to novices.

Managerial human capital has its roots embedded in the human capital theory. This theory proposed that both individuals and society can gain from economic benefits based on investments in people. While prior experience, training, intelligence, values and so forth are some of the key dimensions considered important for human capital, education has by far received the most significant attention. This becomes an important factor when resourcing is considered in emerging markets where the capability maturity is not that high. For organisations considering internationalisation, hiring talent in unknown markets based on their human capital capabilities becomes important.

With businesses becoming more of an ecosystem play pivoted on internal and external networks, social capital has seen increased

16. Constance E. Helfat and Ron Adner, "Corporate Effects and Dynamic Managerial Capabilities," *Strategic Management Journal* 24, no. 10 (2003): 1011–25.
17. Constance E. Helfat and Margaret A. Peteraf, "Managerial Cognitive Capabilities and the Microfoundations of Dynamic Capabilities," *Strategic Management Journal* 36, no. 6 (April 1, 2014): 831–50.

attention from a research perspective. Managers, through their formal and informal networks, can sense opportunities, risks and threats and are able to acquire information, knowledge and resources. In emerging or transitional economies, where institutional maturity is low compared to the Western developed economies, social capital has an increasingly higher value. Guanxi, in China, is the informal network among managers that helps them both personally and professionally. Similarly, studies have shown how, in Africa, managerial social capital is leveraged to influence community leaders. Entrepreneurship literature has articulated the importance of the social capital of founders to secure much-needed funding.

The growth of Indian IT Services organisations like Infosys, TCS, Tech Mahindra and so forth are good examples of firms leveraging dynamic capabilities. As the ecosystem has evolved, such companies have moved their value proposition from pure-play offshoring and labour arbitrage to focus on value-added services. Through technology investments and capability building, such companies have expanded their service offerings to include consulting, systems integration, products and so forth. The education industry has moved from the traditional classroom environment, leveraging technology, to the online portfolio. Alliances with global universities have helped in broadening the learning and research opportunities as well as access to a broader base of faculty and students.

Application of Dynamic Capabilities

Strategic Human Resource Management has so far been closer to the RBV than Dynamic Capabilities. The static orientation has, therefore, not kept pace with the agility of change needed to be successful in the unstructured world. A feature in the much-acclaimed journal *Human Resource Management Review* in November 2021, titled "Dynamizing human resources: An integrative review of SHRM and dynamic capabilities research",[18]

18. Paula Apascaritei and Marta M. Elvira, "Dynamizing Human Resources: An Integrative Review of SHRM and Dynamic Capabilities Research," *Human Resource Management Review* 32, no. 4 (December 1, 2022): 100878.

aims to bridge this gap. The authors state their belief that such an integration is key to the sustainable long-term growth of an organisation, as it ensures agility and the capacity to transform. Environmental dynamism is a given in today's world, and thus, organisations cannot afford to stay stuck with their proven successes.

While SHRM practices may not by themselves impact organisational performance, they enhance the dynamic capabilities and thereby influence performance and competitive advantage. What are some of the things that successful organisations do to strengthen their dynamic capabilities? Their hiring strategies promote diversity of talent, training practices broaden their skill base, stronger social networks internally speed up the transfer of knowledge and compensation practices strengthen trust and belief in fairness.

The existing human architecture of the firm, unless continuously evolved, may pose the biggest difficulty to organisations as they drive changes of large magnitude. An organisation's need for different skills and capabilities would imply letting go of a part of the workforce and replacing them by hiring talent with the desired skills and capabilities. This is a reality when organisations are driving digitalisation, like in the IT services sector or privatisation, such as railways, airports and other public sector enterprises. Such changes demand different processes, requiring different employee networks and behavioural repertoires. These shifts need to be driven through greater alignment of the HR strategy to the overall enterprise strategy, or else their impact is marginalised.

A key element of building dynamic capabilities is how organisations orchestrate their resources. Considering talent as a resource, a growing interest for organisations has been towards acqui-hiring, which refers to buying another organisation to get access to the skills and expertise of its staff, rather than for products, services or markets it operates in. There is evidence of growing leverage of acqui-hiring, particularly in the technology space where such organisations are invested in getting access to emerging or relevant deep technologies, which otherwise they would find difficult to build organically. Apart from building deep tech capabilities, acqui-hiring also helps in establishing an entrepreneurial culture.

Large organisations often have a dedicated M&A team that is scouting the market for both opportunistic and intentional acqui-hiring. As a part of the process, significant effort is put through due diligence to understand the routines and processes in the targeted organisation to help integrate it into the parent organisation once the deal is made. While sensing and seizing are important, a deeper understanding of the routines helps in the overall alignment and reconfiguration of the resources. How organisations integrate the acquired talent also varies. Often, organisations choose not to integrate the talent immediately but ring-fence the acquired entity for a while with some broad alignments at the leadership level. They could also continue to operate from a different workspace that minimises the transition impact on individuals. The acquired talent could also have specific aspects in their original contracts which may not align with the practices of the parent organisation. Some of these clauses could be ring-fenced again or phased out and aligned over a period.

CONCLUSION

Through this chapter, we journeyed through different frameworks leveraged by HR professionals across different industries over a fairly long period of time. Each of these has a different origin. Some of these have also evolved with time to their current versions. And yes, these are not the only ones. There are some more frameworks that have been in use, too.

Is there a need for one encompassing framework in HR? To help have a point of view, let us look at learnings from the way the existing frameworks are used today. There are a few common themes.

Any framework needs to balance between simplicity and rigour. Different situations demand different levels of rigour. The more simplistic ones, like the SWOT analysis, provide a direction and a broad perspective. Any individual in the organisation can initiate a SWOT like the TA leader at Zentra Technologies. Compare that with the Design Thinking framework. It requires active brainstorming in a small group. At the other end, the PCMM framework needs to mobilise a big part of the organisation. But the rigour is way beyond a SWOT.

Frameworks not only bring alignment on the 'what' but also on the 'how'. The core of the Design Thinking framework is customer empathy. The process starts with investing time to build a strong understanding of what the real problem for the customer is that needs to be solved. Similarly, the GPTW Framework demonstrates the need to thrive in a culture that lives the core values, builds trust and transparency and values all employees.

Finally, most of these frameworks are not limited to HR but are applicable across domains in an organisation. This ability makes these frameworks more universal and compelling to the leadership in the organisation. The 7-S Framework, through its seven elements, the SWOT analysis and Design Thinking, demonstrate this flexibility. The concept of environmental dynamism and its impact on decision-makers in organisations has been exemplified through the dynamic capabilities approach. There is a deeper embedding required in the way an organisation does things through processes, routines and practices. This leads to the desired reconfiguration of resources towards sustaining competitive advantage.

The connections that these frameworks establish between business strategy and HR plans and priorities have been pursued in this book. Thus, more than building the case for one overarching HR framework, it is best to leverage the existing ones in HR, keeping in perspective the above themes.

3
Talent Strategy on The Ground

It is all well for us as experienced professionals to write on the basis of our own experiences with multiple companies across different stages of their lifecycles. However, any work like this cannot be inured to the trends in the industry at large. To research the same, we followed the classic approach:

1. Literature review
2. Practitioner survey
3. In-depth interviews

The literature review is summarised in the previous chapter on frameworks. Subsequently, we designed a questionnaire and surveyed HR and Business Executives from across different industries. Furthermore, we carried out personal interviews with some participants. In this chapter, we will look at the salient points from the survey. The insights from the individual one-on-ones are distributed across the book either as explicit illustrations or as strengthening our perspectives.

The survey essentially tried capturing the following:

- Company ownership: Is it listed or private? If listed, is it a small cap/ mid cap/ large cap. If private, is it a start-up or an MSME organisation?
- Industry vertical: Software product, IT services, FMCG, financial services, Pharma and so forth.

- Location: Headquartered out of India/ Rest of Asia/ US/ Europe.
- Business position of the organisation: Market leader/ Challenger/ Mature and stable/ Mature and declining/ Startup.
- Role played by the participant: Business leader/ HR leader/ Other function leader/ Consultant.
- The top challenges faced by the organisation. The participants chose three from among the following:
  - o Revenue growth
  - o Profit increase
  - o Market share improvement
  - o Customer delight
  - o Internationalisation
  - o Quality
  - o Business model transformation
  - o Rapid product development
- The phrases frequently used in my organisation. The participants chose one statement from the following:
  - o We are an employer of choice.
  - o We are employees first.
  - o We have a high-performance work culture.
  - o We are an inclusive employer.
  - o We attract and retain the best.
  - o We have a very balanced and attractive C&B.
  - o Our talent helps us to win.

These questions helped capture the background of the participants. Then, we had a series of questions on their strategic planning process:

- Involvement in the strategic planning process (from anchoring the process to being informed).
- Frequency of strategic planning process (broad strategy with annual planning, just annual planning).
- Is strategic planning accompanied by an HR strategy?

- Reasons for developing an HR strategy.
- Frameworks used for developing HR strategy (The choices included strategy development and deployment frameworks, including HR scorecard, SWOT, 7S, design thinking and OKRs. The latter may not be strictly about strategy, but having them as choices gives us a better understanding).
- The processes governed by HR strategic planning (Workforce planning, employee cost management, talent attraction and value proposition, organisation structure and so forth.)
- How is the HR strategic planning documented and reviewed?
- How is progress on HR strategic plans measured?
- Outcomes from the strategic plan.

These questionnaires and responses are enclosed as an Annexure.

We had more participation from HR leaders in India-headquartered companies that are market leaders from the software industry. However, we think that the following insights are relevant for all organisations.

Insight 1: Everyone is transforming, including market leaders

All strategy needs to be aligned with business needs. In this section, we gathered the respondent choices on what are the top challenges being faced by their organisation. They can choose any three from the following:

The top challenges facing my organisation are:

- Revenue Growth
- Profit Growth
- Market Share Improvement
- Customer Delight
- Internalisation
- Quality

- Transformation of business model
- Rapid product development

Figure 3.1: Top Challenges

We expected revenue growth and profit growth to be the leading choices. However, what we found was that the first choice was the transformation of the business model, followed by revenue growth followed by market share improvement.

This was intriguing because we expected market leaders to continue doing what they are while the challengers or companies turning around should be transforming. The survey pointed to different trends:

	Market Leader	Challenger	Mature+	Mature -	Start-up
1	Transformation	Revenue growth	Transformation	Transformation	Product development
2	Profit growth	Transformation	Revenue growth	Revenue growth	Revenue growth
3	Revenue growth	Market share	Market share		Market share

The top challenge being faced by market leaders is transformation. This is in line with the accelerated rate of change in business. In just twelve years, the market leadership in smartphones in India has gone from Nokia to Samsung to Xiaomi to OnePlus, with Apple steadily gaining market share. Becoming a market leader and staying as one requires staying ahead of the curve of market forces. In many industries, that determines business growth.

Employees in challenger companies have identified revenue growth as their primary choice. That may be the most obvious one, but are they thinking enough about how to increase the revenues? It may be possible not by trying harder but by trying different things.

Transformation and revenue growth are the top drivers for mature organisations. Both realise the need to change from their stable position to grow faster. Start-ups, however, are often enabling transformation. For them, it is still about rapid product development that, in turn, would drive revenue growth and market share. And valuations, of course.

The following table illustrates how the priorities can vary based on industry verticals, too. While the size of the sample within verticals may preclude conclusions, the variations in the top three are intriguing.

Telecom	Tech Services	Software Products	Financial services	FMCG
Transformation	Revenue growth	Revenue growth	Transformation	Market share
Customer Delight	Transformation	Rapid product development	Market share	Rapid product development
Revenue+ Profit	Profit growth	Transformation	Product development	Transformation

For executives in telecom, delighting the customer comes ahead of even revenue growth. Rapid product development is a priority not just for Software products but also for financial services that are fast becoming digital. We did not have enough input from companies with a manufacturing orientation.

So, whatever the industry you are working in, you need to be worried if you do not hear about a need for transformation!

Insight 2: Successful companies take HR strategy more seriously

The following table represents the rigour with which HR strategy is reviewed in an organisation classified by the market positioning of the organisation.

	Company Position (Percentage Responses)					
HR Strategy in my organisation is	**Challenger**	**Early-stage start-up**	**Growing Market Leader**	**Mature and stable**	**Mature but declining**	**Total**
Documented and reviewed regularly at the HR Head level	18%	8%	32%	17%	0%	22%
Documented and reviewed regularly at the CEO/Board level	36%	38%	60%	52%	33%	50%
Documented but forgotten	9%	0%	0%	4%	0%	3%
Neither documented nor known.	5%	31%	2%	4%	67%	8%
Not documented, but elements are known	32%	23%	6%	22%	0%	17%
Grand Total	**100%**	**100%**	**100%**	**100%**	**100%**	**100%**

This tells us that:

- In 92% of the market-leading organisations, HR strategy is documented and reviewed at the CXO level. 60% by the CEO.
- CXO level review happens in 69% of the mature organisations, too. However, in 30% of such companies, there are unknowns around the strategy.
- 46% of employees in challenger organisations say that their HR strategy may not exist or exist informally.
- The same holds for start-ups, but unless one is in the technical unicorn, their talent strategy may be still evolving, so it is understandable.
- In 67% of the companies that are on the decline, HR strategy is neither documented nor known.

We can make two inferences here. The market leaders have mature processes, and so they do HR strategy as part of the bureaucracy. Or, they take talent seriously enough to make long-term plans for it. If serious, then does the strategy get reviewed?

	Company Position (Percentage Responses)					
HR Strategy in my organisation is	**Challenger**	**Early-stage start-up**	**Growing Market Leader**	**Mature and stable**	**Mature but declining**	**Total**
Not reviewed at all	5%	23%	2%	4%	33%	7%
Reviewed and measured at a defined cadence	18%	31%	56%	48%	33%	42%
Reviewed, but measures are not clearly defined	36%	15%	31%	22%	0%	27%
Reviewed in an ad-hoc manner	41%	31%	11%	26%	33%	24%
Grand Total	**100%**	**100%**	**100%**	**100%**	**100%**	**100%**

We find that 42% of all companies have their strategy reviewed at defined frequencies.

27% do the reviews but are not clear about all measures. Some kind of review happens, and this applies even to 31% of the market leaders.

That said, we find a 38% difference between market leaders and challengers in terms of rigour of talent strategy and reviews. Maybe an organisation trying to compete should start looking more at talent as a competitive edge than just a tool to enable their revenue growth.

To approach talent strategically, you need to have a plan and review it based on the measures. Our data shows that there is a great scope for improvement among all organisations, even if some seem to detest the bureaucratic nature of the same.

Do the focus areas for strategy change with the type of the organisation?

MARKET POSITIONING	# 1 PRIORITY	# 2 PRIORITY	# 3 PRIORITY
Challenger	Workforce planning	Talent attraction	Employee cost management
Early-stage start-up	Workforce planning	Performance management	Talent attraction
Growing Market Leader	Talent attraction	Workforce planning	Organisation structure
Mature and stable	Workforce planning	Talent attraction	Organisation structure
Mature but declining	Employee cost management	Organisation structure	

Options included processes like learning and development, total rewards, performance management and so forth. However, as the table above shows, strategic planning is still about aligning the organisation structure, workforce planning and hiring to meet business needs. Organisations trying to reduce employee costs still look at the hierarchy and headcount plan.

There was no option to choose "employee engagement" or "employee retention". We suspect that would have gained a lot of attention from management across the board.

Start-ups are the only type of organisations that have chosen performance management, possibly because of the pressure to deliver to shortened timeframes.

Most organisations are transforming. This cannot be achieved by just hiring quality talent but also through learning and career development strategies. When they are not chosen, one suspects that even today, in many organisations, what passes for talent strategy is glorified workforce planning.

This points to a systemic weakness. In the book, we share a framework that expands beyond workforce capacity.

Insight 3: Formalisation enables success

We have seen that in challenger companies, as well as those on the decline, there is a lot of informality around the HR strategy. What is the incentive for going formal?

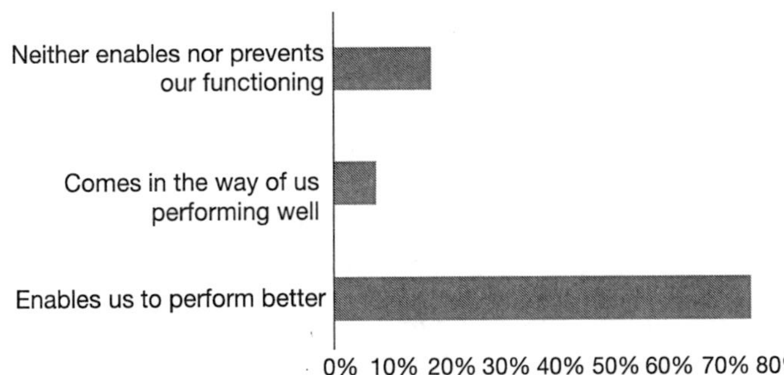

Figure 3.2: Impact of a Formal Process

More than 75% of the participants have said that a formal process enables them to perform better, while 17% have said that it neither enables nor prevents. The high percentage means that even those who don't have a formal process feel they will benefit from it.

Formalisation of HR Strategy	Enables us to perform better	Neither enables nor prevents our functioning	Comes in the way of us performing well
Documented and reviewed regularly at the HR Head level	71%	17%	12%
Documented and reviewed regularly at the CEO/Board level	94%	2%	4%
Documented but forgotten	33%	67%	
Not documented, but elements are known	53%	31%	16%
Neither documented nor known.	40%	60%	
Grand Total	**75%**	**18%**	**7%**

- In 94% of organisations where the strategy is reviewed at the CEO/Board level, it is felt that it enables superior performance. The corresponding number drops to 71% when it is reviewed at the HR head level. There is a one-fourth gain in the credibility of the formal strategy when the business leadership is involved in the process.

- As the seriousness with which the strategy is documented and reviewed reduces, the less effective the strategy itself becomes. Many are comfortable with the view that formalising the strategy is not really required as long as we know the components. However, these numbers clearly show that formalising it is the first step towards creating credibility with executive leadership.

Assume that two organisations have created a formal strategy. Then, does the frequency of reviews have an impact?

Frequency of Reviews	Enables us to perform better	Neither enables nor prevents our functioning	Comes in the way of us performing well
Reviewed and measured at a defined cadence	93%	5%	2%
Reviewed, but measures are not clearly defined	69%	10%	21%
Reviewed in an ad-hoc manner	60%	36%	4%
Not reviewed at all	44%	56%	
Grand Total	**75%**	**18%**	**7%**

Regular reviews enhance the performance effectiveness by 25% while reviewing without clear-cut measurements is the same as reviewing in an ad-hoc manner.

Insight 4: HR's self-appraisal is more liberal than what their peers think

The next axis we examined was the feedback of business leaders vs the feedback from HR leaders.

The first question was whether HR leaders participate in the strategic planning process.

My organisation actively involves HR in Strategic Planning						
ROLE	**1**	**2**	**3**	**4**	**5**	**Grand Total**
Business Leader	24%	8%	24%	30%	14%	100%
HR Leader		4%	20%	43%	34%	100%
Other	7%	13%	33%	33%	13%	100%
Grand Total	9%	6%	23%	37%	24%	100%

This table shows an intriguing dichotomy in perceptions between the business leaders and HR leaders. The ratings are on a 1-5 scale, going from lower level of involvement to higher level of involvement.

- 43% of business leaders say that HR is actively involved in strategic planning, while 77% of HR Leaders say that they are actively involved.
- A full 32% of business leaders say that HR is not actively involved in the strategic planning process for the business.

This shows differences in perception between the business leaders and HR leaders on the involvement in the business planning process.

The dichotomy extends to the question of whether an HR strategy accompanies the business strategy.

ROLE	Yes	No	Not Sure
Business Leader	30%	54%	16%
HR Leader	79%	14%	7%
Other	53%	27%	20%
Grand Total	**58%**	**30%**	**12%**

(Other here refers to leaders from other functions like finance, marketing and so forth.)

Only 30% of business leaders say that an HR strategy is crafted after the business planning, while on the other hand, 79% of HR leaders say they do the same. This is a big difference.

The next table explains the major reason for the same. Unless an HR strategy accompanies the business plan and is reviewed by the business leaders, a business leader does not really know whether such a strategy exists. A formal process may exist within HR, but when it is contained within HR, others might still look at it as an informal process.

Formalisation of strategy	Documented and reviewed regularly at the HR Head level	Documented and reviewed regularly at the CEO/ Board level	Documented but forgotten	Not documented, but elements are known	Neither documented nor known
Yes	22.22%	74.60%		3.17%	
No	15.63%	9.38%	3.13%	43.75%	28.13%
Not Sure	38.46%	15.38%	15.38%	23.08%	7.69%
Grand Total	**22.22%**	**48.15%**	**2.78%**	**17.59%**	**9.26%**

When the strategy is documented and reviewed regularly at the CEO level, it gains visibility. The entire organisation, and not just the HR, agrees that there is a strategy. On the other hand, when it is contained within HR, nearly 40% of the participants say that they are not sure if there is an HR strategy.

Interestingly, even the choice of key HR processes governed by the strategy is different for HR and business.

	Role (Percentage Responses)			
STRATEGIC PRIORITIES	**Business Leader**	**HR Leader**	**Other**	**Grand Total**
Compensation and benefits	0%	4%	7%	3%
Employee cost management	3%	11%	13%	8%
Inclusivity and diversity	5%	7%	0%	5%
Learning and development	10%	0%	27%	7%
Organisation structure	13%	12%	7%	12%
Performance management	18%	5%	7%	10%
Talent attraction and value proposition	28%	23%	27%	25%
Workforce planning	23%	39%	13%	30%
Grand Total	**100%**	**100%**	**100%**	**100%**

As we had seen earlier, workforce planning and talent attraction are the most popular processes for strategic planning, in excess of 50%. However, there are key differences between Business and HR at the next level.

For business leaders, performance management, organisation structure and learning and development take the 3-5 positions. These three account for 41% of the choices.

For HR leaders, organisation structure, employee cost management and diversity come next. Not only does HR put greater weight on workforce planning, but it also assigns far less importance to performance management and L&D.

For leaders from other functions (finance, quality and so forth), L&D is as important as talent acquisition. Possibly due to leaders in finance, employee cost management and compensation also become important.

So, we can discern three different priorities after factoring in workforce planning and talent acquisition. HR executives, business executives and executives from other functions all have a different pattern.

The solution lies in dialoguing and going beyond what is obvious—workforce planning, talent acquisition and employee cost management.

Insight 5: No framework dominates the scene

1. What are the frameworks used for detailing HR strategy?

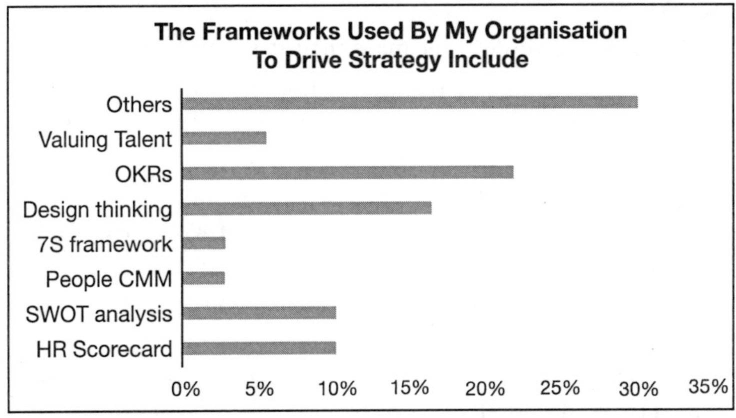

Figure 3.3: Frameworks Used to Drive Strategy

There do not seem to be one or two popular frameworks. 30% use a homegrown framework. Even an HR scorecard is used only by 10% of organisations. 7S is another one which is used. Therefore, strategy definition is done using a variety of frameworks.

On the other hand, design thinking is used by 16.4% of companies to collect inputs to craft strategy. Similarly, 21.8% use OKRs for strategy deployment. OKRs and Design thinking, of course, are more prevalent in software technology companies. In the course of our conversations, we also came across the "where to play, how to win" paradigm frequently.

2. What are the participants saying?

Let us look at the flavour of feedback from executives working in different types of organisations.

Growing Market Leaders

A few years back, strategic planning for both business and HR used to be long-range. However, so much volatility and changes in the environment have resulted in constant changes within the organisation. Hence, there is a need for more dynamic strategy planning for just the quarter or year while keeping the long-term in perspective. The methodologies for strategy planning are multi-fold and built on systems thinking.

HR strategy is about three main thrusts in my organisation:

1. Digitisation: Learning portal, HR queries using AI, claims and expense management, employee experience, including virtual onboardings and so forth.
2. Talent Analytics: One source of data worldwide and ready now data with no latency.
3. Enabling a culture of focusing on outputs and working from anywhere.

It's a robust process of strategy articulation and cascades into HR leader goals. It covers all critical elements, takes stock of overlaps and dependencies and has a defined program plan. It is also reviewed at the highest levels of the organisation. It probably needs better articulation and communication with business leaders.

Our business has relatively short cycles, and HR strategy tends to get buffeted by these changes as well. This, in turn, affects the overall employee experience. We are still trying to figure out how to solve that.

Stable and Mature

HR is at the table for key decisions. HR could be more in leading mode, not participative mode. HR is not working with the business but following what the business decides.

I would like to see it more broad-based and involving more folks than less. Define metrics and responsibilities of stakeholders for common understanding.

Challenger

As with almost all Indian IT services companies, the bulk of the staff is seen as a cost element, with anything being done impacting the bottom line. Cost structures don't really permit a more generous strategy. However, the organisation should, for starters, get away from doing the bare minimum to retain the specific resource.

Enterprise HR strategy needs to be articulated better. Now, it's defined at a more local leader level.

Currently, it follows a cliched approach. I think a better approach will be to focus on one or two strategic priorities and really get them done.

There is no grand HR strategy; it is an element of business planning and very much integral. HR projects are signed off and given independence to execute once signed off. Would prefer this mechanism rather than a big set of PPTs :-)

Early-Stage Start-up

Fairly evolved—we have a road map and OKR philosophy. Employee focus is quite high. Sometimes left out of the product discussions.

Need Advisory inputs.

Mature and Declining

Can't be in the head of the promoter who uses jargon.

Presently, it is more focused on layoffs and restructuring. I would like to see more strategy on L&D, where the workforce is created to be future-ready, creative and innovative. This can't be done alone by L&D but also requires inclusive participation from the leadership team-walk the talk. In fact, HR strategy should be centred on creating an environment for innovation, collaboration and creativity for sustainable growth.

We have looked at a lot of data. It does have some shortcomings in terms of coverage. When we look beyond that, what are the takeaways?

- There are variations in how companies define and implement HR strategy.
- Business leaders and HR leaders view the role of HR's participation in the strategic planning process differently.
- The understanding and appreciation of business leaders correlate with the strategy being reviewed by the CEO/Board.
- Successful strategies are reviewed in a cadence.
- Strategic priorities and the importance of HR processes vary from industry to industry.
- Not having a commonly understood and articulated strategy is a risk for HR because there could be misalignment in the top priorities.
- Workforce planning and talent acquisition have the mindshare. There are opportunities to take the strategy beyond into the realms of L&D, performance management and so forth.

ELEVATING FOR EFFECTIVE STRATEGY

As part of the research for this book, we reached out to many senior executives in both business and HR to gather their perspectives. People management is typically divided into functional areas like talent acquisition, learning and development, performance management and so on. One of the assumptions we had was that there is likely to be a strategy for each functional area, which, when consolidated, yields the organisation's HR strategy.

Our first insight from these discussions was that reality was a little different. As our survey showed, most organisations consider workforce planning and talent acquisition as the primary focus area for strategic planning. There are many dimensions to this, which we can articulate as:

Workforce capacity: Organisations need to build their workforce capacity. Capacity building is a combination of planning the workforce and acquiring talent. Given the business areas and numbers, companies forecast their headcount. Traditionally, this used to consider talent acquisition, internal growth and attrition numbers. Larger organisations also need a location strategy for getting the best returns, both inside the country as well as globally. Annual workforce planning is performed in line with strategic questions of:

(a) Should we continue to do the same work using full-time employees? Or are there parts that can be outsourced? If outsourced, how do we ensure a favourable cost and quality equation?

(b) How do we staff up full-time employment? Do we hire all talent based on a ready fit? Or do we do some of that and primarily grow talent from within? In either case, how do we approach the cost and quality equation?

(c) The workplace is becoming a man-machine hybrid. Chatbots can handle repetitive queries and address level-one problems. Cobots are taking over the tough-to-do work on the shop floors. How do we strategise to get a return on investment from technology?

We also noticed that executives outside HR were more concerned about learning and development and performance management. How does HR incorporate this into strategic priorities? We shall include the following:

Workforce capabilities: Two organisations may have the same total headcount. However, they don't have to achieve the same results because the capabilities behind the numbers could be very different. Progressive organisations expect their workforce not just to enable meeting business goals but actually to become a competitive edge. This becomes accentuated when industry-wide transformations happen, like cloud technologies or sustainable energy. The strategic questions are around the adequacy of:

(a) Capability to meet near-term business goals across all functions.

(b) Capability to prepare to meet medium-term business goals.

(c) Getting the people with the right capability in the right role.

Any organisation that chooses to focus on the first and excludes the second runs the risk of becoming redundant.

Workforce capability subsumes the practices of learning, leadership development and career development.

Workforce Performance: Right numbers with relevant capabilities are critical. However, by itself, it does not guarantee superior performance. For continuous performance improvement, we need to answer questions on:

(a) Do we have the right mechanisms to convert business goals to individual objectives?

(b) Do we have an alignment of our reward with performance?

(c) Do we have the optimum structure to achieve our goals? Do we have the right people in key roles?

(d) Do our employees collaborate with each other? What about our leaders?

(e) Does our culture enable high performance?

HR needs to focus on these drivers to deliver superior performance. To be effective, an HR function needs to revisit the assumptions behind these practices at least once in two to three years. Given that the marketplace and organisation evolve continuously, these practices are always in focus.

It is said that culture plays a bigger role in influencing business outcomes than strategy itself. In every industry, for every market leader, we could have five or more contenders, each aspiring to become a market leader. This aspiration drives some of the capability strategies (developing sales skills, for instance).

Culture is a massive topic. For the purposes of this book, we would like to highlight the different themes which impact performance and not take a deep dive into each. We will be examining the themes of culture, teamwork, as well as total rewards and performance management with an organisation performance lens.

Figure 3.4 illustrates this line of thought. Organisations are founded on a purpose and have their values. For existence, the company needs to be profitable and grow year on year as far as possible, which leads to the business strategy.

The business strategy is converted into the talent strategy using the pillars of capacity, capability and performance. End of the year, we have the outcomes with three possibilities:

- Objectives have been achieved.
- Objectives have been partially achieved.
- Objectives were unsuccessful.

In the first two, the HR organisation looks at ways and means of either improving upon success or ensuring success on all objectives. When faced with failure, they need to reimagine how they intend to achieve the business goal because there is not much that can be improved upon.

What are the traditional HR processes and practices subsumed under capacity, capability and performance? Figure 3.5 details this.

What we heard was that these are not reviewed on a year-to-year basis (and it would be foolish to do so), but on the basis of leadership assessment of how well an organisation is doing. There would be multiple change programs that emanate from a directional change.

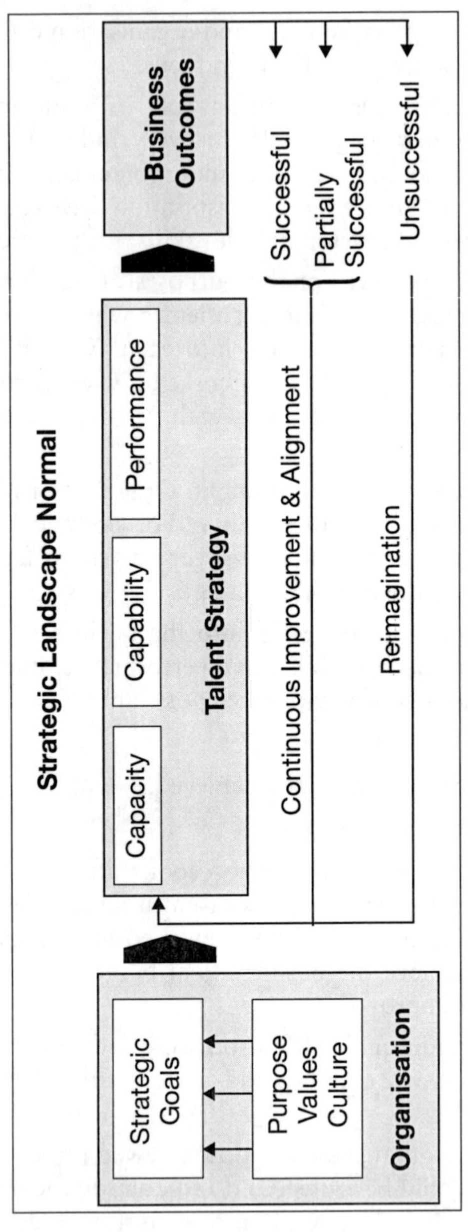

Figure 3.4: Strategic Landscape Normal

The theme that interconnects the previous three is how HR function plans for itself. HR has to confront questions on the following to be truly effective in achieving these strategic outcomes to be truly effective:

- Operating model
- Technology and analytics leverage
- People skills
- Collaboration and business alignment

We will dedicate each of the following chapters to the themes of capacity, capability, performance and transformation. Let us get started with capacity.

CAPACITY	CAPABILITY	PERFORMANCE
Workforce Planning Outsourcing Offshoring Talent Acquisition Quantity Hybrid Models	Talent Acquisition Quality Learning and Development Leadership Development Career Planning Skill Management	Performance Management Compensation and Benefits Reward and Recognition Team Building Employee Engagement Culture Building

Figure 3.5: Theme-Process Map

4

Starting with Organisation Capacity

In 2012, *Fortune* published an article that was excerpted from the book *The Greatest Business Decisions of All Time*.[1] It listed calls such as Apple bringing back Steve Jobs, Johnson and Johnson's famous Tylenol recall and Tata Steel's 1993 decision to take a radical approach to downsizing. Those in the world of business are very familiar with the transformational impact of Steve Jobs' return and the value exemplar of Johnson and Johnson. Why was Tata Steel's decision in the same league?

In the early 1990s, Tata Steel was India's largest private-sector organisation. The organisation produced two million tonnes of steel. However, the productivity numbers were abysmally low. They were producing 100 tonnes of steel per person per annum. The global leaders in steel production were at 10x that number at that time. Tata Steel embarked on modernisation to upgrade its technology.

At its peak, Tata Steel employed more than 80,000 full-time employees. They had nearly 3000 employees as secretaries and office boys. Their ethos and their standing meant that they could not go ahead and issue thousands of pink slips. Such a decision would not have been in line with the persona of Tata Steel.

1. Fortune Editors. "The Greatest Business Decisions of All Time." *Fortune*, June 10, 2014, accessed June 18, 2022. https://fortune.com/2012/10/01/the-greatest-business-decisions-of-all-time/.

Instead, they introduced a voluntary retirement scheme whereby they pre-paid the salaries of employees who opted for it till their date of retirement. They convinced the unionised workforce to give up their lien on inter-generational employment guarantee. They also conducted competency-based assessment centres for the management staff and eased the exit of those found redundant.

This meant that by 2006, Tata Steel's headcount had shrunk to 38,000. Nearly half the workforce had left voluntarily. The organisation ended up becoming the lowest-cost producer of steel in the world.

This is a great illustration of how companies look at their headcount. There is little value in looking at absolute numbers. The value lies in:

- Evaluating the workforce using standard ratios.
- Benchmarking it against the competition for improvement opportunities.
- Deriving productivity numbers.

Business As Usual Workforce Planning

Let us begin with a recap of how organisations typically used to do workforce planning.

We consider an organisation, say GAL. GAL has revenues of 1000 million rupees and profitability of 10%. The organisation employs 2000 people. It is planning to grow by 5% next year. Will you automatically increase the headcount by 5%?

This is a typical question faced by organisations. We cannot give a straight "yes" or "no" to the 5% headcount increase.

First, we look at the internal measures. We include management span of control as well as teeth-to-tail ratio.

Let us say the GAL has 400 people in management and supervisory roles, and it employs 300 people in business-enabling functions.

Then, the management span of control is 400/2000 = 20%.

Teeth to tail ratio = 300/2000 = 15%.

Are these the right numbers?

First, we use general ratios to understand these numbers. 20% proportion of managers means that there is one manager for every five employees. It is said that the management span of control of 1:7 or more is desirable. The data also says that 15% of employees are in business enabling functions. Is this the right number? Again, it is perceived that any ratio higher than 10% is worth examining.

However, the higher ratios could be unique to the industry. Here is where the benchmarking with competition could help.

GAL has a revenue productivity of 5 million rupees per person. Is this a good number or not? It depends on the industry benchmarks. Another related measure is the percentage of workforce cost on all costs.

The benchmarking would help us decide on the following:

- Is the organisation is overstaffed, understaffed or adequately staffed?
- For the 5% increase in revenues, should there be a proportionate increase in headcount or less?
- Is there a case for increasing management and corporate roles?

This is how basic workforce planning happens. By default, good organisations always try to improve their productivity numbers, and so the final percentage headcount increase is usually arrived at after much debate.

This is the simplest scenario. As long as the organisation is hiring from an existing talent pool and it has a good reputation there, the talent acquisition strategy does not change much either. It becomes another productivity game to improve cycle time, conversion and so forth.

Reality is never so simple. Let us say that the organisation is also looking to grow the business by entering into another line of business. These could be:

- Adjacent products: From instant noodles to instant soups. (Not a big change)
- From services to developing own products (Big change)

- From commodity business to branded business (Big change)

When an organisation goes from noodles to soups, it might need new people and maybe new skills. However, they won't have trouble attracting talent, especially if they are doing well with the noodles.

Let us look at an organisation going from commodity business to branded business. Assume that they are doing it for expansion and not as a turnaround strategy, in which case it is an even bigger change!

Eventually, a bunch of challenges spring up:

- Will it be possible to seed the branded business with people from the commodity business? (Unlikely)
- If we are going to hire from the market, what is the strategy? What companies do we target, and what are the market compensation levels? Where do we peg our salaries?
- What is the Employee Value Proposition (EVP) for new employees? Why should someone who is working in a branded industry leave their job and embrace the opportunity?
- In the scenario of the compensation being higher than that of the existing business, what would be the best way to handle the differences?

Frequently, an organisation in this situation would bring in the seed team from outside at market salaries and then build the business out, in which case, again, the following challenges need to be thought through:

- Successfully onboarding and retaining the core team
- Creating an incentive for growth
- Identifying points of synergy with existing business

The temptation would be to implement the same policies, but to be successful, the organisation needs to be willing to be selectively flexible.

It is possible that in the new product line, they would need to look at the span of control and teeth-to-tail ratio more commensurate with that of a new business.

Therefore, as long as an organisation stays in the business it is used to, workforce planning is about optimising the workforce productivity. Till maturity is attained, newer business lines are consciously held to softer standards, allowing them to grow. At the same time, the HR strategy across the spectrum of processes needs to be examined for necessary customisation.

One of the CXOs we spoke to said that the quality of strategy depends on the kind of questions that the organisation seeks to address. As far as workforce strategy is concerned, the following questions set the base:

1. Do we have the optimal workforce in terms of cost?
2. Do we have the right operating model factoring in outsourcing, remote working and technology?
3. Does the existing workforce provide us with a competitive edge through superior capabilities?
4. Is our workforce motivated to deliver best-in-class performance?

Workforce costs and operating models are highly interconnected. Workforce capabilities are a function of both the quality of hires as well as agility of development. Performance management systems and incentives may deliver competent performance, but it takes motivation to deliver discretionary effort.

Let us explore the core thinking behind the questions listed above.

1. Is pink the colour of workforce optimisation?

To any observer of business, the headlines would be familiar. When an organisation is not doing well compared to its peers, it undertakes a restructuring. One of the first steps typically reads like these:

In October 2019, the Teaneck-based IT services firm Cognizant announced the "2020 Fit for Growth" plan. As a part of the plan, it would lay off 12,000 mid to senior-level employees, of which 5,000 will be reskilled and redeployed. The rest 7,000 will leave the firm by mid-2020.[2]

The 7,000 employees were from the mid and senior levels.

IBM plans to cut about 20% of its European workforce, with the heaviest blow to fall on technology jobs in the UK and Germany, as it prepares to roll out "NewCo," the organisation told labour representatives in the European Union.[3]

Bloomberg reported that the 10,000 job cuts in Europe would be complete by mid-2021.

Often, such announcements are accompanied by statements that, to quote Professor Will Sutton, use words like:[4]

- Adjusting to shifts in demand
- Fitness plan
- "Non-essential" employees
- Offboarded
- Rationalising
- Rebalancing the level of human capital
- Re-engineering plan
- Reduction in force
- Smart sizing
- Special forces philosophy
- "We've decided to go in another direction."

---

2. Swathi Moorthy, "Cognizant's '2020 Fit For Growth' Plan: 7,000 Mid, Senior Level Employees Laid Off," *Moneycontrol*, November 1, 2020, accessed June 18, 2022, https://www.moneycontrol.com/news/business/cognizants-2020-fit-for-growth-plan-7000-mid-senior-level-employees-laid-off-6044001.html.
3. O'Ryan Johnson, "IBM Plans Massive European Layoffs Ahead Of 'NewCo' Spin-off: Report," *CRN*, November 30, 2020, accessed June 18, 2022, https://www.crn.com/news/channel-programs/ibm-plans-massive-european-layoffs-ahead-of-newco-spin-off-report.
4. Bob Sutton, "A Compilation of Euphemisms for Layoffs," *Work Matters*, November 16, 2018, accessed June 18, 2022, https://bobsutton.typepad.com/my_weblog/2008/11/a-compilation-of-euphemisms-for-layoffs.html."

Such phrases are concealed in such announcements and focus primarily on reducing their headcount and letting go of people in thousands. Is this strategic?

Any capable organisation continuously reviews the following elements before taking action on recruitment and promotions:

- Capacity, capability and performance of the workforce
- Benchmarks performance against best-in-class organisations

In this case, how do thousands become redundant overnight?

Layoffs are largely a defensive move intended to shake up an organisation and, at the same time, achieve payroll savings. It is possible that an organisation wants to exit a business that does not make sense and, in the process, has to let go of people. However, in most cases, such layoffs are an admission that the organisation needs to cut costs and rationalise the workforce either as a signal or as part of an expected outcome from a business reorientation. In the short term, the organisation may gain a few dollars and even exit some poor performers. However, tactical layoffs are never a one-off. In the words of Wayne Cascio:[5]

> [C]ompanies that conducted large-scale layoffs significantly underperformed—compared with those that conducted few or no layoffs—with respect to profit margin, return on investment, return on equity, market-to-book ratio and industry-adjusted total return on common stock.
>
> Circumstances do matter, though. Companies that fired people because of financial difficulties fared worse than those that fired offensively, as part of a general restructuring. But neither group fared as well as stable employers that avoided layoffs. In terms of employee productivity, several authors have reported that productivity declines following downsizing, but savings in unit labour costs offset the declines, with market value being unaffected.

5. Wayne F. Cascio, *Employment Downsizing and Its Alternatives* (SHRM Foundation, 2009), https://www.shrm.org/hr-today/trends-and-forecasting/special-reports-and-expert-views/documents/employment-downsizing.pdf.

This has been borne out in my personal experience too. Organisations can be shaken up by layoffs, and then it becomes a band-aid to boost earnings once in a while, even as the lingering effect of ongoing layoffs compromises the ability to innovate.

To prevent the impact of such one-time layoffs, organisations adopt the philosophy called "upgrading", wherein low performers are let go annually. The idea is that continuously reviewing contributions and taking action increases the quality of the workforce with time. This probably is the right idea, assuming that the organisation also upgrades the quality of the incoming workforce in parallel. However, things get muddied when quotas are set, like "Every year we remove our bottom 5%". Without objectively comparable measures, such exercises become political and vitiate the environment.

2. Soup to nuts or core and context?

There exist other workforce strategies that don't quite have the brutality of large-scale layoffs. Here, organisations proactively review their workforce costs and identify different modes of operationalising work. Staying with a Q&A approach, what would be the questions to lead to an optimal workforce?

- How do I decide whether to do the work in-house or use a third party?
- In either case, what gives us the best results in terms of costs and quality?
  - o Full-Time Employees (FTEs)?
  - o Outsource?
  - o Technology like robotics and Robotic Process Automation (RPA)?
- Considering global sourcing and hybrid work model, where should the work be sourced from?

If you create a RACI chart, HR is primarily responsible for hiring FTEs. However, workforce strategy requires a deeper involvement with the entirety of the above three questions.

However, beyond the FTEs, these questions are typically not in the realm of HR alone. Some may look at it and say that to become strategic, HR should take accountability for those aspects, too. Reality is more complex. Operating model decisions are taken based on cost and quality. For cost, finance gets involved, and for assuring the quality, the relevant function gets involved. The moment someone moves from headcount to an outsourced workforce, the line item becomes an expense, so it has to be budgeted for and conclusively proven to be less expensive than having full-time workers do the same. How are these calls taken?

Core or context?

Even into the 90s, some Indian organisations used to have full-time employees handle all work; workers in security, canteen, driving and so on used to be on the organisation's payroll. Today, it would be very difficult (but not impossible) to see organisations have employees who play those roles.

Outsourcing providers gained on such a premise— "It's best to manufacture and sell world-class products. Why burden your bandwidth by running auxiliary services? This is our speciality, and we will cover it for you." Suppose you are working for an organisation making washing machines. It is extremely challenging to establish a causal linkage between the quality of security services to the quality of machines produced. In this case, security services become contextual to running the business. When it is so, would the organisation pay attention to employing security staff, creating a career path and providing for their workplace, benefits and so forth?

Hence, you outsource the security function and make such services contractual on the basis of Service Level Agreements. It is not that this would always result in a lesser cost; however, it does help HR to focus their attention on the workforce that designs and manufactures washing machines.

Traditionally, large manufacturing organisations, especially in the automobile industry, focused on manufacturing a few key parts and then had vendors deliver the components. Large auto manufacturers have an ecosystem of vendors who focus on specific components. The core vs context segregation included not just headcount but the components of the vehicle as well. In this case, the organisation focuses on the critical parts like the engine and is comfortable outsourcing the rest, which helps focus management attention again. The organisation chooses to keep the headcount smaller and of a higher level of capability than a large workforce with many semi-skilled or unskilled workers.

Similarities can be seen in HR processes, too. In the recent past, many elements of the talent acquisition process, like aptitude tests, psychometric testing, background verifications or resume screening, are done by third parties, while the recruiting team focuses on stakeholder management, candidate experience and the selection process efficacy. Here, technology also enables oversight of the outsourced work.

Have you checked the packaging of biscuits to see where they have been manufactured? If not, you would be surprised to find that the product is not manufactured by the organisation at all! They typically have one partner per region to source the finished product from. They essentially take the view that their role is to set the standards and audit for quality. They then focus on branding and marketing.

As everyone knows, Apple devices proudly say, "Designed in California". However, these often have chips made by Samsung and are assembled in China. Does this mean that manufacturing is not core to Apple? Do people buy Apple devices only for the design and not build quality?

The Apple decision retains the logic used by our security vendor earlier. Many organisations can do a great job of hiring and training security folks. However, they choose to let a provider specialising in security do it. In this case, Foxconn or any other partner has developed a deep expertise in bringing high-quality devices to the market. They are able to deliver to the specifications of Apple successfully. Semiconductor performance, manufacturing quality and design are all core to Apple. However, Apple has found a way to operate by bringing together its in-house design and marketing capabilities, Samsung's semiconductor manufacturing capabilities and Foxconn's handset assembly capabilities.

Starting from housekeeping to semiconductor design, organisations do not follow the soup-to-nuts philosophy of doing everything in-house. Transactional processes are not core and are easily outsourced. Even complex electronic manufacturers find a way to bring together capabilities from across different organisations, each of whom could choose to focus on one area.

While core vs context is a fascinating strategy theme, it is not in the scope of this book. However, let me share the classic framework by Geoffrey Moore.[6]

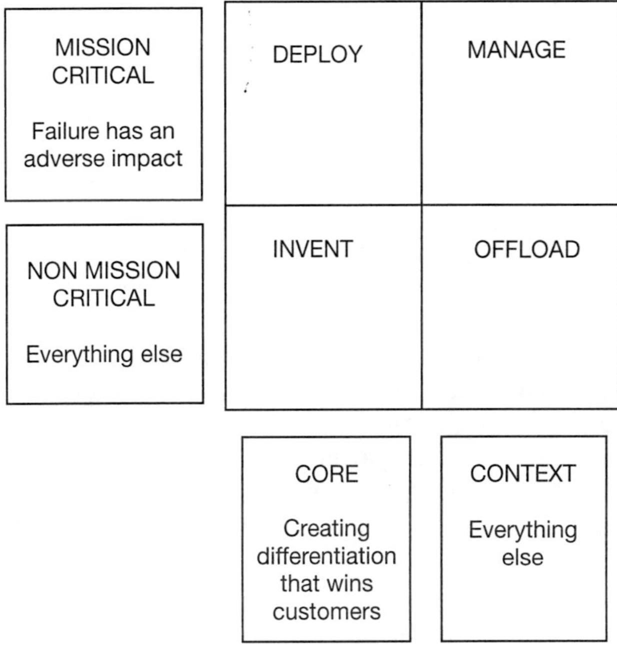

Figure 4.1: Core vs Context

This matrix flows as follows:

The yardstick used here is that core is what creates differentiation with customers; product design and performance do, but payroll and security don't.

- Invent: As an organisation starts with a new invention to create a competitive differentiation. At this point, it is not mission-critical as the business does not rely on it.

6. Geoffrey Moore, "Core, Context, and the Future of Work," *LinkedIn*, August 6, 2021, accessed June 18, 2022, https://www.linkedin.com/pulse/core-context-future-work-geoffrey-moore.

- Deploy: Once the product crosses a threshold, it is important to gain differentiation. The organisation has to deploy the product ahead of the competition. It is core and mission-critical.
- Manage: After a while, competition catches up. The product is still bringing in revenues, so it is on the critical path, but it has become context.
- Offload: After some time, it moves into maintenance or support mode. The organisation can decide to pass it on to a third party for management.

This framework would be familiar to every user of Microsoft Windows. Windows 8, 10 and 11 coexist. Right now, you can buy machines with Windows 10 and 11. However, in time, Windows 11 will be the only version sold with all new machines and a pathway will exist for users to migrate up from Windows 10. However, Microsoft progressively removes support for the earlier versions and works on the next version at the same time. With rapid product development and faster cycles, more and more organisations are choosing to focus on creating competitive advantage by focusing on the Invent and Deploy stages. Based on the capability of their partners, they choose to involve them in the Manage and Offload stages.

The cost angle makes it more attractive. From the 1980s, China and other Asian countries started by offering cost advantages in manufacturing that were not available in the West. With time, the cost advantage became a cost, quality and scale advantage, which is unbeatable. This arrangement helped the organisation and the outsourcing provider focus on their core competencies, leading to mutual success.

This led to the establishment of global supply chains. With time, this concept extended to information technology work and what is now called IT Enabled Services. These essentially started off as extended discretionary workforce services. If an IT function needs a Java programmer for three months, the IT services organisation will be able to provide the same.

On-site contracting received a boost from offshore contracting. For the cost of one contractor in the US, the organisation could actually buy the contract equivalent of three people in India. The cost advantage was unbeatable.

All models evolve with time. Similarly, technology outsourcing has evolved to:

- Buy out deals where the outsourcer takes work and related headcount on their rolls and manages SLAs.
- An organisation has a multi-level arrangement, headcount onsite, captive centre offshore and third-party partners both on-site and offshore. Sophisticated analyses are done to decide who gets to do what kind of work.
- An R&D organisation could use the core vs context and do all their product development set-up in-house but outsource all their application work to a third party.
- IT becomes the context for the outsourcing organisations but core for the outsourcers. Subsequently, more work was outsourced, including customer support, infrastructure management and regular business processes.

This is where the cost equation morphs into one of talent availability. Sure, the relative payroll costs are still in favour of hiring in India. However, suppose you need five hundred engineers in digital technology next year. Given these are skills in high demand, it is going to be very difficult to hire them all in the home country. So, you need to go to a country like India, where there is a higher availability of people with skills. It is not as if the competition for talent is going to be less, but the odds of hiring are better. You can also convert this into a talent development challenge by hiring a few with depth and then building a team around them for mentorship and training.

From a staffing perspective, let us look at software engineering talent alone. The management consulting firm Zinnov has done a lot of work in global development centres. They publish a report on the best countries to set up a centre of excellence on the basis of the availability of talent and its cost.[7]

---

7. Nilesh Thakker et al., "COE Hotspots of the World 2023," *Zinnov*, April 11, 2023, accessed June 18, 2022, https://zinnov.com/global-capability-center-setup-location-analysis-2023-report/.

As you know, China, India and the US are the three big countries in terms of availability of software engineering talent. Many countries in Eastern Europe also have software engineering talent, but not at a similar scale. Thus, Zinnov has broadened the shortlisting criteria to include:

- Talent availability
- Software ecosystem maturity
- Ease of doing business
- Cost analysis

If a client from the US is planning to set up a centre of excellence in software engineering, the top five countries are India, China, Canada, Poland and Mexico.

This is an illustration, and similar analyses and rankings exist for BPS, R&D, product engineering and so on. A few years ago, I was part of an executive team crafting a business case for investing in Israel. Israel is supposed to have outstanding engineering talent, but not at scale. However, the driver for the investment was that Israel's engineering excellence catered to the global market, and thus, such impact can be manifold.

HackerRank, a website that offers coding challenges, has more than 1.5 million developers. They published a ranking in 2016 on the basis of how well developers are able to address the challenges posed. According to this, the top five countries are:[8]

- China
- Russia
- Poland
- Switzerland
- Hungary

Similar lists exist for all industries. For example, the top five countries in garments include not only China, Germany and India

8. Lori Janjigian, "These Are the 10 Best Countries for Computer Programming - and the US Didn't Make the List," *Business Insider*, August 31, 2016, accessed June 18, 2022, https://www.businessinsider.in/enterprise/mobile/these-are-the-10-best-countries-for-computer-programming-and-the-us-didnt-make-the-list/articleshow/53953309.cms.

but also smaller countries like Bangladesh and Vietnam. When you go shopping for clothes next time, just look at the labels on the country of origin. You will be surprised at the variety!

An HR professional needs to understand the dynamics of costs and talent availability in a connected world and use this information when deciding on sites.

This is where global companies face many interesting workforce strategy challenges. I had worked with a software product organisation that had grown on the basis of acquisitions both in the US and elsewhere. The organisation had more than five software development locations in the US and more than twenty locations worldwide. One day, they realised that the real estate costs of maintaining multiple offices were not worth spending. So, they decided to rationalise. The US was simplified into three offices, one for each time zone.

Then, the European operations were consolidated into Prague, and they had offices in Australia, China and India. Would you consider this as:

- Financial strategy to reduce expenses?
- Operational strategy to simplify operations?
- Talent strategy to develop a more homogenous culture?

It is a combination of all three and, at the same time, the decision included looking at the following people-related costs:

- Relative payroll expenses across countries
- Relative skill levels across locations and replaceability
- Proximity to large customers
- Handling the employee actions. Do we offer separation? Relocation? Who should be allowed to continue to work from home?
- How do we transfer knowledge? How do we build a cohesive culture with time?

There you go. You start with what looks like a basic office consolidation exercise, which quickly becomes a strategic workforce exercise.

Location strategies are not necessarily the domain of multinational corporations. Even within India, there are specific hubs from which the companies operate. A quick analysis of the top ten IT companies reveals:

- All of them have operations in Bangalore, NCR, Hyderabad, Chennai and Pune.
- They have also followed a regional strategy, with at least one office in the North, West and East; Mohali, Bhubaneswar and Mumbai, for instance, even when headquartered in the South.
- The emerging smaller locations include Mysore, Coimbatore, Cochin, Trivandrum, Vizag and so on.

Initially, some organisations experimented with a differential salary based on location. While there is consensus upon an allowance based on location, having different basic pay itself based on location has not worked. So, if all centres are at the same cost, what decides where they grow? It should be on the basis of:

- Availability of Skillset: In Bangalore, for instance, you get employees with diverse skill sets.
- Cost of Retention: Because of the availability, most companies have centres in Bangalore. This leads to demand outstripping supply and, hence, a higher employee turnover.
- Proximity to Client Locations/Captive Centre: Organisations, especially in R&D services, have 50-100 member offices in places like Noida or Hyderabad just to align with their clients.
- Physical Infrastructure: For instance, space in Export Processing Zones, though this particular factor is becoming less important in a hybrid work environment.

Do companies plot such parameters before deciding on location? From my experience, they consider these, but the decisions are often made more tactically. A business could be seeded on the basis of its leader's preferred location and build on from there. In one of the organisations I had worked with, the sales and marketing team first got moved from Bangalore to Delhi, as the leader was based there. Then, when the leader shifted out, the employees from Delhi were relocated back to Bangalore on grounds of synergy and colocation. However, it did destabilise the team twice, as some of the core team members decided not to relocate during each move. Government concessions also have an impact on where plants and offices are set up.

3. Do you go to work, or does it come to you? Or both?

As early as 1995, the manufacturing organisation I worked with had e-mail services. The access was limited by time. The office staff were expected to send all files by mail twice daily using a dial-up connection. However, fax machines were still the most popular medium of internal and external communication in the mid-90s. Fax machines were expensive and were installed only in offices. Without widespread internet, laptops were just fancy devices and even landline telephones were used mostly inside office spaces. Thus, work meant coming to the office.

As of 1999, at work, all I had was:

- A desktop
- Landline phone

Basically, work meant office and home was restricted to personal and family time. At home, I used the landline only to inform the office in case I was late or taking an unplanned leave.

But by 2003, I had:

- A mobile phone
- A laptop
- A dial-up internet connection at home

Essentially, in the period between 1995–2000, enterprises were transformed by broadband connections and mobile telephony. Within the next five years, work became something that could be accomplished from anywhere. Soon, people started carrying the ubiquitous blackberries. From home, I could:

- Dial into a conference call
- Attend to work, email and code

Unlike the olden days, when a suitcase was used to carry important papers home, the connected laptop meant work could be done anytime and anywhere. With enhanced bandwidth capacity, you could also attend audio and video conferences from anywhere.

The 1997–98 article "Free Agent Nation" by Daniel Pink[9] explored the possibilities of individual experts freelancing using these technologies. The author later published a book with the same title. This was just before the dotcom wave and presented the freelancing possibilities as an evolution out of corporate life, discussing how people could earn a living by doing what they are good at without putting up with the drudgery of corporate bureaucracy or politics. He also classified the free agents into soloists, temps and microbusinesses.

The reality, of course, hasn't played out as aspirational as Pink thought. The number of successful soloists has, by and large, remained constant, with more and more people joining their ranks as an end-of-career measure. Younger professionals keep moving between consulting and having a full-time job in a freedom vs security trade-off. Temporary workers have become ubiquitous across industries and knowledge work.

While many of us may not remember Pink's book, we would know the phrase coined by New Yorker editor Tina Brown for knowledge workers increasingly pursuing work, "a bunch of free-floating projects, consultancies and part-time bits and pieces while they transacted in a digital marketplace."

The terminology 'gig work' she used has now become widely popular, becoming another theme for the future of work studies. Digital marketplaces exist for knowledge work, but in the recent past, technology has allowed digital marketplaces in commodity work.

Ola Cabs, for instance, is a digital marketplace. Drivers choose their work in competition with other workers on the basis of having the fastest response and proximity. Let us expand

9. Daniel H. Pink, "Free Agent Nation," *Fast Company*, December 31, 1997, accessed June 18, 2022, https://www.fastcompany.com/33851/free-agent-nation.

the concept a little bit. You ask for a ride and get three options based on the following:

- A time window of five to ten minutes
- Newness of vehicle
- Customer rating of the driver

You may be able to pay a small premium based on what you are looking for and not just the time of day. Choices have an impact. They are even more critical when looking at engaging talent through marketplaces. You look at profiles based on experience, relevance and price and make a decision on who to go with a premium or not.

You could say that job portals like LinkedIn or Naukri are 1.0 of a talent marketplace focused on employment.

Portals like GLG and FlexingIT are 2.0 of marketplaces that deal with freelancers.

So, what kind of questions must HR ask when deciding on gig work? At an assignment level, it is easy; "I have this specific deliverable (training/coaching/coding), and I need to find the best person for the same". It is more of a challenge when taking the long view.

- How are we going to staff this function? Will we set aside a certain portion of work on a flexible basis?
- If so, what areas would these be? Will it be on the basis of expertise?
- Would we identify specific people for the same and treat them as preferred partners?
- What is the premium I am willing to pay not just for quality but also for reduced costs? If I find more competent people in Bangladesh than in India, then am I good to go with them?

In HR, of course, this is nothing new. Most L&D functions have staff for management and administration, while the training itself is done by preferred partners. Compensation benchmarking surveys are done by consulting organisations against organisation employees.

However, technology makes some work locations neutral, and that is where talent marketplaces come into play. A friend of mine has a start-up in the healthcare space in the US, and he gets his web development done out of Lithuania. The digital marketplace expands choices and opens access to a global audience but also increases complexity.

Small organisations typically used to hire who they can and improvise. This does not seem to be the constraint that it used to be. One of my friends runs a mid-sized firm in New York. His development team of 20 sits out of Trivandrum. Another friend who I have mentioned above runs an even smaller start-up focusing on healthcare. He found his developers in Lithuania through the internet.

Many of the illustrations so far focus on two basic questions:

- Employee or contractor?
- Where should either be located?

Telecommuting/teleworking is a phrase coined by Jack Milles in the early 1970s. While working as Director for interdisciplinary research at the University of Southern California, he began formal research on telecommuting and teleworking, terms he coined in 1973. He led a lot of studies on the present and future impact of information technology and created standards by which major telecommuting projects are judged.

The basic principle of telecommuting is that work is something you do, not travel to, which can be rephrased as "Work is what we do, not where we are".

In the initial days, there was hardly any work that could be done without commuting to work unless it was externally oriented, such as a field sales job or telesales.

It is not unusual to see sales heads of even mid-sized firms operate out of their home if it is closer to the markets than the operational HQ.

From there, with the advances in communications, pretty much any work that could be done from an office could be done from home as well. However, this became a work-life choice, especially for women employees or those having caregiver responsibilities.

In India, as the tech sector grew, the commuting time increased. In the 2000s, MNC product companies encouraged work from home options. After all, when the sponsors in the US are comfortable with having teams in faraway India, why should it bother the Indian managers if their teams work from home in the same city? Work from home options were available and were opted for based on specific personal needs. However, a default work from home mode was not encouraged for full-time employees. Informal estimates suggest only about 5% to 10% of total work time was handled from home annually.

The 2020 pandemic changed the dynamics, with almost everyone with a staff job being forced to work from home. From an experiment, this became the only way of accomplishing work with safety.

Information technology and technology-enabled organisations to grow their business during the pandemic. TCS, for example:

- Grew its top line by 3.5%
- Retained its profitability
- Added 40,000 employees

This was accomplished by more than 90% of employees working from home. TCS physically did not have a few big offices but nearly 400,000 individual rooms wherein employees were seated in front of a computer. Thus, they were successfully able to adapt to this model overnight. This is not to say that all organisations should become telecommuting ones, the more interesting takeaway is the TCS plan of 25 by 25.[10]

What is this 25 by 25?

To quote *Business Today*, "By this model, the company believes that by 2025, only 25 percent of its associates will need to work out of facilities at any point of time. Also, the employees will not need to spend more than 25 percent of their time at work."

10. Nevin John, "75% TCS Staff to Work from Home by 2025, R&D to Occupy Vacant Office Space," *Business Today*, November 20, 2020, accessed June 18, 2022, https://www.businesstoday.in/latest/corporate/story/75-tcs-staff-to-work-from-home-by-2025-r-d-to-occupy-vacant-office-space-279170-2020-11-20.

This is expected to save costs on office rentals, commuting and other infrastructure-related charges. While TCS has outlined a bold plan, other companies are looking at this model as well. Increasingly, the term "hybrid workplace" has come into mainstream conversations. The related strategic questions are:

- What percentage of the workforce do you have in offices currently? Is that required?
- If you can reduce, what end-stage percentage would you like to have at any point in the office?
- What would be the policies governing the hybrid workplace?
    - o Should everyone work for a set number of days at the office?
    - o Would some be marked as full-time office employees and others as flexible?
    - o How would you create a consistent workplace culture when not everyone is present all five days of the week in the same place?
    - o How do you foster collaboration in a hybrid model?
    - o How do you enable managers to be comfortable with the new model without being overburdened?

Many organisations moved to flex-time in the 90s, by which employees could choose to arrive and go based on their biorhythms as long as they were in the office during a certain time (10 am to 4 am) and put in 40–45 hours at work. Now, we are talking about flextime and flex place. Anyone going for the hybrid workplace would be advised to go through the Microsoft research on "The Next Great Disruption is Hybrid workplace—Are we ready?" whose key observations include:[11]

- Flexible workplace is here to stay
- Talent is everywhere in a hybrid workplace

To quote from the report, "Remote job postings on LinkedIn increased more than five times during the pandemic, and

11. "The Next Great Disruption Is Hybrid Work—Are We Ready?," *Microsoft*, March 22, 2021, accessed June 18, 2022, https://www.microsoft.com/en-us/worklab/work-trend-index/hybrid-work.

people are taking notice. Forty-six percent of remote workers we surveyed are planning to move to a new location this year because they can now work remotely. People no longer have to leave their desk, house or community to expand their career, and it will have profound impacts on the talent landscape."

This, in turn, brings out more complicated questions for HR. The remit was to ensure the safety of employees at work and commute all along. If more and more work is going to be done from home, an organisation has to put up with some of the expenses. More importantly, what about workplace safety? Will domestic violence, for instance, be considered within the scope of companies? During the pandemic, Unilever rolled out a set of initiatives to support women employees to help handle the problem for their employees as well as extended staff. The hub and spoke of office model is illustrated below:

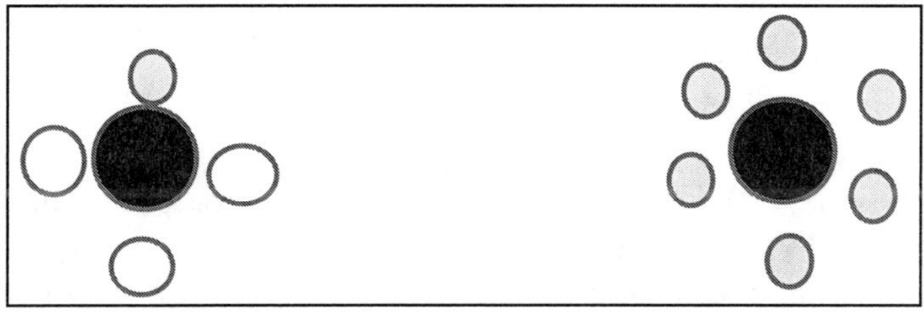

Figure 4.2: Hub and Spoke Office Model

Here, the black box stands for the head office, white for secondary offices and grey for a satellite or home office. Traditionally, companies were not bothered about the grey part, which was optional. However, post-pandemic, many companies are experimenting with reducing their office footprint so that the office is a place for collaboration. Work happens simultaneously in home offices as well as the head office. There need not be many small offices unless the customer needs it.

The future could be a series of satellite offices with a core to which people can come around the clock of their choice.

4. The Automation Wave

So far, we have been asking questions about the kind of work, the type of workforce and the nature of the workplace. That leaves us with another question that is becoming increasingly relevant and could be a primary fork.

For this work, should I employ people or use automation?

Robotics in manufacturing work has been prevalent for more than 40 years. In fact, as early as 1962, General Motors had started using robots on the shop floor. Initially, robots were used for mechanical jobs like holding parts, moving, welding and such.

In the 80s, it was even felt that since robots can work continuously and do not form unions, a group of robots could entirely man the factory of the future, with the cost of technology being offset by increased productivity. That hypothesis did not really come through. However, with the reduced cost of technology, Industry 4.0 is here. This is based on technology:

- Internet of things
- Mobile devices
- Advanced human-machine interfaces
- Smart sensors

It could be said that the adoption of technology on the shop floor is a far bigger decision than just workforce-related. In countries like Germany, there is a sophisticated use of workplace automation. For a long time, China was relying on relatively lower labour costs. However, these have increased with time, and there is a shortage of people willing to work on the shop floor. The adoption of robots has accelerated in China in the recent past. One-third of the robots being installed are in China. It is estimated that 20 million or 8.5% of the global manufacturing workforce will be replaced with robots by 2030.[12]

It is not just the shop floor. The warehouse also has become a playground for custom-built robots. Amazon typically used to have people classify items, put them in containers and move them around in warehouses. This meant that many could be walking 10-12 miles a day carrying loads, the kind of work that impacts their wellbeing.

---

12. "Robots 'to Replace up to 20 Million Factory Jobs' by 2030," *BBC News*, June 26, 2019, accessed June 18, 2022, https://www.bbc.com/news/business-48760799.

A wide adoption of purpose-designed robots has meant that both people who load items into boxes and those who stack them onto shelves are now stationary, with robots doing the heavy lifting. This has definitely reduced the risk of workplace accidents. At the same time, it is felt that it has increased the workload on the individuals to pick and stack faster, leading to different kinds of accidents. Eventually, though, the warehouse might end up as a highly automated workplace which is very productive and, at the same time, reduces the number of employees. Amazon was even said to be piloting delivery by drones.[13]

Robots are increasing on the Indian shop floor, too. According to an article in the *Mint*:[14]

- Mondelez India has a unit that can pack 6300 chocolate bars per minute.
- Bosch's factory near Bangalore has co-bots (robots working with humans).
- M&M has a "robotic weld line" at its factory in Nashik, which now caters to many of its products.
- A Trivandrum-based organisation, Genrobotics, has developed a robot to clean the sewers, hopefully eliminating people from doing this dangerous work.

Industry 4.0 is a theme that is playing out across physical locations like warehouses, factories, hospitals and even restaurants. That is not to say white-collar work won't be impacted. The *World Economic Forum's* Future of Jobs Survey 2020 reports that the following white-collar jobs have diminished the most in the US in the previous decade.[15]

---

13. Jason Del Rey, "Amazon's Warehouse Robots and Their Complicated Impact on Workers," *Vox*, December 11, 2019, accessed June 18, 2022, https://www.vox.com/recode/2019/12/11/20982652/robots-amazon-warehouse-jobs-automation.
14. Leslie D'Monte, "Robots Are Coming for India's Shop Floors," *Mint*, September 10, 2019, accessed June 18, 2022, https://www.livemint.com/technology/tech-news/robots-are-coming-for-india-s-shop-floors-1568135022807.html.
15. "The Future of Jobs Report 2020," *World Economic Forum*, October 9, 2023, accessed June 18, 2022, https://www.weforum.org/publications/the-future-of-jobs-report-2020.

In descending order, these include:

1. Computer operators
2. Executive secretaries and administrative assistants
3. Word processors and typists
4. Switchboard operators and answering services
5. Machine feeders and off bearers
6. Telemarketers
7. File clerks

As can be noticed, there has been a significant decline in clerical roles having to do with data entry, scheduling, taking notes and so forth. This is just the prelude to the reengineering of administrative work.

Chatbots came first. These are the ubiquitous pop-ups that you see when you open any commercial site. Often given a name and image to humanise, these handle the first-level queries anyone will have. They automate the administrative work handled by customer support organisations.

When you are writing a mail on Gmail, you will find that the app completes a sentence as soon as you have keyed in a few words. This is conversational AI that learns from human mail exchanges and tries to predict.

We also have applications like Amazon Alexa that are voice-based and can have simple conversations. AI-enabled bots have transformed customer support across many verticals. Then comes RPA (Robotic Process Automation), which is a different usage of technology.

Let us take recruitment. Automation has made sure that a resume is captured digitally and can be shared electronically with hiring managers. However, there still is a human interface required to:

- Map resume to the job indent.
- Screen the resume (where technology is not implemented).
- Share the shortlist with the hiring managers.

- Schedule face-to-face discussions, including tests and interviews.
- Make travel and stay arrangements for outstation candidates.
- Communicate with candidates after the process.
- Fix compensation and release the offer letter.
- Trigger background verification actions.
- Stay in touch with candidates till they join.

The existing process has been made digital. However, it still needs human intervention to navigate the steps. Of course, most of this work is done by outsourced agencies, thereby reducing the cost.

This is where Robotic Process Automation comes into play. RPA relies on a set of tools that automate repetitive administrative processes. RPA tools can work across multiple IT systems. For instance, a RPA can:

- Read the job requirements from the recruitment system.
- Source from job portals for resumes that fit the requirements.
- Store these profiles in a folder for access.
- Check for suitable slots and schedule an interview.
- Trigger background verification.
- Communicate with selected candidates and address their generic queries.
- Collect documents required for joining.

RPA can accomplish most of these steps with some customisation and much less human interaction, making the cost of the process lower. More importantly, the error rates are crushed because the machine does not get bored or tired.

Initially, a rule-based RPA will have a lot of exceptions that get escalated for human interaction. With time, recruiters can enhance the capacity of RPA, enabling them to handle more strategic work.

From a workforce planning perspective, the continuum for many tasks seems to be:

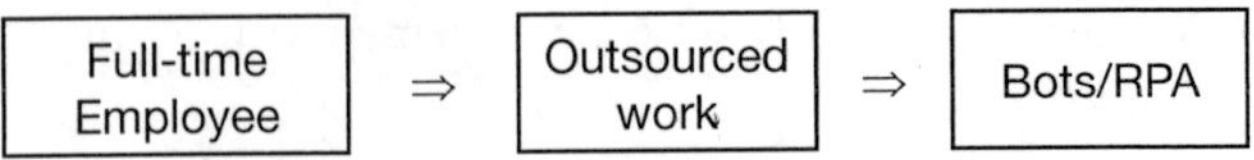

Figure 4.3: Task Deployment Continuum

For a comprehensive workforce strategy, one needs to be asking the following questions on a regular basis:

- Is the given process being handled at the optimum cost-quality ratio?
- Is it possible to enhance both by leveraging technology?
- If we leverage technology, what are the jobs that would still be handled by people?
- How do we redesign work after implementing technology?

Workforce Capacity: From Homogeneity to Hybrid

Advances in business models have resulted in organisations having a hybrid workforce with FTEs, outsourced workforce and offshore work.

Aggregators have helped to unlink work from a job and parcel it out on an assignment basis. In the past year, the emergence of gig work has been subsumed by the hybrid work location, wherein in addition to flexible time, employees are being encouraged to have flexible workplaces and schedules where the office may be a hub of work but not the centre.

Chatbots and RPA are helping reimagine what work needs to be done by humans on an ongoing basis.

We are at an interesting time as many of these trends are becoming mainstream. A simple headcount planning exercise has now become complex, spanning countries, time zones and technologies.

However, it is not a smooth one-way transition. Gig workers for companies like Uber have been organising and requesting for their welfare. Courts across the world, from California to the UK to France, have judged Uber drivers to be employees requiring benefits and healthcare, not just transactional gig workers.

Legislation and worker rights will continue to influence the organisation's decisions on the workforce.

An Organisation's Experiment

One of the MNCs operating in a documentation-heavy environment had a typical problem in one of its centres in India. The back office set-up required its associates to:

- Extract individual pages from bulk PDF files, rename them as per team requirements and segregate them based on the type of notices.
- Schedule appointments for visa interviews and communicate with the applicants.
- Monitor several websites for changes in the regulatory environment.

This work is critical to the clients. The representation has to be timely and accurate. The organisation had graduates manning these processes. However, they were faced with high attrition.

The organisation then decided to widen the pool of hiring. Instead of offering jobs in a routine manner, they wanted to take work to people who needed it the most. To begin with, they identified the skills required to perform these roles. These were simple enough:

- Ability to read, write and talk in English
- Positive attitude

Given that the work involved people working alone, these were visualised as work from home jobs. The organisation piloted the hiring of differently-abled people to perform the documentation roles. They looked out for people in the smaller villages and towns around the city that have good internet connectivity. The firm worked through employee references as well as leads on deserving candidates from NGOs.

In the initial phase of this program, the organisation could hire and train 20+ qualified differently-abled individuals with hearing impairment, speech challenges and other physical disabilities. Selected candidates were trained in the activities to be performed. The firm also conducted a series of upskilling programs to enhance their skillset, knowledge and aptitude. Each of them was also assigned a peer coach to demonstrate the allocated tasks and administer review and feedback to the individual performing the role.

Once they got past the initial challenges, they were able to learn at a fast pace driven by focus and determination. The initial success has encouraged the organisation to expand the program in the coming days.

This has helped the organisation to:

- Eliminate the impact of employee attrition on client satisfaction.
- Take jobs to those who will find it valuable, creating a more committed team that is not easily put off by some of the repetitive but critical tasks.
- Adapt the work from home model effectively.
- The firm has expanded the D&I concept to the differently abled and leveraged it effectively.

This is a great illustration of how an organisation can use multiple trends (globalisation, hybrid work, diversity and inclusivity) to imaginatively enhance its workforce capacity.

5
Workforce Capability: Talent Quality

In the last chapter, we looked at workforce capacity, which was about having a workforce at the best possible location with an appropriate model of engagement and at optimum cost. Having the best workforce capacity is the first pillar of a winning HR strategy. It needs to be accentuated by workforce capability, which acts as a multiplier of capacity.

Workforce capability is a function of two broad themes:

- Organisation capability
- Employee capability

These are not mutually exclusive. There is a significant body of work around both themes. To quote from the HBR article by Dave Ulrich and Norm Smallwood in 2004:[1]

> These capabilities—the collective skills, abilities, and expertise of an organisation—are the outcome of investments in staffing, training, compensation, communication, and other human resources areas. They represent the ways that people and resources are brought together to accomplish work. They form the identity and personality of the organisation by defining what it is good

1. Norm Smallwood, "Capitalizing on Capabilities," *Harvard Business Review*, August 1, 2014, accessed June 18, 2022, https://hbr.org/2004/06/capitalizing-on-capabilities.

> at doing and, in the end, what it *is*. They are stable over time and more difficult for competitors to copy than capital market access, product strategy, or technology. They aren't easy to measure, so managers often pay far less attention to them than to tangible investments like plants and equipment, but these capabilities give investors confidence in future earnings. Differences in intangible assets explain why, for example, upstart airline JetBlue's market valuation is twice as high as Delta's, despite JetBlue's having significantly lower revenues and earnings.

In the article, they go on to outline eleven capabilities of well-managed organisations, including talent, learning, leadership and so forth. The capability for any organisation is a combination of:

1. Investments in tangible resources like technology, infrastructure, etc.
2. Processes that underpin the organisation.
3. Investments in intangible resources, which is mainly people.

For this chapter, we will skip the first two and focus on the capabilities delivered through people and people processes. What are the typical capabilities delivered through people in an organisation?

Sales and Business Development

- Hunting Capability: To go out and get new business opportunities.
- Farming Capability: Continue generating revenues from existing businesses.
- Branding Capability: To differentiate the work being done by the organisation from others.
- Product Development Capability: To research and sense market requirements and movements and proactively develop products that cater to the same. Depending on business strategy, move into areas of higher margins.

- Customer Service Capability: Provide a responsive service to existing clients so that they continue to be satisfied users.

Manufacturing/Production

- Quality: Develop a product of the desired quality.
- Cost: Ensure the product is manufactured at or below the target cost.
- Speed: Align the production and inventory to market needs.

These are essential for all business organisations. Enabling these would be the ability to manage cash flow, working capital, pricing and the talent supply chain.

You might look at these functions and see an organisation chart. The sales organisation, for instance, would have:

- Sales executives (Everyone refers to them as hunters, but nobody designates them as one!)
- Account managers (Farmers)
- Brand and marketing specialists
- Customer support executive (Not always part of the sales organisation)

Every mature organisation has these roles as well as job descriptions, KRAs and so on. However, with the same HR infrastructure, companies deliver very different performances. Some are market leaders, while some are laggards.

JDs and KRAs identify the capacity and are not different for roles across companies. Who plays these roles and how they play can deliver very different capabilities, resulting in different results.

Let us look at the Indian Premier League in Cricket. The IPL is, in some ways, a controlled talent experiment. All eight teams (as of 2021) are provided with the same salary budget of 85 crore rupees. Teams are allowed to choose between eighteen to twenty-five players. All teams can field a maximum of four overseas players in a match. The resources on the field are the same twenty overs per team.

All teams have batters, bowlers, keepers and all-rounders. So, their JDs, KRAs and budgets are similar. Given that, as of 2021, across thirteen seasons, you would think that each of the eight teams would have won at least once. In practice, though, the following teams have won:

- Mumbai Indian: 5 times
- Chennai Super Kings: 3 times
- Kolkata Knight Riders: 2 times
- Hyderabad Teams: 2 times
- Rajasthan Royals: 1 time

Three teams (Punjab Kings, Delhi Daredevils/Capitals, Royal Challengers Bangalore) are yet to win a title, while just three teams have won 77% of all titles.

This, obviously, is because they have been able to leverage very similar resources more effectively. In other words, with the same capacity, they have derived greater capability.

TALENT ACQUISITION FROM THE MARKETPLACE

Organisations traditionally focus on the following two processes for improving capability:

1. Scan the talent marketplace and choose the best available talent. Within this, the two approaches are:

   (a) Hire early and develop from within.

   (b) Hire across the board and assimilate.

2. Develop capabilities required for business through training, mentoring and coaching.

Competency frameworks, as seen in an earlier chapter, act as the linchpin for these processes.

The traditional approach looks at the outside world as a dynamic marketplace and the organisation as a fixed entity. Employees are promoted when positions open up at a senior level. However, peer-level vacancies are mostly filled by recruits from outside. If there is a vacancy in market research, for example, the organisation will hire from the market even though qualified candidates are available in the analytics function.

The emerging practice is to treat an organisation's talent as an internal marketplace, which is the first port of call and go to the external marketplace only if the internal marketplace is inadequate. The internal marketplace is synchronised with the external market.

The effectiveness of the synchronised marketplace relies on

- Using position-specific hiring mechanisms with predictive validity.
- Management of internal talent in line with strategic expectations.
- Learning and development to continuously develop talent.

Compensation and performance management align capability to performance. We shall be looking at workforce performance subsequently.

Let us first examine the strategic questions of talent acquisition.

1. What is our primary mode of acquisition? Hire at entry levels and develop or hire laterals opportunistically?
2. How do we ascertain that the people we are hiring are of the desired quality?

Talent acquisition is generally split across two domains in most organisations.

- Campus Hiring: ITI craftsmen, diploma holders, Engineering graduates, Chartered Accountants and MBAs are all hired from campus/entry level. Typically, campus recruits are hired on the basis of potential. Since campus hires can join only at particular times, campus recruitment is more medium-term and needs mature development processes. It is also a process that needs a certain volume of hiring to deliver a return on investment.
- Lateral Recruitment: The organisation goes out and hires from the market based on the urgency of requirements, skill availability and functional expertise that comes along with experience. While potential is important, relevant prior experience is critical. In some companies,

leadership hiring is carved out from lateral recruitment to align better with sensitivities.

GROWING CAPABILITIES FROM WITHIN

Consulting organisations like McKinsey and Bain follow the entry-level hiring model extensively. There was no pool of management consultants to hire from 75 years ago. The cadre has to be created, leading them to the campuses. Subsequently, these companies also differentiated themselves as firms that offer extremely bright and hard-working young professionals who analyse and provide effective solutions. A partner with McKinsey once told the New Yorker that they are the biggest employers of Rhodes and Marshall scholars on the planet outside the US Government![2] The value lies not so much in domain knowledge, which is what experience brings, but in an ability to look at a problem with fresh eyes mentored with expertise from work done for many clients in similar situations.

Consider the IT services industry in the 1990s and 2000s. Going into the 90s, India did not have a pool of software developers, which meant that there was a great demand for people with experience in the beginning. A running joke in Bangalore was that an employee would attend walk-in interviews over the weekend and resign by Monday, as he would have joined a new organisation. When the demand for a skill is high, poaching by paying higher salaries is not a sustainable strategy, especially when everyone starts playing it. In such a situation, it makes sense to grow your own talent by investing in development rather than paying a hiring premium.

So, organisations like TCS, Infosys and Wipro primarily hired from the campuses. Since the American work visa needed a four-year qualification, the focus was on engineering. The industry was:

- Growing anywhere between 50% to 100% annually.
- Nearly 50% of the workforce had less than two years' work experience.

2. Nicholas Lemann, "The Kids in the Conference Room," *The New Yorker*, October 11, 1999, accessed June 18, 2022, https://www.newyorker.com/magazine/1999/10/18/the-kids-in-the-conference-room.

Even twenty years back, one could see ads from some leading colleges talking about how a certain organisation has hired 1000 (yes, one thousand) students. How does one run fast-growing organisations by hiring freshers in thousands?

This, in turn, was enabled by running large academies or the terminology that became popular "universities". Freshers were selected not for their coding abilities but for their analytical skills. Then, they were taught facets of coding (while being paid for it) and were assigned to projects. This isn't new. For decades, National Defence Academy, Indian Administrative Services and Tata Administrative Services have been running on this model.

When is this model most effective?

1. When a new cadre has to be created. IAS or NDA inherited existing mechanisms, but with selective hiring year after year, they have successfully created a cadre of qualified officers.
2. There is a demand-supply mismatch between opportunities and the available talent pool.
3. The job is standardised and repeatable. This helps the organisation to define the competence and performance thresholds and control using it.

However, by the time MNC consulting organisations started setting up their office in India, the available talent pool had grown from the initial days. Accenture, Cap Gemini and so forth were able to bootstrap on the basis of primarily hiring an experienced workforce. As established companies, they had to hit the ground running and start delivering from day one, which was possible by hiring skilled employees. With time, the talent supply chain matured to accommodate both entry-level and lateral hires.

Almost all mature organisations have a campus hiring program. The percentage hired from campus could vary anywhere from 5% to 30% of total hiring numbers annually. The percentages are higher when:

- The management and leadership of the organisation have primarily joined from the campus.

- The talent development systems are in place, including not just the initial training but the coaching required to enable the potential of the young recruit.
- The business growth is primarily organic.
- The business is built on one primary capability—consulting, accounting, legal and so on.

Let us expand on these points. Hindustan Unilever takes pride in having strong talent management processes and developing leadership from within. Of their leadership team of ten people, eight have experience in excess of twenty years and one has more than fifteen years. A few of them have been with HUL right out of campus.[3] The organisation firmly believes in growing talent from within and would like to attract young people. The organisation also has a famed system to identify high-potential talent and groom them through assignments to leadership positions.

When the business growth is organic, it is possible for in-house talent to go ahead and take up business responsibilities for adjacencies. For a HUL person, it is possible to go from cosmetics to food products, for instance. However, when an organisation is going from infrastructure to digital, it may need to hire a new line of talent all the way from leadership positions.

Any large organisation can set up training academies for freshers and get them to leverage the existing body of knowledge using knowledge management mechanisms. Once such an academy is in place, it is a question of arriving at the numbers needed for business the next year and going ahead with the hiring plan.

It is also said that homegrown workforces are more loyal and result in a cohesive culture. The flip side, of course, is that they tend to be internally focused, especially when successful and struggle with rapid change. We can see more of that subsequently.

So, any organisation needs to decide on a strategy for talent acquisition at the entry level. The proportions will vary based on the organisation's capability to invest and develop them.

---

3. "Our Leadership," *Unilever*, September 18, 2023, accessed June 18, 2022, https://www.hul.co.in/our-company/our-leadership/.

Further on, the organisation also needs to ensure there are enough retention mechanisms to retain them for a longer time.

Organisations with good training programs run the risk of becoming hunting grounds for other organisations. It would take at least a year for an entry-level employee to be fully productive. Having made the investment, the organisation needs to recoup the investment by retaining them. The following approaches exist in India:

- Have a legal agreement signed with the employee through which they agree to stay with the organisation for a 12 to 18-month period. These act as deterrents, though the legal defensibility of such mechanisms is a moot point. Also, they create a perception that the employee should look forward to leaving after that period!
- Have a part of compensation tied to the employee completing 18 months. This is like deferred compensation, which has the effect of tying the employee to the organisation. This is easier to administer.

In any case, organisations recruit at entry levels with a buffer for attrition and so balance the losses out. The other challenge of late has been the rapid changes in the business environment, which makes campus recruitment a clunky process. In 2019, for instance, many organisations made job offers on campus. However, the onset of the COVID-19 pandemic meant that some of such organisations were in no position to add new recruits. This, in turn, led to some rescinding offers or rescheduling the joining date. While eventually, most organisations end up honouring their offers, the unpredictability of the joining date reduces employment stickiness.

HIRE PRE-TRAINED TALENT

When an organisation needs a person with some experience and skill, it looks at the available talent in the market and selects the most eligible candidate that it can afford. This 'just in time' process or hiring is termed lateral hiring.

More mature organisations model the following as their need to hire is in larger numbers:

- Projected growth rate
- Headcount needed to service the growth
- New headcount to be hired = ((Headcount needed factoring in for growth)- (Present headcount) + (Attrition rate* Present headcount)) * (1- productivity improvement percent)

We are merging a few paradigms here:

1. Headcount forecast
2. Forecast to protect against attrition
3. Reduce the numbers attained by the desired productivity improvement. So, if we need to hire 100, adjusted for a 5% improvement in productivity, we shall hire 95 new employees.

How do we break it down into levels?

1. Identify the role for each vacancy.
2. Decide on the percentage of positions to be filled by promotions and internal movement.
3. Arrive at the final number based on each level.
4. Decide on whether every attrition needs to be replaced and, if replaced, by someone at the same level of experience or someone with a lower level of experience.

Suppose an organisation needs 20 additional branch managers:

- They review the pipeline and find eight internal candidates who are presently assistant branch managers and can be made managers.
- Then, they need to only hire 12 branch managers from outside. Of course, there will be a vacancy for assistant branch managers, which will again be an independent decision to hire or promote. When they keep going on this path, they will get to entry-level requirements.
- Suppose there is a vacancy for three branch managers arising out of attrition. A similar process of decision-making is arrived at. However, the hiring is made only after the employee actually quits.

ATTRACTING QUALITY TALENT

We just saw how the capacity is arrived at and the decisions taken leading to promotions and external hiring.

As far as talent acquisition is concerned, most organisations measure the following:

- Number of new hires from each channel (Consultants, job boards, referrals and so on)
- Cost of selection from each channel
- Offer conversion rates from each channel

These are measures that still indicate the efficiency with which new capacity is added. What about capability? How do we know whether, accounting for all new hires, the organisational capability has improved, declined or stayed the same?

It is not unusual for organisations to look at the quality of hire. However, the measures used for the same are typically:

- Early attrition rate
- First-year attrition
- First year performance review

These are post-hiring measures, and there really seems to be no way of objectively measuring the quality of hire, much less capability. In their absence, many fast-growing organisations are filled with people saying that while they passed a tough test, the newcomers are having it easy.

In a discussion, I remember hearing a senior consultant from one of the Big 4 say that they grow headcount to the extent they can be developed. So, if one principal can groom four consultants a year, they won't hire eight consultants. This could compromise the business, but they were willing to do it for the sake of people's capability.

A proxy measure most often used is the quality of institutions or organisations the candidates are hired from. For campus hiring, organisations try to hire from the most reputed institutions. If in technology, it has to be a few leading IITs and if management, a few leading IIMs plus three to four other institutions. The US has its Ivy League colleagues, as does every country. The quality of the institution is taken as the surrogate for capability.

So, the first strategic choice is made by organisations to attract talent from top colleges. For that, they need to have policies and practices that enhance the attraction to prospective college hires. The better the reputation, the more the ability to hire top students from top colleges. According to a Universum survey in 2020, the following five organisations were rated as the best ones to join from campuses in India:[4]

- Google
- Apple
- Deloitte
- Microsoft
- Amazon

Similarly, HUL, McKinsey and Bain are rated as the best employers post management qualification.

So, many organisations that want to grow their talent from within invest in becoming the employer of choice on relevant campuses.

This leads us to two of the big strategic questions for HR heads:

1. Are you selecting based on past credentials or future performance?
2. What do you do to attract such talent?
3. How do you select for performance?

One of the organisations I had worked with had very clear specifications for the kind of talent it would hire from campuses. We were very particular about the campuses, the performance in high school, intermediate and college, followed by performance in the analytical test. When the organisation grew, there was a need to expand the hiring pool. However, many managers were not comfortable with expanding the pool as they felt it would compromise quality.

There was a study launched to identify the drivers of performance. Historical data was taken on the campus recruit's:

4. "Country Rankings," *Universum*, April 29, 2022, accessed June 18, 2022, https://universumglobal.com/rankings/india/.

- College
- Academic performance of the candidate in the school
- Academic performance of the candidate in college
- Performance in aptitude test
- Performance in tests after initial training

These parameters were correlated against on-the-job performance for statistical validity. What we found was that almost all pre-selection indicators that were perceived as being critical were not statistically valid. All selected candidates underwent a boot camp for three months, and their confirmation of the organisation's roles was based on their performance on a test that assessed them on their learnings in the past three months. This score correlated with their final performance.

The logic is quite straightforward. Their performance in school or college is from writing exams in an academic setting. The test after selection was in an organisational setting, testing them against the standards expected at work. Hence, this correlated well.

HIRING QUALITY → HIGHER PERFORMANCE

The last decade started with an interesting research finding that was shared by Google. In an interview with the *New York Times*, their then-HR head, Laszlo Bock, said that:[5]

> We found that brainteasers are a complete waste of time ... How many golf balls can you fit into an airplane? How many gas stations in Manhattan? A complete waste of time. They don't predict anything. They serve primarily to make the interviewer feel smart.

Candidates' past academic performance wasn't predictive either, Bock said—a stunning admission for an organisation that's notoriously stuffed to the gills with PhDs.

"Google famously used to ask everyone for a transcript and GPA and test scores, but we don't anymore, unless you're just a

5. Thomas L. Friedman, "How to Get a Job at Google," *The New York Times*, February 22, 2014, accessed June 18, 2022, https://www.nytimes.com/2014/02/23/opinion/sunday/friedman-how-to-get-a-job-at-google.html.

few years out of school," Bock said. "We found that they don't predict anything."

After two or three years, your ability to perform at Google is completely unrelated to how you performed when you were in school, because the skills you required in college are very different," Bock added further. "You're also fundamentally a different person. You learn and grow; you think about things differently."

The bottom line, he said, is that Google's earlier hiring practices simply weren't effective. When Google studied its employees' performance and compared it to how the same employees scored in interviews, there was no correlation.

Such findings made organisations re-examine their hiring specifications. Google, for instance, started using competency-based hiring more extensively.

More such analysis has led to organisations not insisting on a four-year college degree for being considered for employment. Not just Google but also Apple, Siemens and Netflix do not insist on a four-year degree like they used to. A lot of hiring happens for programming jobs, and these organisations would rather hire on the basis of demonstrated coding skills.

This is in line with published research, "The Validity and Utility of Selection Methods in Personnel Psychology: Practical and Theoretical Implications of 100 Years of Research Findings" by Hunter and Schmidt, a 2016 paper.[6] They reviewed research from across the past 100 years and identified what usually passes for hiring specifications like:

- Educational background
- Years of experience
- Unstructured interview performance

These do not have a high predictive validity. The five methods that do are:

6. Frank L. Schmidt and John E. Hunter, "The Validity and Utility of Selection Methods in Personnel Psychology: Practical and Theoretical Implications of 85 Years of Research Findings.," *Psychological Bulletin* 124, no. 2 (September 1, 1998): 262–74.

- Work sample tests
- Cognitive ability tests
- Structured interviews
- Job knowledge tests
- Personality questionnaires

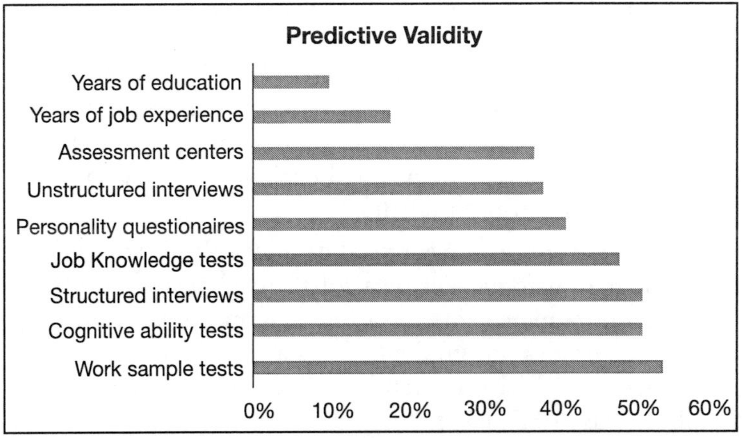

Figure 5.1: Predictive Validity of Hiring Methods

Directionally, a lot has changed in campus hiring in India too. Most campus jobs are for programming jobs. While a few organisations test the aptitude of the candidate, almost everyone tests the programming skills of candidates. Structured interviewing is also becoming more prevalent.

Most organisations have a GPA cut-off of 7 or 8 while shortlisting candidates. However, as much as the academic percentages used by the organisation I mentioned earlier, the GPA scores have less to do with predictive validity and more to do with administrative capacity.

Basing your hiring on predictive validity allows flexibility. The aforementioned organisation I had worked with had focused on hiring for a set of colleges based on their reputation and avoided the rest. But as the demand for talent increased, aptitude and coding tests have ensured that even when widening the pool, the same organisation has been able to maintain revenue productivity and customer satisfaction. They have been able to use the levers of selection and development in consonance to deliver sustained capability without compromising on profitability across the years.

Being dogmatic means that one is stuck to a specific talent pool and then fights for it. The phrase "war for talent" has gained currency ever since McKinsey framed it. There is a talent shortage, and recruiting organisations wage a war with their competitors. In India, it is seen as the *sine qua non* for product development organisations to hire from what is called tier-1 colleges—IITs, BITs, NITs and the like. It is not uncommon for recruitment heads of smaller companies to say they don't go to tier-1 but to tier-2 colleges as a way of saying that we still go for quality. Being dogmatic has tied organisations into a tough fight for a limited pool of talent.

Last year, a message went viral on LinkedIn. It was written by a gentleman who worked as a software engineer with Zoho, a product development organisation. The intriguing thing was that the person did not graduate from a tier-1 college, was not an engineer and had not even attended college. He had only completed class 10 and was working as a security guard in Zoho.

A manager saw a spark in him and mentored him after office hours. With time, he picked up coding skills and was so good that he ended up transitioning into a software engineering role. In most organisations, this would have been a pipe dream.

However, Zoho is an organisation that has consciously built its talent from within. Instead of doing the rounds of tier-1 engineering colleges, the organisation experimented with hiring students who had completed school but had no financial ability to go to college. The organisation started with hiring from Corporation Schools in Chennai, shortlisting candidates after an aptitude test. Subsequently, potential candidates were put through exercises to assess how they would handle real-life situations. Then, they were selected and put through a two-year program that taught them not only coding but other functional skills as well.

In the words of Raj Vegesna, Zoho's chief evangelist, "That's a fundamental idea behind the Zoho University. It started with six folks in the first batch. Now, here we are in 2019 we now run two batches. Each batch is now, I think, 200, 250 people. About 1,800 of our 7,000-employee base came through Zoho University."[7]

Close to 25% of their staff have been hired not from tier-1 or tier-2 colleges but right out of school. Has it hurt them? In 2019, they earned 110 million dollars on 610 million dollar revenues. While the organisation is privately held, it may be worth multiple billions. Their unique approach has led to excellent retention rates that have helped business success.

The challenge really is about re-examining assumptions, doing experiments proactively and creating differentiators. Instead of debating only on the salary package, strategic clarity will emerge with discussions on the following:

- Brand vs affordability
- Hire vs develop
- Pedigree vs attitude

Hiring for shop floor jobs is not a lesser challenge. There is a tacit need to hire people from socio-economic backgrounds who deliver performance and retention without trouble. A large manufacturing conglomerate hires shop floor workers either from the family members of existing employees or from specific villages from where employees had been hired in the past. One might question whether it is diverse enough, but they are basing it on what works for them.

Coimbatore has a lot of textile mills. The yarns need to be handled with dexterity and without breaking. It is tough and monotonous work. The organisations found that it is best done by teenage girls. Even after legal permissions, how do you hire young girls to work on the shop floor? The better ones hire them from needy families from rural areas on a fixed-term contract. However, it is not just work because anxious parents would want to ensure the safety of their daughters. Progressive organisations provide:

7. Brent Leary, "Raju Vegesna of Zoho: High School Grads Get Tuition Free Training through Zoho University – and 1800 Get Jobs with the Company," *Small Business Trends*, July 28, 2020, https://smallbiztrends.com/2019/01/zoho-university.html.

- Hostel accommodation and food
- Weekend trips to the city, including occasional movies
- Exposure to vocational training
- Practices to prevent harassment at work

While the young girls invest their valuable time, the girls are also being trained for a job after leaving the fixed-term contract. They can pick up a graduation or vocational skills like Nursing. The Coimbatore-based KPR mills, for instance, have helped with the higher education of 27,000 employees.[8] It is true that there are also organisations that are exploitative, but the best ones have a more integrated agenda.

THE INTERNAL TALENT MARKETPLACE

Quality of hire decisions holds good for all hiring. However, there is an emotional side to hiring for leadership roles. When it is accepted that there are no internal candidates, leadership hiring from outside is less of a challenge. It is tougher when there are internal aspirants. What if:

- We have internal aspirants who may be good but not ready yet. There is talent outside that is more ready for the role. Should we promote the internal aspirant or hire the external candidate?
- If we do an external hire, what will the internal aspirant do? What if they quit?
- We may need to pay a premium to hire from the market. What if this disturbs team equity?
- Even if we hire based on validated mechanisms, how do I enable the success of the new hire?

These questions are often interconnected. I have seen CEOs wrestle with such questions for days when hiring for senior roles. In more than one organisation, I have also seen the angst among employees and hiring managers when, for similar roles, a new

---

8. "KPR Mill's Education Initiative for Women Employees Yields Excellent Results," *The Textile Magazine*, June 3, 2021, accessed June 18, 2022, https://www.indiantextilemagazine.in/kpr-mills-education-initiative-for-women-employees-yields-excellent-results/.

join is paid more, even in comparison with proven performers. The following scenarios are only too familiar.

Step Up/Step Down

An Indian organisation with a commodity core was expanding into branded business. They hired the business head, Kumar, from a reputed MNC. They paid him market wages, significantly higher than peers in the core business. The plan was to have the executive come in, hire the sales team, set an incentive plan and let them loose.

However, it turned out differently. Having worked in large organisations, Kumar could design the process but was not prepared for the implementation challenges. Hiring team members for an organisation with an unknown brand was much tougher than doing it for a market leader. He faced the same problem in the market, too. He could not walk into retailers and decide on shelf space. While the relationships stayed, the balance of power had shifted. He now had to conceptualise ways to promote the product to the market.

Put simply, he had gained his premium for his big organisation pedigree and experience. However, his role needed him to play an entrepreneurial role, for which he was not ready. He was required to make the market. His comfort zone was in managing the market. Eventually, the employment relationship ended within a year, despite Kumar's best efforts.

This is not a one-off. Getting the fit just right for key roles takes effort and multiple learning loops. For key leadership and business roles, smaller organisations start by looking at expensive talent from top organisations. With time, they calibrate, especially after a few right hires.

This is an extension of the quality of hire challenge. As long as organisations follow a rigorous process using validated instruments, the outcome should turn out to be good. We were hiring an India business head for one of the organisations I had worked with. The APAC head, who was the hiring manager, clearly said that we should be looking for candidates, not from market leaders but challengers because that is what our organisation was. The hiring pipeline had to be more open and not skewed by brand names.

A second big theme is hiring from India-headquartered organisations vs hiring from MNCs, each with a cultural legacy. An HR manager in an India-headquartered organisation is likely to have been exposed to cycles of policy design and would have had access to CXOs. More time would have been spent on designing and implementing policies. Conversely, while the quality of work exposure is increasing in MNCs, the HR role is still more of a communicator and integrator. HR acts as the face of the organisation to its employees and as an integrator of the local leadership team by building relationships. Exposure to leadership happens in one-off meetings or calls, and an impact made in such settings acts as multipliers or disablers of career growth.

When hiring from an MNC, Indian organisations need to be aware of the strengths (relationship building or stakeholder management) and the opportunities for improvement (policy design or corporate role).

MNCs should look for an ability to build multiple across-the-board relationships when hiring from Indian companies or at least have the potential to develop this skill.

What does the research say about lateral hiring?

The most difficult part about lateral hiring is that the value of all relationships built by an employee is reset to zero. New hires have to start all over, build new relationships and then grow. Research by Harvard Professor Boris Groysberg says that performance is portable for some jobs but not all.[9] To be specific:

> Our research shows that stars whose jobs require them to cooperate and collaborate with other workers have a hard time maintaining performance when they move to a new organisation. So, if you're a manager, you might want to think strategically about what positions you can hire a

9. Boris Groysberg, Linda-Eling Lee, and Ashish Nanda, "Can They Take It with Them? The Portability of Star Knowledge Workers' Performance," *Management Science* 54, no. 7 (July 1, 2008): 1213–30.

top-notch outsider for, and which ones you're better off developing talent for inside the organisation.

If you do hire outside talent for a highly interactive job—which sometimes happens—give them adequate time to get up to speed, and provide them with mentorship and structure. Don't be too quick to get rid of someone who needs to re-establish his or her network in order to succeed. Instead, focus your efforts on helping those individuals to build the network they need. Careful integration is the key.

However, many organisations do not seem to have that long a view. It possibly stems from the fact that in the talent market, a person doing the same work in a comparable organisation has a similar compensation. To get the person to make the move, a premium has to be paid, which works out to be around 20% to 25%. The person making such a move will land at a higher level of salary than internal peers as well as aspirants. Such a difference is seen as paying a newcomer more to do the same job that existing employees are already proficient in, which creates friction in the system. To overcome this, leaders try to prove their decision right and set higher expectations from the newcomers right from day one. The newcomers could be thrown into the deep end even before they are ready.

According to research done by Professor Mathew Bidwell of Wharton University, lateral hires:[10]

- Are paid 18% to 20% more.
- Get significantly lower performance evaluations than internal candidates promoted into such roles for the first two years.
- They have higher exit rates.
- However, if they stay beyond two years, they can get promoted faster than internal candidates.

To summarise, hiring laterals is absolutely essential. However, to be effective, you need to:

---

10. Matthew Bidwell, "Paying More to Get Less: The Effects of External Hiring versus Internal Mobility," *Administrative Science Quarterly* 56, no. 3 (September 1, 2011): 369–407.

- Have a validated selection process.
- Implement the process without being biased by the academic and corporate pedigree of the candidate.
- Be patient. Whatever premium is being paid to the candidate is not their fault, and that should not create an artificial urgency for the candidate to outperform.
- Consider internal aspirations objectively. Especially when selecting for higher level roles, the internal aspirants need to be in the process, and feedback clearly shared with them if they do not qualify.

The last point finds expression in organisations as internal job postings. The jobs are first posted internally before being shared with the outside world. This is good practice. However, IJPs are often undermined by the organisation culture. It takes us back to the basic question—who is responsible for the employee's career growth?

- Is it the organisation?
- Is it the manager as exhibited in practice?
- Is it the individuals themselves?

Internal job postings sit at the intersection of all three. The organisation will have a requirement in which an employee may be interested in furthering her career. However, the employee's manager may have an upcoming project and would like to retain the employee who is experienced. Then, each participant in the process has to make a trade-off:

- The employee should make a trade-off between not getting the job and leaving the organisation for a similar job elsewhere.
- The organisation does a trade-off between the cost of a suboptimal project and the cost of losing an experienced employee.
- The manager does a trade-off between retaining the employee for the project and managing the risk of handling the project with a newcomer.

These trade-offs create stress in the system and often are decided by what is perceived to be business requirements and not employee aspirations. As such, in saving the short term, companies risk long-term disengagement and turnover.

As we have seen, companies are giving employees the choice of how they want to engage with the company (full-time, part-time and so on). Progressive companies have also been flexible with how employees use their time at work. 3M has been a pioneer with the 15% rule, whereby an employee is free to spend up to 15% of their time on projects that excite them, even outside of their work domain. Google, similarly, has a 20% rule reinforcing flexibility. These practices allow employees to pursue their interests and work on projects that they find interesting.

In many organisations, there are task forces and cross-functional teams focused on problem-solving. Employees either volunteer or are nominated for these opportunities. These, again, offer employees an opportunity to build their collaboration and problem-solving skills.

One can look at these as traditional and modern approaches to career paths. In a traditional approach, the organisation or the manager owns the people. They decide on jobs, assignments, career growth and job rotation. This assumes that the organisation's talent is the organisation's resource and is delinked from the external talent market.

The consulting major Deloitte conducted a survey of 10,000 organisations and discovered that more than two-thirds of the respondents found it easier to find a job outside their current company than within it.[11]

The modern approach assumes that:

- Employees not only join an organisation to manage their careers but also stay in charge of their growth within the organisation.

---

11. "Are You Overlooking Your Greatest Source of Talent?," *Deloitte Insights*, accessed June 18, 2022, https://www2.deloitte.com/us/en/insights/deloitte-review/issue-23/unlocking-hidden-talent-internal-mobility.html.

- The organisation provides opportunities for learning and development. It is upon the employee to utilise these within job requirements.
- The organisation shares not some but all open positions with the employees. Employees who apply would be treated on par with external candidates and go through the hiring process. There could be minimal gating criteria, like time spent on the present job, but no other barriers.
- The opportunities to work on cross-functional teams and task forces would be shared transparently, and interested employees can apply and get chosen.

The modern approach considers the organisation's talent as not just a consolidation of job holders but as a consolidation of skills and abilities that are relevant to the present and future. These are then converted into a marketplace by combining the short and long-term requirements with employee aspirations. By expanding opportunities in the internal marketplace, the employee is inclined not to look to the external marketplace for opportunities. This philosophy is the "talent marketplace".

Schneider Electric is a 25+ billion Euro organisation employing nearly 1,40,000 globally. They faced the challenges from a traditional model, as mentioned earlier. They found that a considerable number of people leaving the organisation were not able to find jobs internally. Attrition in the women workforce meant reduced diversity as well.

In 2020, the organisation launched the Open Talent Market (OTM) globally after piloting it and internal debate and discussions. On OTM:[12]

- All jobs were posted.
- All assignments were posted.
- Employees posted their skills and abilities.

12. "6 Tactics Schneider Electric Used to Amp Up Internal Mobility," May 26, 2020, accessed June 18, 2022, https://www.linkedin.com/business/talent/blog/talent-management/schneider-electric-internal-mobility.

- Algorithms did cross-matching and shared with employees' jobs/gigs, which would be in their line of interest. AI is also intended to eliminate selection biases.
- Employees made themselves available as mentors and also sought mentoring. Mentoring was not just top-down. Seniors could opt to be mentored on digital skills, for instance, by relatively younger colleagues.

Initial trends show that at least half the white-collar workforce had signed up on the system. Mentorships had started, gig assignments were being fulfilled, and the organisation was on track with its objective of creating an employee-owned career marketplace.

Unilever is another organisation that has rolled out an internal talent marketplace called Flex for its white-collar workforce. The organisation was able to redeploy resources in the middle of the pandemic from businesses with a lesser load, like food solutions, to those that saw a spike in workload, like sanitisers. The organisation was able to reallocate 10,000 employees within six to eight weeks. As many as 3000 were actually working across national borders, which would have been difficult to envisage without a hybrid working model. Flex is also based on the purpose an employee has and the kind of experiences they would like to build his career upon.[13]

An internal talent market is at the leading edge of how digital is helping re-imagine the workplace. This is enabled by breaking down the monolithic job into a set of manageable skills, competencies and experiences.

To recap, we plan numbers and hire the best talent either from the market or from inside the organisation. Where relevant, external hiring from campuses and their proportion is decided upon.

Acquisition into a role is the starting point for workforce capability. We require continuous development to make sure the talent always stays current and highly capable.

---

13. David Green, "How Unilever Has Created a Culture of Internal Talent Mobility," March 7, 2021, https://www.linkedin.com/pulse/how-unilever-has-created-culture-internal-talent-mobility-david-green/.

Once we have streamlined the process of talent acquisition and allocation, we need to:

- Identify the necessary competencies and skills needed for the business to succeed.
- Select key roles and ensure the incumbents are best in class.
- Create a pipeline of diverse talent for continuing success.

Let us explore strategic approaches for achieving these outcomes in the next chapter.

6
Workforce Capability: Development

As we have seen, hiring quality talent is critical for superior performance. However, it needs to be supplemented by continuous learning.

The traditional approach to learning and development had the following monolithic structure:

- Organisations mapped their roles onto a competency model.
- Training programs were usually mapped onto the competencies. Mostly classroom with some online learning and the occasional developmental assignment.
- Training needs were identified by the manager based on the role played by the employee.
- A training calendar was created on the basis of forecast needs.
- Feedback was taken on the programs for improvement.

The overarching assumptions were that L&D was the owner of development and that all competencies were equal. However, these assumptions have evolved with time. The changes are as follows:

- Some competencies are more important than others. An organisation may choose, for instance, to enhance:

(a) The product knowledge of sales executives
(b) Design thinking skills in solutions roles
(c) People management skills in managers

A report from 2016 talks about 31,000 employees from Infosys having completed workshops in design thinking out of a planned 70,000. This was obviously driven by the organisation trying to layer a design capability on top of IT solutions and was given high priority and visibility. Based on customer feedback, business growth expectations and employee retention numbers, competencies can be prioritised and addressed using a programmatic approach.[1]

Two changes have realigned the individual training needs:

1. Individuals own their development. While the needs are identified, it is up to the individual to go ahead and utilise the opportunities provided for development. In some organisations, weightage is assigned to individual development as a part of personal goals.
2. If employees need to own their development, there should be greater cognisance of demands on their time. Accordingly, more and more content is being made available digitally. An employee can learn far more skills by:
   i. Multiple MOOCs that come with a recommender algorithm
   ii. Access the content 24/7, including through tablets and phones.
   iii. Get certified in different skills from universities. The organisation lays out the priority areas and then reimburses the cost of being certified.

In this set-up, the organisation sets out the broad contours for development but leaves enough scope and choice for learning.

1. Sonam Choudhary Francis, "Design Thinking @ Infosys," *LinkedIn*, March 8, 2018, https://www.linkedin.com/pulse/design-thinking-infosys-sonam-choudhary/.

LEARNING: FROM WHAT WE DELIVER TO WHAT PARTICIPANTS DELIVER

Multimodal delivery has become the norm. It is fashionable for many organisations to say that they follow the 70/20/10 principle in development—70% happens on the job, 20% from development assignments and 10% through classroom training. This hasn't been statistically validated, but at the same time, it reinforces the fact that training alone is not sufficient.

Traditionally, employees used to attend a workshop and then go back to work. Whether they learnt or could implement anything from such learning was all up in the air. Subsequently, the Kirkpatrick model of training evaluation was adopted widely. From just looking at training program feedback, organisations began focusing on the institutionalisation of learning.

Also, earlier, the different mechanisms of development used to be isolated. Mentoring was for middle managers, coaching was for leaders and training was for early career executives. Let us look at an illustration from the ATD Awards 2019 under the Sales Enablement category for the German software giant SAP's initiative to develop sales capability:[2]

> The Academy for Sales Leaders program is a four-and-a-half-day, on-site workshop designed to equip frontline sales managers with the skills and tools they need to become better innovation leaders and coaches, drive innovation in their teams, and successfully develop team members.
>
> The program consists of pre-and post-activities that bookend the workshop experience. Pre-workshop activities include readings, videos, and e-learning curricula.
>
> Four days prior to the start of the workshop, attendees are invited to a WhatsApp message group, so they can begin to connect, socialise, and network.

The workshop component focuses on these areas:

2. Alex Moore, "2020 Excellence in Practice Award Winner: SAP," *Association for Talent Development*, July 20, 2020, accessed June 18, 2022, https://www.td.org/magazines/td-magazine/2020-excellence-in-practice-award-winner-sap.

- Building a high-performing team and leading in the exponential economy
- Experience the customer side of the business and their strategies
- Engaging customer C-level executives
- Running your business

On the last day of the workshop, participants give final pitches and presentations that are recorded and uploaded to an internal video platform for future reference and review.

After the workshop, ongoing learning reinforcement consists of "flash drills," a series of questions that continue for four weeks. There is also a facilitated call 60 days post workshop, and at 90 days post workshop there is a Digital Transformation Plan check-up and opportunity for participants to share success stories.

This structure is becoming the new norm. While the in-person workshop is still the key component, around it, we have:

- An e-learning platform that facilitates asynchronous, offline learning.
- Social connection between participants.
- A capstone project or its equivalent to put the skills learnt into practice so that the participants take away the memories of applied skills in addition to knowledge.
- Continued coaching and feedback for at least three months after the program.

This is a good illustration of how learning is viewed as integral to business, leading to these changes.

More and more business-led learning interventions have not shied away from investing but would like tangible success outcomes. The same program in SAP was deemed successful because:

> The success of the program has been significant. The teams reporting to Academy participant managers outperformed others who reported to sales managers who did not participate in the program. Double-digit improvement in win rates, average deal close value, pipeline opportunities, and pipeline value were realised.

As it happens elsewhere in HR, technology has helped transform learning experiences. Gamification (converting a learning challenge into interactive games) is a strategy that is used with a younger workforce. Cognizant wanted to build its workforce capability in pharmacovigilance from the ground up. Their strategy, as mentioned in ATD awards, is:

> The PV Genesis program is a seven-day classroom training with a series of 20 modules. Some are instructor-led, others are self-paced, and much is gamified.
>
> Since its inception in 2009, 5,185 Cognizant associates have been trained using the platform, with an average of 48 trainees per month over the last three years.
>
> As evidence of the gamified training's success, it has elicited a schedule adherence of greater than 90 percent, a first-pass yield of 80 percent, and has received 85 percent satisfaction. It has also expanded from a single client to eight major clients.[3]

So, the questions we need to ask are:

- What is the competency roadmap for our business priorities?
- What is the learning strategy to be used for delivering a tangible and sustainable outcome?
- How are we enabling employees to own their development? What are the investments in this?

These questions shift our focus from favouring activity to favouring results.

THE LEADERSHIP DEVELOPMENT ALCHEMY

We have discussed workforce learning in detail. What about the top talent and their leadership development?

There are many estimates of the amount spent on leadership development. The figures for the US alone range from 40 billion to 70 billion dollars. Ever since GE was seen

3. Jennifer Homer, "Tech Leader Focuses on Future-Proofing Employees," *Association for Talent Development*, July 20, 2020, accessed June 18, 2022, https://www.td.org/magazines/td-magazine/tech-leader-focuses-on-future-proofing-employees.

as an exemplary organisation and their leadership development centre at Crotonville was identified as the magic ingredient for enabling leaders to navigate diverse businesses, from financial services to aeronautical engines in far-flung countries, leadership development gained a life of its own. Prior to that, leadership development was part and parcel of management development. Organisations are expected to not just name successors but establish a pipeline for senior roles. While the mechanisms may be different, leaders are also employees who require support to perform their roles better. However, leadership development aligned with:

- Assessments
- Succession planning
- Executive coaching
- Developmental assignments

All of which add up to a lot of money, leading to a sense of exclusivity. Ace sportsmen and endurance sports heroes are opted in for delivering seminars.

The traditional models of leadership development are widely prevalent. However, do they deliver? Like everything else, organisations that answer the following questions get better RoI:

1. What is our focus area? Quite often, the leadership competencies are defined in such a way that the ideal leader is a combination of Roger Federer and Ratan Tata. When we have abstraction at the centre, the development efforts don't deliver. On the other hand, focusing on specific outcomes and behaviours leads to better outcomes.
2. Strength focus vs weakness focus: Strengths orientation has gained momentum in the recent past. Long back, I coordinated the 360* feedback exercise for the leadership team in an organisation. I found a particular trend intriguing. It is not as if leaders who were the stars had strengths across the board. They also had weaknesses. However, they were rated very highly by everyone for their strengths. Aligning responsibilities to strengths produces a quantum improvement in business results.

3. Outcome orientation: One of the approaches an outbound training provider used was to leave a group of leaders on the road with a little money. They had to find a way to return using their abilities. Another popular program includes trust walks. The space is filled with interesting approaches. However, these don't work unless there is time to reflect and change. The leadership coach Marshall Goldsmith used to say that there is no linear relationship between the time spent with him and being successful as a leader; rather, what actions are taken based on the time spent have a greater impact. This becomes all the more important as the focus is on the level of an individual, and if they are not growing, then they are quite likely to be regressing.

This begets the question most employees ask. Who is a leader? Shorn of repartee, the CEO is seen as the numero uno and the reference for all leadership programs. The CEO is a leader. Then, everyone who is reporting to the person also holds a position of responsibility. They should also be leaders. If we need to create an impact on the business, then the way to go is by following the hierarchy as evidenced by the organisation chart. Is this the best way, or is there another way of looking at leadership talent? Leadership development is an outcome of the organisation chart. But, is this the right approach?

Sandy Ogg, the founder of CEOworks and former CHRO of Unilever, advocates the talent to value model. In this, the organisation:[4]

1. Identifies the value agenda. Essentially, there are two scenarios. In the first scenario, the business continues the momentum as usual. However, in the second scenario, the focus lies on bending the value curve, signifying a turnaround or acceleration strategy.
2. Identifies the roles that create value. Straightaway, instead of the hierarchy, we start looking for key roles in the

4. Sandy Ogg, "Connecting Talent to Value," *SHRM*, accessed June 18, 2022, https://www.shrm.org/executive/executive-events/strategic-hr-forum/Documents/Sandy%20Ogg.pdf.

organisation. In a services organisation, the account manager of their biggest account may or may not be very high on the hierarchy. However, that person could be playing a role in generating high value. Focusing on value leads us to fewer, more critical roles.

3. Once the roles and capability needs are identified, assess the incumbents /aspirants on their suitability for the role. The accent is not on "potential" but more on the here-and-now readiness.
4. Map the role-talent risk. Based on the talent assessment, map into categories ranging from "change now" to "being creative about the shape of the role to maximise impact."
5. Follow through with role coaching, wherein the context of the role and talent are taken together and can be dynamically altered based on deliverables.

In his work with Blackstone Investments, Ogg found that 22 out of 180 most successful portfolio companies managed their talent decisions with an eye to linking critical leadership roles to the value they needed to generate. Prioritisation and focus matter.

It is not to say that talent to value is a silver bullet. However, the approach clearly aligns talent development with business outcomes. Ensuring the right roles are identified and mapped to the right talent is far more concrete than general, feel-good leadership development.

SKILL CENTRALITY

A recruiting note was posted by the founder of Bharatpe, a digital payments firm, in July 2021. The post said that the organisation was looking for 100 engineers and they were offering:

- Choice of a superbike: BMW/JAWA/Royal Enfield etc.
- Gadgets package: Bose headphones, Apple iPad, Harman speaker etc.
- WFH chair and table.

- Opportunity to watch the T20 cricket world cup in Dubai.[5]

This was in addition to a fairly attractive compensation package. In a tweet, the founder of Ola joked that he was looking for affordable engineering talent in Silicon Valley. There is a general consensus that in India, we are staring at great demand for computer science skills from across different industry verticals, and the supply is nowhere close to keeping up with it. Also, IT services companies like Infosys have communicated that they are returning to more development of talent from in-house.

The effect of the pandemic is unusual but by no means unprecedented. Every decade or so, the economy slows down and then turns around. At the point of turning around, most organisations look for people, creating a demand-supply skew. What we are seeing is part of it, influenced by the pandemic.

However, this is on top of major transformations happening in the industry itself. To mention two:

1. Digitalisation by itself is creating a huge space for global organisations. If you take retail, we have Amazon, which is primarily digital and trying to strengthen its footprint and Target, which is primarily physical, creating a digital footprint. There is a need for computer science talent to:

(a) Create the e-commerce user interface.

(b) Manage infrastructure to run the website.

(c) Develop the applications to run the sales and warehousing systems and analytics to fine-tune the strategy.

2. The automotive industry is in the middle of a big transition from fossil fuel to clean fuel. The cars will run on batteries, and the battery can be powered by solar or fuel cells. This would, in turn, need talent to design the vehicles, powertrains and sustainable batteries. Automobiles rely on semiconductors and code to perform effectively. All this needs a lot of design

5. Livemint, "BharatPe Starts Giving BMW Bikes to IT Professionals as Joining Bonus, Extends Offer," *Mint*, July 29, 2021, accessed June 18, 2022, https://www.livemint.com/companies/news/bharatpe-starts-giving-bmw-bikes-other-perks-to-it-professionals-extends-offer-11627559450874.html.

skills. The skill shortage is amplified by the fact that there is no pipeline, even from the engineering campuses. There, you have students pursuing mechanical engineering, electrical, electronics and computer science specialisations. Traditionally, mechanical and electrical engineering used to be sufficient for the automotive industry. However, for battery-operated vehicles, the engineer needs to be proficient in:

(a) Mechanical engineering applications.

(b) Electrical engineering applications, especially having to do with battery performance management.

(c) Programming the software that monitors the performance of the vehicle.

So, the nascent EV industry has to relook at not just manufacturing processes but also the talent pipeline right from the entry level.

For a long period, business had moved away from skills and focused more on management and leadership. After a certain level, career options ended for anyone preferring to be a specialist. The focus was more on administering value, which in turn meant efficient management. Many companies looked to manage costs to boost market value, and executive compensation was tied to the same. Research and design were relegated to the background in most large organisations.

However, as seen elsewhere, it is possible to create value of a greater magnitude by building a business on innovation, and innovation does not come from efficient management or leadership:

- In a software organisation, value is created by the programmers and architects.
- In a product organisation, value is created by product designers.
- While market research and sales are important, value in FMCG companies is created by the chemistry teams who develop the new products or flavours.

Workforce capability strategies then need to be fine-tuned to not just critical roles but also critical value-generating skills.

Everyone knows the skill requirements for what an organisation currently needs, which used to suffice when the rate of change was slow. We are living in times of accelerating change. In this scenario, knowing not just the skills of today but what is going to be essential tomorrow is equally important.

GE is a conglomerate with a mix of businesses. You may not think of them as coders. However, their then-CEO Jeff Immelt said in a discussion in 2016:

> If you are joining the organisation in your 20s, unlike when I joined, you're going to learn to code. It doesn't matter whether you are in sales, finance or operations. You may not end up being a programmer, but you will know how to code.[6]

GE's business then may not have needed all employees to know coding. However, operating in Industry 4.0 needs all employees to be programming literate, if not on joining, at least as they grow.

Such transformations are not new to business. I had started working in a personnel department, where the GM (Personnel) had his cabin, and only his secretary had a standalone PC. You needed to remove your slippers before entering the work area. We had specialised computer operators then.

If I were to be a new join today, then I would have picked up computer skills right from school and some coding skills in college. I would very likely start in an HR or people function role, where I would not only get a personal laptop, but that laptop would be the primary means of connection to the entire organisation and the rest of the world.

In 1991, if someone had told me this, I would have been scared. However, things kept changing and not just me, but everyone else adapted too. It is very difficult to see a static shelf life in any profession.

---

6. Jackie Wattles, "GE CEO Jeff Immelt Says All New Hires Will Learn to Code," *CNNMoney*, August 4, 2016, accessed June 18, 2022, https://money.cnn.com/2016/08/04/technology/general-electric-coding-jeff-immelt/index.html.

This brings us back to the core strategic questions on workforce capability:

- How do we track our capabilities and skills?
- Do we know what are going to be our skill requirements in the long term?

  (Assuming short-term is a known challenge)
- How are we going to enable our workforce for such futuristic skills?

There are many solutions to the first question. Some organisations use assessments and certifications to baseline their skill levels. There are also organisations that create their own proficiency levels and assign people to jobs on the basis of demonstrated proficiency, which is assessed at periodic intervals.

Establishing skill requirements for the long term needs more foresight. In organisations that deal with iron and steel, for example, plant modernisation is a big program that runs for years. You can see organisations having a roadmap to upskill operators to operate the new machinery. How do they adapt to the digital world?

Tata Steel, for instance, undertook the journey by:[7]

- Identifying the adoption of Industry 4.0 as a business objective in 2016.
- Setting up a Digital Value Assessment team.
- Including digital as a lever in business improvement programs.
- Carrying out a selection process from engineers below the age of 30. The chosen ones were designated as mentors to senior leadership, including the MD.
- Organising visits by executives to digital native organisations in the US.
- Rolling out a "Digital for all" program to all employees and making it mandatory. These were 101 programs, where focused sessions were held with labour unions

7. "Redefining The Future Of Steelmaking," *Tata*, November 2020, accessed June 18, 2022, https://www.tata.com/newsroom/business/tata-steel-plants-redefining-future-steelmaking.

and blue-collar workers to allay any fears they may have had about digital.

- Setting up an Analytics and Insights centre to support the business.
- Utilising technologies like RFID and AI in the workplace
- Collaborating with an executive from TCS to drive the digitisation work for TCS.

These enablers, in turn, led to the organisation utilising digital technologies for different core processes, which led to different units of the organisation being recognised as the World Economic Forum's Advanced 4th Industrial Revolution Lighthouse.

Many of these steps would be familiar to practitioners of change management. It is also illustrative that they had a roadmap and used different channels, including training, experience, mentoring and so forth, to align the capabilities to outcomes. Therefore, at an organisational level, the adoption of new paradigms is not about skills alone but cannot be done without the skills.

Finally, that brings us to what an organisation looks for in its employees, especially if alternative models of staffing can take care of spikes. The question becomes—how do I create an agile workforce?

This again brings us back to the hiring principles. In addition to analytical ability and communication skills, it has also become imperative for an organisation to focus on the learning ability of the employee. Hiring becomes more focused on the learning flow in a career than fixed highlights. Even now, we are hiring on fixed points like college, graduation, years of experience and so on. In future, the focus needs to shift to the nature of experiences, currency of learning and utilisation of opportunities. The organisation can provide learning exposures, but success goes to the employee who can learn fast and get to implementation.

TO SUM UP

Organisational capability differentiates between organisations with the same capacity.

Capacity can be grown by adding new employees and developing existing ones.

Hiring can be more here-and-now or long-term with entry-level hiring. Companies use both with ratios determined by their ability to develop talent.

Focusing on the quality of hiring and aligning processes to the quality is a decision that enhances capability.

Lateral hiring is successful with careful selection and patient handling.

Internal talent markets are here to stay.

Learning is moving from top-down, gap-based to bottom-up, individual-based.

Capability is being driven more and more by the skills of the workforce. Change management approaches work to reorient to emerging challenges.

The ability to learn is becoming a key factor for hiring.

Will the desired performance happen once we have the right capacity and capability? Or do we need to focus on additional strategies for the organisation to be successful? Let us discuss these questions in the next chapter.

7
The Differentiator: Workforce Performance

We have implemented a strategy for workforce capacity. We have also identified the levers for workforce capability building. What follows next?

As we see in many sports leagues, the management of the teams usually does a good job of identifying and staffing the positions. However, drawing on the Indian Premier League (IPL) again, the difference between a CSK and another team is how the team converts potential to performance.

Many HR professionals, when asked about their contribution to an organisation's performance, focus on the performance management process, which is an example of availability bias. Performance management is an important process. Normalisation or check-in discussions, the act of performance reviews and managing the outcomes is one of the most intense experiences an employee and manager can go through. Doing that process well takes a lot of effort. However, is it all that an HR can do?

The impact of HR practices on firm performance is an ongoing area of active research. Becker and Huselid, in 1998, created an index for HR sophistication based on 17 policy characteristics.[1]

1. Brian E. Becker and Mark A. Huselid, "High Performance Work Systems and Firm Performance: A Synthesis of Research and Managerial Implications," in *Research in Personnel and Human Resources Management*, ed. Gerald R. Ferris, vol. 16 (JAI Press Incorporated, 1998), 53–101.

Using this, they estimated that one standard deviation change in index leads to an 11% to 13% change in market value per employee. This especially happens at two stages—when the organisation goes from having an unstructured HR system to one that is structured and when it truly differentiates at a higher level of maturity.

Jeffrey Pfeffer, in his 1998 book The Human Equation,[2] writes that the following seven practices are found in most successful organisations:

- Employment security
- Mature hiring using different methods based on the positions
- Decentralised and self-managed organisational structure
- High compensation, dependent on organisation performance
- Extensive training
- Egalitarian culture
- Transparent communications

It can be debated whether causality is contextual and not absolute. We have seen organisations offering secure jobs yearn for a high-performance culture while those that perform well by market standards struggle to retain employees when the job market booms. What needs not be debated is HR's influence on multiple drivers of organisational performance rather than just the performance management process. Let us pick a few that are more tangible for detailing:

1. Organisation design and structure
2. Leadership alignment
3. Strategy flow down
4. Team collaboration

2. Paul Lawrence and Jeffrey Pfeffer, "The Human Equation: Building Profits by Putting People First.," *Administrative Science Quarterly* 43, no. 4 (December 1, 1998): 956.

5. Performance management, reward and recognition
6. Employee engagement

A typical HR professional might look at this and say that they spend most of their time on items five and six, with some actions taken around four. However, the involvement of HR in items one to three differentiates a high-performing HR organisation from an average one. The broader the scope and longer the timeframe of influence, the more strategic the function is.

For the purposes of this chapter, we can take one to three as areas of influence and four to six as areas of ownership. Let us elaborate further.

ORGANISATION DESIGN AND STRUCTURE

In an interview, the CEO of Wipro, Thierry Delaporte, said that the structure he inherited had seven sectors, which broke down into thirty-one industries, nine geographies and twelve business units. He had twenty-seven unique profit and loss units reporting directly to him, and this organisation had more than 800 KPIs. Delaporte observed that it took attention away from the client. He said that he broke this down into two global business lines and four geographies, shrinking the P&Ls reporting him into just four. The early signs are that the structure is working well.[3]

Organisation design is a niche responsibility. The pain points of organisation design are felt by the business leaders, making it a common mandate for a CXO to reassess the organisational structure. The big transitions often involve:

- Going from a functional structure to a business unit structure.
- Going from a structure based on geography to one based on products.

---

3. Shilpa Phadnis and Sujit John, "Simpler Structure, Transforming Employees: A Frenchman Sitting in Paris Turns Wipro Around," *The Times of India*, October 18, 2021, accessed June 18, 2022, https://timesofindia.indiatimes.com/business/india-business/a-frenchman-sitting-in-paris-turns-wipro-around/articleshow/87091176.cms.

- Differentiation between how the customer-facing functions and business-enabling functions are organised.
- Organisation into market-focused verticals and capability-oriented horizontal units.

Such changes accompany the organisation's evolution or a need to change the status quo. Recognising the importance of an outside-in perspective for objectivity and alignment with market trends, organisations usually refrain from assigning this responsibility to an internal department. Instead, mature organisations usually hire big brand consultancies for their organisational structuring work.

Even so, organisational structure is one of those areas that differentiate HR's role from being present at the table to one who executes orders. HR's traditional role does not offer an opportunity to study the structure and evaluate options from an external perspective. However, HR can participate in the process to moderate it and bring in objectivity by being an observant insider.

One of the organisations we had worked with had completed an organisational restructuring using a branded consultancy. Their recommendation was seen as coming from an expert, making it more acceptable, and it was soon implemented. A key recommendation was to create a new vertical structure. The organisation identified new leaders, assigned them responsibilities and communicated the new structure. The new leaders had to take over the client relationships from existing managers, who had the expertise and owned the relationships. Existing managers had to move to a Centre of Excellence role, whose KPIs were not clear. Chaos ensued. The organisation faced problems of:

- Clarity in roles and responsibilities.
- Clarity in performance goals and objectives.
- Career path.
- New manager onboarding.
- Conflict resolution and team working.

In all of this, HR had to play a key role along with the leadership team. As you would recognise, this is change management 101. Many of these problems could have been mitigated if HR was involved right from the beginning. Designing an organisation and creating and naming the boxes is all cerebral work. However, it is people who are going to bring these boxes alive and how they feel ultimately decides whether the structure will work or fail.

Many organisations seem to undergo reorganisation once in three to four years, even if it is just to shake things up. It would be great for an HR professional to keep surfacing the issues on:

- What is our organisation structure trying to achieve in terms of innovation, productivity, capability, market share and so on?
- Is it successful? Are there areas where organisational restructuring would help? These typically take the shape of creating new leadership roles and functions and consolidation of existing functions and units.
- Have we become more bureaucratic? Is it because of too many layers in the structure?
- Are we failing to focus attention on lucrative markets because of our structure? Do we have enough leadership capability in future growth areas?

In larger organisations, HR can have organisation diagnosis and design as one of the strategic capabilities.

HR can influence the formation of boxes and flows in the organisational structure. HR can also leverage objective selection mechanisms for identifying the right candidates to play these roles among the contenders.

Organisation charts typically cover the top two to three levels of an organisation. There are many roles that are not visible on the chart. An organisational hierarchy aligns the rest of the organisation to the chart, and creating it is one of HR's primary responsibilities. These hierarchies give every employee a level, title and career path to aspire to.

Constituting an organisational hierarchy is a fairly routine process. In smaller organisations, it happens on the basis of experience and seniority. A defined hierarchy is one of the actions taken as the organisation reaches a threshold size. Unique roles are identified and stacked after a points-based evaluation of some kind. Lines are drawn at the most optimal points so that different levels are identified, which are used for benchmarking salary and also for promotions. A competency framework can then be developed based on the roles.

So, what are the strategic questions here?

1. **When should one go in for a formal hierarchy?**

   Often, it is done when the manifestations of not having a structure are already creating issues around fairness. Do it too early, and you risk the threat of the structure not being implemented. A large organisation did a thorough job designing the required organisation but postponed the implementation because they feared the impact of change on business continuity. When business slowed down, the organisation had to quickly let go of many mid-level managers who may not have been in the same position if the hierarchy had been changed.

   When rolling out a new hierarchy, an organisation identified outlier employees in its workforce who were doing a role less than what their level required them to. Reducing their level seemed to be one obvious solution. However, the organisation chose to give them a time window to move to a commensurate role. This decision provided a soft landing and increased the acceptability of the new hierarchy.

   Thus, change by itself should not be feared from doing the right stuff, as long as you manage the change with flexibility and human touch.

2. **How many levels are appropriate?**

   In general, there are individual contributors and people managers. Depending on the sophistication and complexity of the product, there would be three to four levels of individual contributors and, depending on the number of employees, four to five levels of management. This essentially means across a career span of 25 years, an employee can hope to get a promotion every four to five years—more easily at first and then with stiffer gating criteria.

Many Indian organisations are still driven by the unvalidated hypothesis that employees want some progression every three years. This leads to grade inflation, wherein by using prefixes such as Assistant and Senior, levels are created. The employee is promoted, but it feels hollow because their roles haven't changed.

As we have said elsewhere, the right answer does not lie in the outcomes but in the process. HR has to examine the organisation's growth, forecast requirements and ensure the organisational hierarchy and promotion policies are ahead of the curve. This should happen systematically, at least once in three years, to identify focus areas. If the organisation is growing fast, new levels may be required. If not, promotions have to be calibrated against growth so that one doesn't have too many managers ending up in leadership roles that can't weather a downturn.

These principles hold good for a traditional top-down hierarchy. Total quality, based on Japanese manufacturing principles, advocates a flat structure. An organisation I had worked with had said that every shop floor function would have a team leader, and everyone else would be a team member. They viewed the organisation as being composed of many teams. While many organisations adapted to this concept, they also had to maintain a hierarchical structure of levels and titles for social acceptance and compensation benchmarking, which ended up defeating the purpose. Tata Motors, for instance, rolled out such a framework but quickly rescinded it.[4] Making logical changes is tougher when it is not fully consistent with societal expectations, whereby people want their titles to reflect their seniority and experience and not competence.

---

4. "Flat Response: Tata Motors Brings Back Designations," *BusinessLine*, January 11, 2018, accessed June 18, 2022, https://www.thehindubusinessline.com/companies/flat-response-tata-motors-brings-back-designations/article64269831.ece.

Technology organisations work in a project mode where, essentially, there are developers and then team leads. The advent of agile methodology has again brought to the fore the total quality concepts. The key difference here is that the market has changed. Let us take computer software, for instance. Even ten years back, there would be a one-time release that would be installed using a CD. Subsequently, the updates and patches would be bunched and released separately. To prevent virus attacks, a separate antivirus software had to be installed. Now, with software on the cloud, the operating system and updates are always on.

The agile principles hold good, especially in mobile apps. The cycle of product releases and updates keeps happening on an ongoing basis. In this scenario, a top-down hierarchy does not cut it. Customer and market insights go alongside software development. There are daily stand-up meetings and weekly sprints. Product development and deployment are done by empowered teams. Some of the leading edge organisations have classified them as tribes and squads.

Agile methodology, empowered teams and organisation as a network have all been concepts gaining currency with time. One could say that organisations of the future would have hybrid structures, with a non-hierarchical, team-based structure for the operating part and a relatively thinner hierarchy at the top. An organisation where leadership is not simply managing a large number of people. Hence, the HR strategy should also look at exploring alternative structures and evaluating their effectiveness.

LEADERSHIP ALIGNMENT

Leaders have a big impact on not just the organisation's success but also on individual functions. In many successful organisations, the leaders collaborate, setting aside individual differences. Getting them to do it takes effort.

It is not uncommon to have a team of rivals at the top. The present CEO, as well as the contenders for the coveted role, for instance, may be collaborating in public but plotting against each other in private. When a set of people need to work together, personal differences, jockeying and perceptions of favouritism are all too common. Trust is the solution, but it gets built over a period of time, and there are cases of falling apart even in long-standing work relations. While it is easy to talk about humility, senior executives also have their outsized egos—not all, but a number critical enough to derail an organisation's agenda.

To be fair, positions at the top are lonely, around which people walk on eggshells and are cautious with feedback; neither is it easy for the leaders to show vulnerability in accepting and working on improvement areas. Also, conflicts bubble up from below and often get portrayed as win-lose conflicts, setting up executives against each other.

In most organisations, the HR head is not just expected to own the HR agenda but also:

- Act as a facilitator for leadership meetings and sessions.
- Be a trusted advisor to the CEO who also keeps the CEO honest.
- A friend of the senior management supporting them on their improvement journey.

Some of this can be achieved by using third-party facilitators as well as experienced board members. Mechanisms like 360-degree feedback help in anonymising multi-level feedback. An HR head can leverage such tools.

Let us take the most commonly used mechanism for getting leaders together, the leadership offsite. This is a good test of the strategic role played by HR. Does the HR head:

1. Work with the CEO in identifying the agenda for the offsite and influence the meeting?
2. Or do they take care of the infrastructure (location), methodology and facilitator identification and let it flow?
3. Or do they just organise the infra and get out of the way?

The ability to work with the leadership team is impacted by what the team perceives the head to be good at. Often, I have seen HR leaders being content with doing point number two above. That is absolutely fine, to begin with, but to be respected, one should move to point number one.

This applies not just to the head of HR but to every business partner who is required to work with a cross-functional leadership team. The success of these roles does not stem just from delivering on the functional deliverables that are explicit, but also the unwritten ones around keeping the leader and team honest.

To be effective, HR leaders should not skirt personality issues at the peer level or highlight those issues to the CEO and sit back. The successful ones confront these issues and work toward a resolution. We will revisit this in the last chapter.

PERFORMANCE MANAGEMENT, REWARD AND RECOGNITION

Hiring arguably has a greater impact on the quality of the workforce than performance appraisal. However, nothing excites the leadership and HR community more than modifying and changing the performance appraisal process.

At its core, performance appraisal is a simple process by which employees know about what they need to do and get feedback on how they are progressing. It is a conversation between a supervisor and the employee. To manage the thread, it is documented in a system.

Let us now look at what different objectives get tagged onto this simple enough process.

Connecting the organisation's goals to individual objectives, which leads to individual performance objectives. These objectives, in turn, can:

- Be assigned different weightages that add up to 100. There also needs to be a minimum threshold and a maximum threshold. One objective cannot be 5% or 90%.
- Be performance-oriented, development-oriented or both.
- Be owned individually or jointly. Joint ownership happens at senior levels.

- Inherit from the individual's manager. An objective that is given 20% weightage for the manager could be broken down into three components for three team members with 40% weightage for each.

Deciding on the frequency of performance conversations:

- Annual/ semi-annual/ monthly.
- Connect to the L&D cycle. While all these don't apply to all organisations, quite often we have:
- Competency assessments in addition to assessment of objectives.
- Training needs for the employee based on their developmental feedback.

Connecting to salary reviews and other consequences:

- Based on the weightages and actual performance rating.
- A relative rank based on everyone's performance.
- Connecting percentage increases to the level and the performance rating.
- And in course of time, connecting performance ratings to promotions.
- Have people on performance improvement plans if their ratings are consistently bad.

There are other procedural issues as well:

- What gets documented, and where does it get recorded?
- What can each participant see?
- Is there anything confidential about the process?
- Is there a formula for calculating the final score?

As evident here, the basic process of setting objectives and having a conversation around them has been bloated to include multiple strategic goals, each of which is important, but the cumulative ask is high. Eventually, all these strategic goals are served from a process perspective, but the impact on the desired outcomes or individual improvement is debatable.

We have made two big shifts in the process in the past twenty years. First inspired by GE and the concept of top grading, everyone aggressively moved into what was known as stack ranking or, more derisively, "rank and yank".

After ten years, many organisations realised that stack ranking has outlived its usefulness and shifted the other way, where ratings don't matter as much as conversations. After years of fighting around normal distribution, this seemed a much better area to focus on. Organisations haven't totally given up on a final rating but have made the process more decentralised and flexible around roles, functions and so forth. This is a big shift from even five years ago when the distributions were near sacrosanct, and exceptions were not possible without executive approval.

That said, what are the questions you need to ask?

1. Why does the organisation have a formal performance management system?

This is not an easy question to answer without resorting to multiple bullet points. However, when implementing, there would always be a need for trade-offs that we need to be aware of. We can say that we want to have a system to document employee performance and connect reward and recognition objectively or that we want to create a cascade of performance from organisation goals to individual goals.

However, being parallelly successful in both is a big challenge as both need piloting and improvement based on feedback. Hence, you need a defined roadmap. You could say that we will establish a culture of objectivity in the first year alongside clear performance goals for the leaders. In the second year, you can expand the performance goals to the level of managers and, at the same time, take action on feedback about objectivity. Setting multiple objectives and treating all of them equally ends up compromising all of them.

2. What would I like the impact of the process on employee satisfaction to be?

This question is the crux of many performance management decisions. Any process that involves identifying 80% to 90%

of the organisation as not being the best is designed to cause unhappiness. Why?

You can do a random experiment in your next staff meeting. Just ask the participants to rate themselves within the group, whether they are below average or above average. Ideally, half should say they are above, and half should say they are below. But does it happen in reality?

Studies across multiple fields, from teaching to driving to telling jokes, reveal that a majority of people think they are above average. A study by the National Centre for Biotechnological Information revealed that 65% of people think they possess above-average intelligence.[5]

This is explained by the phenomenon called "Illusory Superiority", wherein a person overestimates their own abilities in comparison to others. The Dunning Kruger effect explains this well, wherein a person with lower capability overestimates their ability while a person with higher capability, because they know more, ends up underestimating their ability.

Many organisations classify employees on the basis of performance into three or four buckets. While the topmost quartile or decile might rate themselves objectively, everything else is up for grabs. Even poor performers might think themselves to be in the second quartile.

In such a situation, is employee satisfaction a legitimate goal? In our experience, we have seen three buckets (say 10% outstanding, 2% poor and equal for everyone else) get more acceptance than four buckets. However, there will always be people unhappy with how they are rated.

Having better measurability of results is one of the solutions. This seems easier in functions where the outputs are numeric, say on Wall Street or in sales functions. Every employee has a measurable target, and evaluation is dependent totally on

5. Patrick R. Heck, Daniel J. Simons, and Christopher F. Chabris, "65% of Americans Believe They Are Above Average in Intelligence: Results of Two Nationally Representative Surveys," *PLOS ONE* 13, no. 7 (July 3, 2018).

achievement against that target. A higher proportion of the salary is variable and is completely tied to achievement.

It seems simple enough. However, on the ground, no two targets are equal. Goal achievement could often hinge on a variety of factors like territory, promotions, product availability, competition actions and so forth. So, even within the same organisation, there would be different goals for two managers at the same level. Then, we start heuristics, like using past performance as a baseline. Individuals might strategise around maximising their incentive, whether it helps the organisational strategy or not. To prevent this, a rubric is created with quantitative and qualitative factors, and we start becoming subjective again!

Hardly anyone is 100% responsible for their output. The team with which they work also plays a big part in individual performance. What qualifies as average performance in a very good team could very well be excellent performance in a mediocre team. Even within a team, it is difficult to precisely quantify individual contributions.

Given these challenges, there are organisations that are giving up on individual goal-based incentive programs, even in sales functions.

Given the greater dynamism, the modern approach to objectivity is a combination of the following:

- Shorter timeframe objectives
- Regular touch down discussions
- Ongoing collection of feedback
- Enhancing the manager's ability to share feedback

The OKR framework (Objectives and Key Result Areas) seems most amenable as it details the objectives to the level of the individual. It is really useful when working on a project mode.

Yet, as one of our colleagues said long back, "Task allocation is based on my assessment of the capability of the individual. If I perceive the person to be better, I will give them tougher assignments with higher expectations. However, I will consider it when doing reviews." Eventually, it is difficult to eliminate the subjectivity completely, and it may not even be a desirable outcome. Even so, subjectivity in assigning work and self-assessment of completing the same are both factors that impact employee satisfaction.

As in many other areas, an organisation then makes a trade-off between recognising performance and retaining employee satisfaction. Even with zero differentiation between employees, some will be unhappy. Given that, it becomes important for an organisation and managers to focus enough on the process and conversations so that the intent does not get reduced to one of the "merit increase of 10%, I am happy; 8%, I am not" kind of a scenario.

3. What is the role of performance reviews in career growth recognitions?

Over a period of time, performance ratings end up as the surrogate indicator for all the work done by the employee. In countries like India, with a young workforce in demand, performance management gets reduced to a single word, 'appraisal', which does not mean the discussion or even the rating but the merit increase. Someone asking, "How was your appraisal?" essentially means, "Are you happy with your merit increase?". This has even become the subject of memes.

Merit increases are solely determined on the basis of appraisal ratings and so are viewed as the most important input in a year's performance. Appraisal ratings are also used as the barometer of consistent performance when we need to select a few employees from many for promotions, deputations, retention plans and so forth.

This is explained by the "availability bias". We may not exactly know the highs and lows of an employee's contributions relative to another. Appraisal rating is available and, hence, is used widely. The challenge lies in creating more data points and weaving them together. So, the questions really are:

- How do we minimise the noise between delivered performance and rating?
- What other points of data do we collect for selecting employees for different purposes?

The first solution is enriching the quality of measurement. Sometime back, the CEO of an IT services organisation wanted to identify the top performers. He wanted a truer source of performance than the relative rating given by the manager. He ended up using the utilisation percentage as a reference. Utilisation is the percentage of the working hours for which an employee has been billed to a client. The argument is that the higher the utilisation, the more important the employee is to the organisation. The exercise ended up revealing some employees who were stars in absolute performance but not reflected in the manager's subjective assessment. The CEO knew where to look.

Another simple example is how Uber captures feedback after every ride. Food delivery platform Swiggy first asks you about the delivery quality and then food quality. Then they expanded to include different dishes that you have ordered and your rating on the same. They also ask about what you liked—portion, price or taste.

This information acts as powerful real-time feedback. Of course, employee performance is not the same as biryani! However, the idea is being transferred to employee feedback as well. Regular feedback is taken from the team members and clients on the quality of work and working style of an employee. These get aggregated into a quarterly discussion. Such inputs consolidated over an appraisal period and discussed frequently make for a more credible rating.

Suppose you are putting together a high-potentials program wherein you choose 100 employees from across the organisation. What would be the data inputs you use for the selection?

The second solution is to involve validated third-party tools free of managerial bias. Traditionally, such exercises used to rely on consistent performance ratings, potential assessment and manager recommendations. The fallacy here is that the manager assigning the performance review does the shortlisting again. An employee could be on the blind side of the manager and keep missing out.

To prevent this, third-party assessments are used. Assessment centres with a battery of surveys and work simulations are used to arrive at a deeper and more independent judgement on an employee's capabilities. Nowadays, technology has made the process swift. They also produce a more acceptable answer to employees looking to navigate their own career paths inside the organisation.

The third strategy lies in educating managers on the need to have conversations and elevating the quality of such conversations. Culturally, in India, people hold back from having tough conversations. Managers don't realise that avoiding such conversations eventually leads to a moment where the employee will quit or worse. An organisation we had worked for had distributed offices. When we collected feedback, one of the employees in such an office said that his manager just shared the appraisal rating on the system and did not have a discussion. We thought they were in different offices. Turns out they were in the same remote office, where only 20 employees were working!

Organisations are tracking the quantity of conversations and working on their quality. Doing this for front-line managers is a great beginning. However, the act of feedback is also cultural. It is incumbent upon the leaders to initiate the culture of having regular conversations. This would help the practice of having frank discussions stick. An organisation can easily have a multi-year program to first ensure there are conversations, then increase the frequency, then work on the quality and then the ability to be objective.

It does not always have to be one-on-one. Some organisations are also starting to have a postmortem meeting to hold discussions with the team members at the end of every project. This helps surface all the challenges encountered, and every employee can relate to their impact and what they could have done better.

To summarise, if merit increases are the only outcome an employee can look forward to during the course of a year, the appraisal rating becomes very important and needs to be made more credible. However, there should be other equally important elements like career growth, project assignments and so forth to which an employee can aspire during the course of the year. This needs to be a credible and multi-faceted assessment.

All best practices work as long as the organisation stays the course and ensures honest conversations.

REWARDS AND RECOGNITION

One of us was part of the leadership team of a site in an organisation. This was over and above the regular role, and so the team members were not able to devote dedicated time. A recommendation was made to include a shadow team of employees below the age of 30. A proper competition was held, young employees made presentations and were selected by a panel. After six months, the site leadership team agreed that the youngsters had injected the much-needed energy.

There was no monetary component here. People volunteered willingly, and a transparent selection process was perceived as a validation of their potential. A public acknowledgement was all that was needed to recognise them.

Frequently, we make the mistake of thinking about recognition always in "giveaway" terms for something that was achieved. A trophy, scroll or gift certificate all constitute recognition, especially when accorded in front of peers. In this process, we forget what can provide greater internal motivation—being chosen from a peer group for additional responsibility like:

- Membership in a task force
- Mentor to budding leaders
- External consultant
- Team member reviewing award nominations
- Job assignment in a new business, new country and so on

The above are some illustrations. These work for more senior folks, who may not be so enamoured of glitzy functions.

One of us had helped build a predictive model for employee turnover. One of the key insights was that the employees who were recognised more often tended to stay longer. Obviously, timely recognition of a job well done in some form acts as a motivator. So, what should be the relevant questions?

- What are the different monetary and non-monetary forms of recognition we have? Do they cover the workforce adequately?
- What do we recognise? Performance only? Values? Culture?
- How transparent and acceptable is our process to identify employees for recognition? Do we ring-fence the process against favouritism arguments, at least for high-value rewards?

In general, functions with tangible outcomes like sales or production have well-articulated recognition. Chairman's clubs, for instance, have recognition for achieving a quota. Typically, people in business enabling functions feel under-recognised. Therefore, opportunities should be available for all functions.

Progressive organisations are beginning to recognise the display of values. Not only organisation values like customer satisfaction but also contributions to society through CSR or even to ESG.

Most rewards are lag indicators, acknowledging work already done. They are symmetric with effort. Function/peer recognitions at one level and organisational levels at the other. Variable compensation, wherein a percentage of individual pay is connected to organisation performance, is supposed to create another symmetric linkage. It does create a connection, but employees at junior levels don't have too much control over the business outcomes. When the organisation does not do well, it can create angst as well. However, greater value comes from asymmetric rewards.

Stock option grants are asymmetric—they may end up being worthless or make the option holder a very rich person. Given how they have been used, they tend to be bracketed along with compensation and benefits. However, stock options are actually neither—not exactly, anyway.

By nature, options tie up employee contribution with organisation growth. While the initial grants are driven by the position, additional grants are increasingly being allocated on the basis of present and future contributions to the organisation's growth. Organisations that go public successfully, Infosys or Freshdesk, for instance, end up generating wealth for employees in a manner different from regular compensation.

Organisations have tried to recreate the wealth generation possibilities of stock options through bonus plans and such. These are applied mostly at senior levels, and nothing truly compares to the satisfaction of giving your best for an organisation, seeing it become successful in the markets and becoming an employee, a proportion of whose wealth goes up and down with the organisation's performance.

TEAMWORK

A lot of literature focuses on the CEOs and individual employee satisfaction. Leadership, functions or projects, an organisation is composed essentially of teams. Enabling performance needs us to ensure the different teams collaborate within themselves and with each other.

However, there is more to team effectiveness. Quite often, HR gets a request to organise a team-building program, preferably outbound. This is used as a catch-all solution for resolving all team-related issues. What would these be?

- Onboarding newcomers onto the team, addressing old vs new dynamics.
- Interpersonal issues between manager and team members or between team members.
- Misalignment between individual objectives and team objectives. Implementing a normal distribution, for instance, is always a challenge for managers because they don't see people quite the same way.
- Manager style: In the near past, this phenomenon has been given some importance. In engagement surveys, for instance, scorecards are generated for different teams,

and it is possible to compare the outcomes between teams that are engaged and those that aren't. However, the improvement in team engagement is mostly attributed to the people management style used. Managers are coached to become better, which is a welcomed change, but teamwork has more dimensions.

More and more teams are cross-functional, cross-locational or even across countries. These bring in additional complexities of communication style, working style and so forth. Google analysed 180 teams across two years to identify what leads to high-performing teams. They found that it is not the quality of individual team members but how they interact, structure and view their contributions that makes the difference. The five key dynamics that set apart successful teams include:

- Belief that they are doing work that matters.
- Working on something that is meaningful to all team members.
- Clarity of goals, roles and execution plans.
- Dependability of team members in delivering high-quality work on target.
- Allowance to take risks without feeling insecure or embarrassed.

The last point, also known as psychological safety, has been getting more attention recently. It turns out that having the freedom to experiment and be oneself has a lot of positive spinoffs. Google found that "Individuals on teams with higher psychological safety are less likely to leave Google, they're more likely to harness the power of diverse ideas from their teammates, they bring in more revenue, and they're rated as effective twice as often by executives."[6]

While not stated explicitly, these also apply to newcomers to the team as well as new managers. The team should be strong

6. Julia Rozovsky, "The Five Keys to a Successful Google Team," *Google*, November 17, 2015, accessed June 17, 2022, https://rework.withgoogle.com/blog/five-keys-to-a-successful-google-team/.

and yet flexible enough to accommodate people from a different background or environment.

So, without focusing on the effectiveness of teams, organisations won't be as successful as they can be. To enable it, HR should seek answers to:

- How many teams do we have in the organisation, both at the highest level as well as at the functional level?
- What is the responsibility of HR as far as team effectiveness is concerned? Do we work to a framework of excellence? If so, what are the practices to enable teams to be effective?
- How do we have teams with high psychological safety? How do we measure it, and what do we need to do to improve it?
- How do we recognise high-performing teams and leaders who manage them?

EMPLOYEE ENGAGEMENT

If you search for employee engagement in Google, it returns 220 million results. Enter employee experience, and you get 419 million results. Obviously, this is a subject well written about, discussed and debated upon.

So much so that, for many HR functions, instead of business success or market leadership, employee engagement has become the holy grail. *Fortune* and Great Places to Work Institute have created a powerful global franchise. Many companies still consider it an honour to feature on the list.

Let us step back from the powerful trend and examine a couple of questions.

1. Does employee engagement lead to better business performance?

This creates the next assumption that serving employees is as good as serving the business. There are enough illustrations about the impact of keeping employees happy. Right from the original Sears Roebuck Employee-Customer-Profit chain to Shell's study on the impact of engagement on reducing accidents, engagement does play a role.[7]

Fortune went to the extent of working with FTSE Russell to create a hypothetical index of the 100 best employers in the US across 20 years, from 1998 to 2016. Such an index returned 11.66% annually when compared to the indices of all cap or of large-cap companies, which returned nearly 5% less. So, clearly, all research points to having engaged employees leading to better customer, business and stock market impact.[8]

This brings forth the next question.

2. Does good corporate performance lead to engaged employees or the other way around?

Global surveys have traditionally highlighted organisations like Microsoft, Cisco, Google as well as others like Wegman's, as great places to work. However, these have been great performing companies as well.[9] They perform very well because of their strategy, culture and focus. A successful organisation is able to attract high-quality talent, which, in turn, makes the organisation better. Culture and values play a very important part there. However, not every top-performing organisation aspires to be a great place to work.

Big consulting companies or firms on Wall Street have a reputation for long hours of work. They have an up-or-out principle, wherein an employee cannot be stuck in a role but has to keep growing. When GE was reputed for being a great organisation, it wasn't an easy place to work. Neither is Amazon now.

---

7. Erik Van Vulpen, "15 HR Analytics Case Studies with Business Impact," *AIHR*, September 27, 2023, accessed June 17, 2022, https://www.aihr.com/blog/hr-analytics-case-studies/.
8. Catherine Yoshimoto and Ed Frauenheim, "The Best Companies to Work For Are Beating the Market," *Fortune*, February 27, 2018, accessed June 18, 2022, https://fortune.com/2018/02/27/the-best-companies-to-work-for-are-beating-the-market/.
9. "Great Place to Work Rankings," *Fortune*, accessed June 18, 2022, https://fortune.com/great-place-to-work-rankings/.

This leads us to the other point. It is not only by being nice to people and showering them with unique benefits do organisations succeed. However, it is not possible that all great workplaces have assured success. We know of organisations that focused more on being the best place to work, ending up with mediocre business performance. Everyone likes to be a great place to work, and some workplaces are tougher than others, but they attract people who flourish in such a culture.

The organisations that have been extremely successful get there by getting their focus right, and their success attracts people. This is not to say that a workplace has to be filled with hard-charging managers. Far more important is what Reed Hastings of Netflix has outlined as the principles of his organisation.[10]

1. Encourage independent decision-making by employees.
2. Share information openly, broadly, and deliberately.
3. Be extraordinarily candid with each other.
4. Keep only highly effective and talented people.
5. Avoid rules.

It surprises us no end when you ask HR professionals what they are doing, and they say, "Employee engagement activities". Just as organisation performance is not about the appraisal process alone, employee engagement activities are just a small part of engagement. This rests on the false assumption that employee engagement is a measurable outcome that can be increased by get-togethers or fancy offices. Happiness is an individual construct. Yes, events, awards and perks do provide happiness, but these are evanescent. The only enduring source of happiness for most employees is liking their work and the people they work with. How does HR ensure it? This is where another of Netflix's statements is relevant. Their core philosophy is "People over process".

Benchmarking benefits, leave policies and so forth does not create a competitive differentiation unless you also try to pay top salaries. In India, you will find many service organisations

10. "Netflix Culture—Seeking Excellence," *Netflix*, accessed June 18, 2022, https://jobs.netflix.com/culture.

having a lower HR person-to-headcount ratio. It could be 1:300 or less. On the other hand, the technology product companies have a much higher coverage because they pay better and have lighter processes. Surveys, benchmarking and so on might help us treat engagement like a rational process. However, in reality, it is much more emotional than logical. Discretionary effort comes from intrinsic conviction and not external motivation.

In many organisations, a higher than threshold attrition percentage is perceived negatively and leads to HR doing more. All expectations fall on the HR to work more and take remedial actions. Nothing may be further from the truth.

In more analyses than one, we have seen that there does not really have to be a trigger for employees at the entry level to quit. They are smart enough to know what they want and play the market inefficiencies to get a better salary or location. This flies against the assumption that there is always an internal trigger for quitting. Simply put, when there is buoyancy in the market, many people change jobs. Attrition rates are featured prominently in business papers, and HR heads and CEOs make statements on their employee value proposition. While manager maturity is a great focus area, how many will give up an increase of 50% to continue working for a great manager?

There has been hype about resignations, and the demand for digital talent has shot through the roof in 2021. Let us look at the average headcount and attrition rate of four IT Services organisations. IT Services organisations are chosen because such information is easily available.[11]

	TCS	**INFOSYS**	**WIPRO**	**COGNIZANT**
Headcount Q1	509058	267953	209890	301000
Attrition Q1	8.6%	13.9%	15.5%	18%
Headcount Q2	528748	279617	221365	318400
Attrition Q2	11.9%	20.1%	20.5%	22%

11. Financial statements and investor information for TCS, Infosys, Wipro and Cognizant for the April to June and July to September quarters of FY 21–22.

Let us look at the four organisations:

- TCS employs more than half a million people. Yet, their attrition is the lowest.
- Cognizant is the next biggest in terms of headcount. Yet, their attrition also is the highest, 2% more than the nearest competitors and 10% more than TCS.
- Infosys is larger than Wipro. However, both have very similar attrition rates.
- Attrition has increased quarter on quarter for all four organisations. You would think that the biggest organisation would be losing most people. However, based on the rates and some approximate calculations, TCS, which is nearly twice as large as the others, has lost just as many people as the other three organisations.

This is fascinating because, in terms of work content, there isn't much of a difference between them. All of them have big centres across the country.

All of them have significant investments in people development. None of them appear on the list of great workplaces in the country.

Given all this, one would think that TCS has found a better way to hire and retain employees when compared to the competition. Lesser attrition leads to greater predictability of delivering to client demands. In the absence of a common formula, attrition percentages could be different with similar data. Our takeaway is based on the reported number by the company.

Such advantages accrue over a period of time, whether the market is hot or not.

Being focused on attrition management and top 100 lists takes focus away from what really matters.

1. What is the culture of our organisation? Why should it matter to employees?
2. What are we doing, as HR, to embed this culture in the way we do things?

3. Is there transparency around where an employee stands in terms of long-term commitment to the organisation?

It is often said that the most successful organisations are like a cult. Cult of a leader or the organisation itself, where people believe when they say integrity or customer orientation. We have also seen the founders of organisations being very clear about their values, but the bigger the gap between the articulated and the perceived, the more adverse the impact on engagement.

Increasingly, having a purpose is showing up in corporate literature. We have a process way of taking organisational goals and converting them into individual goals. This requires a lot of iterations, and typically, the outcome may not leave a great audit trail. On the other hand, motivating through culture and purpose creates an emotional commitment that resonates more effectively.

TRANSPARENCY AS THE BEDROCK OF ORGANISATION CULTURE

Organisation culture can act as a great enabler of high performance. That by itself has been the topic of a lot of research and literature. However, here, we would like to focus on how an organisation can set itself up, defining what kind of organisation it would like to be.

In organisations with a strong founder, more often than not, the personality and preferences of the founder tend to shape the culture. The cult of Steve Jobs, if you may. However, with time, more and more organisations are being founded by a small group of entrepreneurs. Solo founders come with their own idiosyncrasies. A group of co-founders, on the other hand, have greater clarity on what they would like to do when compared to how they would go about doing it. Inherently, they become more participative because the founders need to assign roles and responsibilities and dialogue on their norms. The absence of uniformly understood norms will end up sabotaging the organisation.

Sahaj Software is an organisation in the information technology and technology consulting services domain. The founders, who had moved on from senior jobs in technology, thought of creating an organisation where work is fun, with no rank-controlled access or privileges and everything is underlined with the ethos of trust.

Sahaj was founded as "A people's collective that stands for a shared purpose— everyone owns the dreams, ideas, ideologies, successes, and failures of the organisation, a synergy that is rooted in the ethos of honesty, respect, trust, and equitability".

These are powerful words, and it is not unusual for entrepreneurs to be idealistic. However, principles alone don't build culture. What is articulated is the intended culture. It becomes real only when practised consistently and even challenging decisions are made, keeping the principles first. Obviously, when you want to be a collective, you would not like any exceptions.

While transparency with business data was easy, there were reservations about complete transparency with the compensation data. Should it not be on a need-to-know basis?

It was possible to say, "We are transparent with everything but compensation". Then, you hyphenate your core principles, which, in turn, has a very different impact on the culture. An aspiring person may think there is a hierarchy where few of the employees have access to salary information while the rest of them don't. It could be perceived that the information on compensation has become a lever of control. After deep deliberations, they decided that salary data would also be open for all employees and the salary review process would involve as many people as possible.

At the outset, transparency in nine parameters out of ten seems a great deal. However, a strong culture is built when it's a ten out of ten. But this requires handling the ensuing challenges in case of compensation, individual concerns of privacy, managers perceiving a loss of control and so on. Even though it is a relatively small organisation, Sahaj made headlines last year for making pay transparent to everyone.

In our experience, we have seen that dissatisfaction with pay or salary increases based on peer comparisons as one of the most intractable issues in employee motivation. Organisations have resorted to policy guidelines saying that 'You cannot discuss your pay with anyone else'. While that is a good policy intent, how do you address the problem? Pay parity perception is one of those fault lines in organisations where policy, market fit, manager capability, appraisal fairness all collide. Given that an organisation has taken it up, we thought it fit to follow through with them.

Let us hear from founder CEO Akash.

CONVERSATION WITH MR. AKASH AGRAWAL, CEO SAHAJ SOFTWARE SOLUTIONS

What are the foundational principles of Sahaj?

Five of us came together to start this organisation. We did not start with what we should do, but what we would like it to be. All five of us have had years of experience in software services and were clear about what we should not do. We wanted to be unique and different from people's perspective.

In most organisations, there is an information hierarchy. The person at the top has access to far more information than the average employee. However, the person at bottom is still expected to be as responsible as if they are owning the organisation. In such a culture, compensation is treated with confidentiality.

Our perspective is that over a period of time, people in technology services organisations have become order takers. Employees are not treated as people. We wanted to reduce this exploitation and support people to make their own decisions. Every individual knows how much they have earned for the organisation.

It is not as if the transparency applies to everyone but leaders. In fact, the compensation for founder/directors of the organisation was decided by a group of 40 employees. For merit salary increases, the budget is communicated. Individual offices decide on what percent hike should be for everyone. Initially, we had the same uniform hike percentage for everyone. Now, the offices arrive at individual increases based on performance and related factors.

There have been cases where team members have said that one of their colleagues is earning less and their salary needs to be bumped up. We look out for people with lower base salaries and ensure that they are given a much higher percentage increase than those who are more senior and are better paid. This is the advantage of transparency.

Salaries cannot be delinked from overall financial information. The financial information in terms of revenues, profits, billing is all shared. All profits are shared on the basis of collective decisions. People decide what percent should go to bonuses and what should be reinvested in business.

How do you build transparency into different dimensions?

We start with the annual business plan. We take everyone through the plan, and they can question anything. We also have regular All Hands discussions, where people can debate on subjects like new office locations, areas of technology focus etc.

We have also tried to remove all barriers to transparency in the organisation. There are no formal roles or levels. People can play different project roles; they can be developer in one place, project lead in another. This again ensures there is no loss of information due to hierarchy.

There aren't many defined policies. There is no limit on paid vacation days.

In fact, we don't use the word "Employee". We prefer using "People".

How does transparency help with business?

When people are treated as another brick in the wall, their ownership suffers, and they merely execute what is given to them.

Our workforce profile is also different. More than half of our people have experience in excess of 15 years. They are leading adult personal lives and so transparency seems more down their alley.

When they think like they own the business, it carries forward into their client interactions as well. When someone can question leadership in his organisation, they also feel comfortable having an open discussion with a leader in a client organisation.

One of our clients had asked us for a proposal for some work. The work would have earned good money for the organisation. However, the project members took stock of what was available and advised the client to carry on with what they already had after making some modifications. In a sense, the employees did what was good for the client and were comfortable leaving money on the table.

Complete transparency and trust with people works positively with clients too. It is a continuum.

How do you scale up with a culture like this?

We have big aspirations. Given how soulless technology services have become for the individual, we think it is possible to create disruption in the industry. Curiosity and pride in craftsmanship are universal. We find that people from outside India are also excited to work in a transparent organisation. Even though our hands are full in India, we have invested into offices in London, Singapore, San Francisco and Melbourne and are taking our story global.

One of the responsibilities of the founders is to grow the next set of leaders and this should help us grow organically.

Our culture is not a rulebook. It is not as if every single person has the same set of attributes. There is room for individualism. However, people who put themselves before the organisation may not thrive at Sahaj.

What role does HR play here?

Other than for recruitment, we have not felt the need for a formal HR function. We are growing through the cohesion of culture. Given that, we may not need the bureaucracy or systems that HR will bring with it.

We do invest a lot in training people in building their capabilities as well as in organisation ethos.

We do lose people, either to higher studies or to big product companies or start-ups. Some need the reassurance of a brand and some want more money. However, our losses are much less than other organisations in our industry.

This is a great illustration of culture being an enabler of high performance. After seven years, Sahaj has stayed true to its founding principles. What happens if they grow to 1000 people? Will they have the same ability? How do you organically scale the culture adding newcomers every year? What if they get listed and the market thinks they have a slow culture, where a decision has to pass through many interactions?

These are valid questions and creating an HR bureaucracy of value statements and presentations delivered by staffers is not the answer. Many large organisations have value statements that are not adequately reflected upon in their trade-offs. The challenge is the internalisation of the founding principles and we think as long as Sahaj continues to do it, they will be successful.

Culture impacts performance. However, too much performance focus can also weaken the culture. Uber, for instance, was a fast-growth start-up chasing growth globally. Business leaders were encouraged to grow at all costs. Growth happened, but from centralisation of power to disconnected employees to gender discrimination complaints, the culture led to toxic outcomes. The company had to get an external assessment and transition to a new CEO to rebuild the organisation. The actions of leaders and their focus influence the culture positively or negatively. When not handled well, organisation culture can derail the company, too.[12]

These days, creators tend to create a universe with multiple characters and story arcs, like the Marvel series of movies. This chapter is also like a universe because each theme chosen deserves a separate book! Quickly summarising what we have covered:

- Superior organisation performance is the desired objective of workforce capacity and capability.
- Performance management, merit increase and recognition are all critical processes. These are HR-managed but not sufficient by themselves.

Effective performance also needs:

- An elegant organisation structure and requisite hierarchy.
- Aligned leadership team.
- Engaged workforce.
- Cohesive teams.

HR organisations should not only manage their processes well but also influence organisational dynamics right from the CEO level. Performance is delivered more from emotional commitment, and so the softer side is equally critical. Aligning organisation growth to employees through asymmetric rewards like stock options should always be on the table.

Organisations are not like the old tales where they live happily ever after once they achieve high performance. Competition changes, business model changes and geopolitical risks, as well as regulatory changes lurk. To stay successful, an organisation needs to adapt and transform.

You might think that capacity, capability and performance included produce superior organisational outcome. While that is true, in our study, we found that organisation transformation as a consistent theme. Whether due to internal reasons or market or

12. Barbara Booth, "A Year Later, What Uber Has Done to Revamp Its Troubled Image," *CNBC*, June 20, 2018, accessed June 18, 2022, https://www.cnbc.com/2018/06/20/a-year-later-what-uber-has-done-to-revamp-its-troubled-image.html.

environmental reasons, most organisations seem to be undergoing transformations. Enabling organisation transformation is the fourth pillar of HR strategy. Transformation is a different, better way of delivering performance. The elements of capacity, capability and performance are equally relevant to transformation strategy.

When do organisations need to transform? Is it to face external threats? Accommodate internal growth? Is it possible to handle transformation proactively?

We will address these in the next chapter.

8

Towards a Better Future: Organisational Transformation

An organisation I have worked with has had a celebrated legacy of over 150 years. From a single paper operation, this organisation reinvented itself multiple times in a range of industrial sectors, including cable, paper products, rubber boots, tires, televisions and mobile phones. For many of us who held our first mobile phone in the 1990s and early 2000s, Nokia was the trusted brand.

Nokia held 40% of the global market share in mobile phones in 2007. It was, by far, the Big Daddy of the industry, powered by its technological leadership. But things changed fast and were best captured by the Burning Platform memo from the then-Nokia CEO, Stephen Elop, to the employees in early 2011. He wrote:

> We ... are standing on a "burning platform," and we must decide how we are going to change our behaviour.
>
> For example, there is intense heat coming from our competitors, more rapidly than we ever expected. Apple disrupted the market by redefining the smartphone and attracting developers to a closed, but very powerful ecosystem.
>
> And then, there is Android. In about two years, Android created a platform that attracts application developers, service providers and hardware manufacturers.

> While competitors poured flames on our market share, what happened at Nokia? We fell behind, we missed big trends, and we lost time. At that time, we thought we were making the right decisions; but, with the benefit of hindsight, we now find ourselves years behind.
>
> How did we get to this point? Why did we fall behind when the world around us evolved?

Eventually, in September 2013, Nokia decided to sell its mobile phone business to Microsoft as part of a 7.2 billion dollar deal. Thereon, Nokia focused its portfolio on three areas: infrastructure, mapping services, technology and patent licensing. The organisation benefited from such clarity and, through various smart decisions, managed a turnaround by 2017.

Risto Siilasmaa, chair of the board, described the journey as "It has been a complete removal of engines, the cabin, and the wings of an airplane and reassembling the airplane to look very different." 99% of the workforce, 80% of the board and everyone barring one member of the executive team, had been turned over by Nokia during this turnaround.

BCG, in its 2017 publication *The Comeback Kids: Lessons from Successful Turnarounds*, described Nokia's post-2012 transformation as:

> ... from walking dead to thriving in a new core business—is unlikely to be Nokia's last. But this success showed that the organisation was able to navigate massive disruptions, reorient itself, and come back even stronger. Today, Nokia is again the pride of Finland and the most valuable organisation in the country. It is well positioned for the next chapter in its long history.[1]

This is a great illustration, but what has it got to do with HR? BCG outlines the five critical elements of a turnaround:

- Develop a clear-eyed understanding of the situation.
- Redefine the organisation's strategic focus on where to play and not play.

1. Ramón Baeza et al., "The Comeback Kids: Lessons from Successful Turnarouds," *BCG Turn*, November 2017, accessed June 18, 2022.

- Restructure to reduce costs and complexity, including changes to the organisation and operating model.
- Build the right culture focusing on speed, innovation and openness to change.
- Invest in digital.

As you may notice, HR has a key role to play in all these critical elements.

Nokia's may be a dramatic illustration. However, when we did the polling of executives (in Chapter 3), we expected revenue growth or profitability to emerge as bigger themes. To our surprise, transformation showed up strongly across the board. On the ground, almost everyone is transforming, if not their entire business, at least parts of it. The transformation could be to:

- React to external changes (Market/Globalisation/Technology)
- Respond to market standing (Competitive with peers)
- Adapt to the organisation lifecycle stage (Progress with growth)

At the same time, broader technological, cultural, legal and geopolitical trends impact organisations and the workforce at large. In an HBR article, "Your workforce is more adaptable than you think", the authors outline 17 different trends reshaping the workforce.[2] These can be broadly classified into:

- Accelerating technological change
- Growing demand for skills
- Changes in employee expectations
- Shifting labour demographics
- Transitioning work models
- Evolving business environment

---

2. Joseph Fuller, "Your Workforce Is More Adaptable than You Think," *Harvard Business Review*, November 24, 2020, accessed June 18, 2022, https://hbr.org/2019/05/your-workforce-is-more-adaptable-than-you-think.

We have covered many of the trends elsewhere in the book. Later in this chapter, we shall take a deep dive into digital transformation.

External Environment: Shifts and Shocks

There are many trends that influence an organisation's need to transform, both from the environment and from within the organisation. Change by nature has to take the organisation from where it is to where it wants to be. Transformation, then, is a strategic approach by which an organisation is able to enact this shift.

When an organisation is proactive, it can shift to the future state on its own time frame. However, not all organisations do. Many get into a crisis by not shifting when there is time. They then receive a shock to the system forcing them to transform in a hurry. An approach that may or may not work.

Let us look at both shifts and shocks in some depth and what HR can do, especially when some shocks arrive unannounced.

Shifts

From the extract, it appears that Nokia was faced with the shock of losing market share and capitalisation. Did it happen overnight? To quote from the same memo, "We fell behind, we missed big trends and we lost time. At that time, we thought we were making the right decisions, but now we find ourselves years behind".

Clearly, there were shifts happening in the marketplace that Nokia misread. Microsoft was also falling behind in catching up with shifts. Then, Satya Nadella took over, and his view, as mentioned in his book *Hit Refresh,* was, "Every person, organisation, and even society reaches a point at which they owe it to themselves to hit refresh—to re-energise, renew, reframe, and rethink their purpose."

When Nadella took over Microsoft in 2014, the organisation was at an interesting crossroads. It was doing well in financial terms, but the numbers did not influence the valuation. Investors were not excited about the future of the organisation as they thought it was not shifting as required.

Nadella recognised this and moved swiftly, making changes. He put his bets on mobile and cloud computing—two vectors that had huge growth potential, but where Microsoft was not the leader. He showed a willingness to partner with competitors and embraced the open-source software community, thereby giving a great boost to the developer ecosystem. His bold decisions included halting Microsoft's smartphone venture by writing off the entire Nokia acquisition. He instead bet on LinkedIn and GitHub. These investments, aligned with Microsoft's core strategy, have boosted its future revenue streams. All this meant that Microsoft's present market capitalisation has crossed 2.5 trillion USD, and its share price has steadily grown over the last five years.

Shifts offer a fertile ground for active HR partnerships. They impact multiple dimensions of the employee experience, which are integral to the success of the shift.

In 2013, I had the opportunity to experience another transformation journey when I moved from Nokia to Adobe Systems. Back then, Adobe was going through a big transformation and moving away from software in a box to the Adobe suite of products on the cloud, something similar to the transformation in Microsoft.

A McKinsey 2015 publication narrated Adobe's transition as follows:[3]

> Over the past five years, Adobe Systems has remade itself as a cloud organisation. It no longer offers its publishing and design tools in the form of physical, shrink-wrapped products to be deployed at customers' sites under a perpetual licence—where customers pay once and can use the software indefinitely. Rather, customers subscribe to Creative Cloud, the organisation's online suite of publishing and design tools, and receive frequent software upgrades as well as a range of new online-only and mobile services.

3. "Reborn in the Cloud," *McKinsey & Company*, July 1, 2015, accessed June 18, 2022, https://www.mckinsey.com/capabilities/mckinsey-digital/our-insights/reborn-in-the-cloud.

This was a big shift in strategy for the organisation, and it required reimagining talent management. It started with mindset changes where mental models had to shift from thinking about product features to thinking about one common customer experience. Teams in Adobe were designed around each product, dispersed globally and more than often self-sufficient with independent roadmaps.

Both organisation design and governance mechanisms had to be swiftly reimagined. One quick way to facilitate communication and collaboration across teams was to invest in internal mobility so that talent could cross-pollinate.

Teams had to look at integrated technology, roadmaps and build transparency as they continuously evolved them. Did this create chaos? Yes, it did. Many leaders who had spent years in the organisation suddenly had to lead differently, while some felt a loss of power when taken out of their comfort zones.

Under the new subscription model, more than four million customers were being billed every month compared to the earlier three million a year. While the revenue recognition mechanism changed for the organisation, customers also had the choice to move away any month. Sustained retention necessitates continuous embedding of value, requiring engineering and customer experience teams to transform to agile ways of working. The existing workforce capacity and capability were not aligned to this. They were enhanced by hiring people who had experienced such environments and training teams to run in the sprint environment. Investing in capacity and capability is not sufficient unless they deliver performance.

The Agile Performance management system meant a shift from once a year to monthly check-ins (sometimes even shorter based on sprint cycles). Performance management conversations are possibly the most difficult experiences for managers. It was manageable annually, but doing it multiple times in a year?

This shift called for overcoming a big mental barrier. Some very interesting insights came in during the first few months, with some employees expressing that they had no performance conversation while their managers thought otherwise. Further investigation revealed that the last few minutes of the regular work review meetings were being used by managers to check on how team members were performing! Managers felt they were ticking off on the performance conversations while employees were expecting differently. The core team had to coach managers and employees to schedule time outside of their work review meetings on a regular frequency for performance check-ins.

Some managers were able to progress, while others were still infrequent with such interactions. A deeper understanding was gleaned from conversations with managers who were still not there. It revealed the reluctance stemming from a feeling of not being adequately equipped. The overall change management was strengthened by deploying learning aids for managers, such as training programs and self-help tool kits. Building capabilities among leaders and managers stretched beyond performance management. Heat maps on individual managers using indicators such as pace of growth in the team through hiring, attrition, engagement scores, exit interview pulse and so forth were created. These surfaced capability gaps that were plugged into different interventions. In other words, enhancing people manager capability was critical to delivering performance in an agile manner of working.

Adobe had high-quality engineering and creative talent in its workforce at that time. It was a leader in its place and thus quite competitive internally. Adobe had realised it would need beyond cerebral brilliance to connect its workforce to one core. Adobe refreshed its leadership behaviour and very clearly called out the role of EQ in leading.

While recognising performance and reward, the organisation had a practice of strongly valuing past credentials, including the institute employees had graduated from. Those from the IITs were valued differentially. Similarly, those in development were rewarded differently from those in quality. But with the pursued transformation, these practices had to change. The India team had to align with the global approach in calibrating performance and reward. Also, engineers were tasked to take end-to-end accountability for the quality of their codes. Thus, the silos between development and quality were pulled down.

Quality engineers were provided the opportunity to transition to development as and when they met the baseline capability requirements.

When I signed up for my Adobe offer in 2013, the share price was still below USD 50. But within 18 months, it surged up to 1.5 times its initial value, signalling a visible shift in trajectory. The story of the power of working together as 'one team' to drive the transformation was getting started. Over the next few years, the share price had more than a 13x increase.

The shift made by Adobe can be explained in a single phrase: "Going from shrink-wrapped to cloud". However, the depth of this shift was so profound that every aspect of HR strategy had to be reoriented. When done proactively, this led to lasting success.

Organisations like Nokia get locked in a success trap that holds them back from making the needed shifts to be in sync with reality. Over a period of time, the gap widens. Transformation through shifts is then no longer possible, and the trigger then zones into a 'shock'.

Shocks

I had once worked for an organisation that was a joint venture between an Indian family conglomerate and an MNC. The JV was in a highly competitive industry, and the organisation was making losses. The founder did not want to carry on and sold his stake to the MNC. Until then, the approach was more benevolent, and the real status of business was not well known. The MNC conducted a complete assessment with a consultant and started with changes to the operating model and organisation structure. This led to one of the longest days of my career, where hard-working men with families were let go on redundancy.

This was a shock to the employees, but the leadership group had seen it coming but not created a sense of urgency. This is not an uncommon case of a shock to the workforce created by delayed strategic actions. What does HR really do in such situations?

The playbook of execution after the shock is clear. You need to reorient the workforce, reduce payroll costs and focus on the essentials when faced with big clients vanishing literally overnight. One of the companies I had worked with created a list of essential people they would like to retain as much as possible because they would be key to the regeneration.

I have sat in business reviews where almost every trend was in red! Since workforce capacity is increased before revenue increases, such failures almost always end up in layoffs and a compromised employer brand. The only role HR can proactively do is to wear the hat of the leadership team member and examine numbers with an independent eye. If the organisation seems to be not doing as well as its competitors or showing declining trends, the HR leader should:

- Examine whether the forecasting capability of leaders needs to be strengthened.
- Examine whether there are holes in the strategic planning process.
- Be wary of any manpower requests that ask for a lot of people before the revenue starts coming in.
- Examine the culture in leadership reviews. Does the founder or CEO not want to hear bad news? Are the stories being spun to look positive? What are the norms of the leadership meetings and reviews? Do they confront or skip around the elephants in the room? If they do skip, how to bring it to the centre? Are they comfortable around conflicts?
- What is the consequence of sustained underperformance?

HR leaders are well equipped to play the conscience keeper because of their independence from the need to paint a rosy picture.

An organisation may be doing most things right and yet be faced with regulatory changes that deeply impact their business. The Goods and Services Tax introduced in 2016, for instance, was a big change for MSME companies. Covid 19 is another big shock for which no organisation had planned.

How leading IT organisations coped with Covid 19 is a great case study of handling an external shock. Many of these companies have a mature disaster recovery process, which has been tested during natural calamities. They can have many employees work from home in the event of a crisis in a location.

They looked at the pandemic proactively, started treating it as a natural calamity and began doing things that seemed logical then—have people come to work on alternate days, disinfect the office regularly and so forth. They got comfortable with a high proportion of the team working from home.

Then, the Disaster Recovery process was rolled out across the organisation, and even those who did not have a laptop got one. In India, they were helped by the fact there was a time window to see what was happening in other countries and take action, keeping in mind the worst-case scenario rather than being guided by optimism. By the time the country was locked down, organisations were essentially in a work from home mode.

There are lessons in this for HR. We do have processes like succession planning to mitigate the impact of leaders leaving. That is internal. We also need to plan for unforeseen changes in the external environment. For instance:

- What if the government declares gender parity in pay?
- Where we depend on work visas, what if that government changes their regulations?
- What if the Government goes ahead with its declared policy on compensation structure?

Unlike Covid, many regulatory changes are often in the pipeline before they are rolled out. It helps to pay attention to what is happening in employment regulation, tax rates and such.

Given the rapidity of business cycles, listed companies have incorporated a risk management process. Someone owns risk management, and the board has a committee to look after risks. They also enlist enterprise risks, and these are outlined with mitigation strategies. Formalising such a mechanism would help HR organisations as well to handle shocks proactively.

Both shocks and shifts are important drivers for the need to transform. While they can impact independently, ignoring shifts often leads to shocks. Many organisations fail to shift when they have the time.

How Organisations Evolve: Life Cycle Stages

Are you working on any of the following?

- Documenting policies that have hitherto been person dependent
- Hiring for a new geography/ business unit
- Creating a formal values and vision statement
- Introducing an organisation performance-linked incentive program
- Planning the succession for key leaders

If you are, chances are that you are responding to a transformation happening within your organisation as it is moving from one stage to another. You do these not because of external shifts or shocks but due to your organisation recognising a need for more formal systems even as you are growing.

Organisations are of various types when viewed according to size, geographic spread, lines of business and longevity. Even if we take any one of them, say Microsoft, and freeze time during the Gates, Ballmer and Nadella eras, each frame would provide uniquely different views. As organisations evolve and grow, they demonstrate some distinct characteristics involving their structure and how they operate.

There is a lot of literature on organisational maturity, including using the frame of biological evolution, product life cycles and so forth.

In their research, Lester, Parnell and Carraher defined the five stages of an organisation's life cycle: Birth, Survival, Success, Renewal and Decline. They went on to demonstrate the linkage of strategy to organisational life cycle stages and how it influences factors like size, structure, power and decision-making. The following table, adapted from "Organizational Lifecycle: A Five-stage Stage Empirical Scale", illustrates the key characteristics.[4]

4. Donald L. Lester, John A. Parnell, and Shawn M. Carraher, "Organizational Lifecycle: A Five-Stage Stage Empirical Scale," *International Journal of Organizational Analysis* 11, no. 4 (April 1, 2003): 339–54.

Life cycle stage	Situation	Structure	Decision-making style	Strategy
Existence < 10 years old	Small, young and homogenous	Informal, single-owner dominated	Centralised, trial and error	Prospector, first mover
Survival > 15 % growth	Medium-sized environment, more competitive	Functional, some formality	Some delegations, begin formal information processing	Analyser, second mover, differentiation
Success < 15% growth	Heterogeneous environment, larger size	Formal, bureaucratic, functional	Reliance on internal information processing	Defender/ segment control
Renewal > 15% growth	Very heterogeneous environment	Divisional, some matrix	Sophisticated controls, formal analysis in decision-making	Analyser/ combination differentiation, low cost
Decline No Growth	Very large, homogenous and competitive environment	Formal, bureaucratic, mostly functional	Moderate centralisation, less sophisticated information processing	Reactor/ product/ service breadth, low cost

Figure 8.1: Life Cycle Stage Characteristics

As an organisation takes off, the focus is on finding the first set of customers and creating a success story to pivot on. This ensuing belief from winning is pitched to attract talent. The organisation's size is small, and the structure is simple. The power to make decisions is with the leader (founder/founders). This is the Birth stage, also called Existence. In this stage, the only HR contribution lies in getting things done the way the founder(s) want.

The Survival stage is when the organisation seeks to grow. Investment in hiring talent brings in the needed specialisations. The structure shows more formalisation, and the focus is to generate adequate revenues to manage operations and plough back the rest into growth. While some organisations get it right and are able to progress to the next stage of evolution, others keep stuttering ahead, still trying to figure out the right strategy to bring in needed stability. Many organisations are worse off and battle for survival. This is a stage to move from informal to formal HR. Policy manuals, an HR calendar and a structured HR department, are all symptomatic of this shift. You would have a hierarchy and organisation chart defined.

The organisations that are resilient enough to pass through the survival stage move on to the next phase of maturity, which is termed the Success stage. At this stage, organisations are managed through formalisation and control. Policies and processes are leveraged for governance. With scale, layers form and slow down the organisation. The senior leadership stays invested in 'strategy', leaving the management to run the operations. Organisations often stay focused on consolidation and stabilisation rather than expansion. In HR, you build on the formalisation. You arguably need to have a consistent approach to allocating limited resources to employees who feel they deserve it. There is a formal appraisal distribution which ties into merit increases, formal policy for promotions and so on. You may also develop competency frameworks and design practices based on that. HR can no longer get things done with senior leadership directly. More managers have a voice, and so committees come into play.

The complexity needed to manage growth reduces the agility required to grow fast. Alignment to organisational vision is diluted, and there are multiple viewpoints on most critical issues. Change becomes difficult. Organisations have two choices from here—renew or decline.

The challenge for HR is to identify and enable a framework that unifies actions, even across the world, while at the same time empowering business and regional leaders to set and achieve aspirational goals. People need to be able to work in a matrix structure without adding to the bureaucracy. HR goes back to the initial model, but at scale, creating an emotional connection with the organisation through communications and collaboration opportunities and strategically leveraging the leaders to build alignment.

Finally, at the Decline stage, the organisation is no longer viable from a financial standpoint. Power and politics start eroding the very core of the organisation as personal goals take precedence over organisational goals. Decision-making is controlled by a limited set of people who may not be best suited for the same. That concludes the lifecycle journey. In our survey, we saw two types of companies that chose transformation. The market leaders spoke about it from a perspective of adapting to shifts, while the laggards focused more on internal transformation. Hiring a new CEO often seems to be the most visible strategy for such turnarounds.

TURNING IT AROUND

There are many companies that, when pushed to irrelevance, end up being sold. Any organisation producing something of value to customers always lives on in some form, even if not as the same entity. Again, this is not a linear, one-way path to decline. Companies sometimes end up making losses before turning around. The one common thread in most cases is the culture, which connects such disparate threads as innovation pipeline, productivity, sales effectiveness, responsiveness and so forth. Let us go back to Nokia and see how one organisation reversed the decline.

Yves Doz, Emeritus Professor of Strategic Management at INSEAD, stated that Nokia's mobile phone story exemplifies a common trait we see in mature, successful companies.[5] Success breeds conservatism and hubris, which, over time, results in a decline in the strategy processes, leading to poor strategic decisions. Once companies embrace new ideas and experimentation to spur growth, with success, they become risk-averse and less innovative. Such considerations will be crucial for companies that want to grow and avoid one of the biggest disruptive threats to their future—their own success.

As Nokia commenced its transformation journey, it declared its shift from a leader to a challenger in 2011. This was very

5. Yves L. Doz, "The Strategic Decisions That Caused Nokia's Failure," *INSEAD Knowledge*, November 23, 2017, accessed June 18, 2022, https://knowledge.insead.edu/strategy/strategic-decisions-caused-nokias-failure.

significant as the CEO called for a 'change in attitude', and the organisation adopted a 'challenger' mindset. The concept of the Challenger Brand first gained attention in 1999 through Adan Morgan, founder of eatbigfish. Brands and businesses that are ambitious to compete with the established leaders in the market must apply a very different approach or strategy, positioning and organisational culture. Nokia realised that, as a challenger, it had to move faster than the market leaders to narrow the gap. This was only possible if they focused on a narrower set of priorities and took advantage of the ecosystem play in others, such as leaving the app development to the development ecosystem.

One of the first things that the leadership at Nokia did once it declared the adoption of the Challenger Mindset was to plan roadshows across the globe to convince and excite its employees on the priorities and the product roadmap ahead. It was a big way to demonstrate that the organisation knew exactly what it had to do and there was alignment at the executive level. This was surely a shift from the days when different parts of the organisation could be tunnel visioned on their own zones without visibility to the big picture.

Nokia realised that the 'Ways of Working' had to change. Decision-making, for example, lacked urgency, and it was fine to take the additional time as the group involved could not reach an agreement. This would no longer work. Product development cycles, which even stretched to 22 months, were speeded up to 7 to 8 months. The organisation had to go faster and harder now. The CEO took on himself to respond to 10 to 20 customer emails every day. Such role modelling shifted the organisation to a different level of customer empathy. Nokia became humbler in the way it started interacting with its partners, carriers and other stakeholders. The internal culture in the organisation started echoing this change. Big budgets had suddenly dried up. More accountability was built in as to how everyone handled organisation money. Flying international to attend an internal hour-long team meeting was once common, but no longer. Leadership teams had to build the new muscle to make tradeoff decisions, be it while hiring talent or areas of investment.

As you see here, the strategy or market orientation may not be HR's primary responsibility. However, certain elements lie under the influence of HR, in partnership with the CEO and leadership team, such as:

- Converting those into measurable outcomes with incentives.
- Creating a culture that enables transformation.
- Developing the capabilities by hiring and competency building.

HR Partnering of Uber Growth: Infosys

As I look back at my 11 years at Infosys, I call it the experience of making a 100,000 people organisation. When I joined the organisation, it had a workforce of about 3000, mostly Bangalore-centric. At the time I exited in 2010, there were over 110,000 employees across the globe. During this time, it had to reimagine itself multiple times. When it was still small with a four-digit workforce, everything was centralised. Processes and policies were simple. Work was done through informal networks at the workplace.

As the growth continued in the early 2000s, Infosys had to spread across multiple locations in India. To function efficiently, some form of decentralisation evolved. More formal processes and practices took shape to ensure that there was consistency across. Some leaders felt that they had lost out on the flexibility of the past, and for everything, 'there was a way' to do things. As Infosys broadened its business footprint it was hiring talent with varied capabilities. Price points for such talent, growth paths and designations had to align with market norms. Infosys realised that the existing grade-based structure was not aligned with its growth. Thus, they adopted a role-based structure. By defining the roles and the competencies required for each role, the organisation believed that it could provide transparency to its employees on career ladders and how they could grow and build their careers. Policies and practices were aligned to roles. In fact, different roles at the same level were billed differently to clients.

While these were strong reasons, the transformation was not as easy as it looked conceptually. In the grade-based system, employees grew based on tenure and performance. However, in the new role-based structure, growth was governed by the availability of a vacancy and individual readiness. Suddenly, employees realised that even if they performed well, they had to wait for a promotion till a vacancy at the next level role emerged. Also, during the mapping, some employees moved a level down. They were employees who had been promoted based on their tenure but were doing jobs that were not big enough. They had been valued over and over again for only what they were good at, but the potential to add higher value was overlooked. Some career ladders only stretched to a certain level. Employees in them were likely to grow at a slower pace and also had to jump out to alternate ladders to experience continued growth.

2003 brought forth a bitter reality as employee engagement plummeted. Infosys had about 40,000 employees then. The need was felt to set up an Internal Communication function to ensure that communication flowed across the organisation in a planned and consistent way. The organisation needed a network of Communication Champions spread across the globe to enable this. A Policy Council had to be set up to ensure broader representation from across the organisation in assessing the need and making fair judgements.

Further on, Infosys transitioned into the Infosys Group as the business footprint widened its scope from a homogeneous space of Application Development and Maintenance (ADM) to a broader range spanning Consulting to BPO. This meant a change in governance and the design of policies and practices that balanced both a common core and specific variations across businesses. Some businesses demanded customised talent offerings, higher reward budgets and retention practices, citing different and higher risk levels affecting their talent. An Executive Committee, composed of a group of senior business leaders, was set up. While there were good reasons for the same, including preparing some of them for CXO positions in the future, it meant an additional layer of decision-makers and approvers. Many times, instead of hastening decisions, this slowed down the entire process.

In mid-2006, I remember being provided the mandate to grow the hiring program by three times on a base of about 8000 hires per year and take the program to five to six countries. As business was scaling up, the intake of talent had to match the pace. However, external regulations on securing VISA saw newer controls emerging, and Infosys realised it had to de-risk itself. This meant hiring from local talent pools in growing numbers in countries beyond India and setting up near-shore centres in proximity to clients. This brought in its own share of shifts in how the organisation was structured, governed and connected on a day-to-day basis. Policies and practices beyond just hiring had to be adapted to manage through a more complex set-up.

We had seen the dynamic capabilities model in an earlier chapter. Organisations today need to continuously transform by building dynamic capabilities for sustained competitive advantage. Infosys flourished by making such changes during my tenure. The organisation has stayed successful since then as well. It could have taken some wrong turns, but the resilience in the system ensured the organisation renewed itself and stayed away from decline.

Having seen the impact of shifts and shocks and the organisational life cycle, let us focus on one theme that offers transformational possibilities to the employee-facing and client-facing organisation—Digital.

The Digital Transformation

In the quarter ending December 2021, production of cars in India fell by 13% year on year.[6] The production could not meet the demand, in spite of mechanical and electrical parts being available. Rather, it was due to the global shortage of semiconductors. It is estimated that a modern automobile has millions of lines of code—GPS navigation, safety cameras and entertainment systems—all relying heavily on computing.

---

6. ET Bureau, "Car Sales Fall 13% in December as Chip Shortage Hurts Production," *The Economic Times*, January 15, 2022, https://economictimes.indiatimes.com/industry/auto/auto-news/car-sales-fall-13-in-december-as-chip-shortage-hurts-production/articleshow/88908171.cms.

Of course, automotive technology is not the classic "digital" transformation that people talk about. At the beginning of the last decade, we had SMAC (Social, Mobile, Analytics and Cloud). With time, digital technologies have enlarged to include:

- Artificial intelligence and machine learning.
- Industry 4.0, which is an omnibus term for iOT, smart sensors and wearables.
- Automation using robotics, both on the shop floor and in the office.

The interplay between computing power, internet bandwidth and reach, cloud storage and app economy has created a world that relies on digital technologies more than ever before for not just automotive, entertainment or education but even fundamental functions such as making a payment. Cash or card used to be the standard question. Now, the options are between cash, card or UPI. If UPI, through QR code or PIN or phone number? GPay, Paytm or PhonePe?

Why is this different from earlier digital efforts? Let us consider the ERP wave, for instance. In most organisations, there was a hierarchy of needs. ERP closely tracked the cash flow in the system, and finance was always the preferred module. While things have come a long way, in HR, ERP was primarily used for employee master data, and the challenges of unifying and centralising HR processes using an ERP are legion. This is digitisation.

What is digital transformation? A simplistic definition would be: "Radically redefining how an organisation makes a difference to its customers by embedding digital technologies across its operating model".

It is not just about technology adoption. Mindset change is required to enable a culture where the status quo can be challenged, and experimenting and failing fast is encouraged. There needs to be greater agility in thinking and action that focuses on skill shifts needed to be 'future-fit'. Finally, outcome thinking pivots on customer experience and value. We will build a better understanding of these as we converse more on digital culture.

Digital transformation has liberated the use of technology in a manner of speaking. There is no need for a hierarchy of users, and cloud technologies have enabled pay-as-you-go. Analytics has enabled the ability to identify patterns in the workforce so that the employee value proposition can finally be customised to the unit of a single employee. Instead of being treated as different entities, HR can actually provide an employee experience that is comparable to what the organisation is providing to the clients.

Such possibilities, in turn, bring up two key questions:

1. How does HR enable digital transformation?
2. How does HR transform digitally?

Transformation by Influence or Capability

As per the WEF Digital Culture Guidebook:

> Organisations with a strong digital culture use digital tools and data-powered insights to drive decisions and Customer-centricity while innovating and collaborating across the organisation. When implemented purposefully, digital culture can drive sustainable action and create value for all stakeholders.[7]

The four pillars listed above—data-driven, customer-centric, innovative and collaborative—have broad acceptance across other attempts to define digital culture. Another research involving Capgemini and MIT has three other dimensions—open culture (involving partnering with external stakeholders), agility, flexibility and digital-first mindset (where, by default, the focus is on digital solutions).[8]

The transformations we have looked at so far, tended to be top-down. The CEO or his team takes a look at the aggregate numbers or the kind of problems that are being escalated to them

7. "Digital Culture: The Driving Force of Digital Transformation," *World Economic Forum*, June 2021, accessed June 18, 2022, https://www.weforum.org/publications/digital-culture-the-driving-force-of-digital-transformation/.
8. Digital Transformation Institute, "The Digital Culture Challenge: Closing the Employee-Leadership Gap," *Capgemini*, 2017, accessed June 18, 2022, https://www.capgemini.com/wp-content/uploads/2017/12/dti_digitalculture_report.pdf.

for resolution. It is not as if the rank and file are not aware of the problems, but they get to see only a thin slice. Necessarily, it is upon the leadership to create the transformation framework and get it accepted across the organisation.

> Last year, while on a consulting engagement with an organisation with over a hundred years of glorious past and still a market leader in its space, I was involved in some candid conversations with the CXOs on their need for digital transformation. The ecosystem was changing, and the executives knew that to stay relevant in the future, they would have to make decisive shifts. As the existing business was still making profits a big decision point was what was the right time to transform.
>
> Being a successful organisation, their key strength had been in retaining talent. Nearly all in the leadership had spent almost their entire careers in this organisation. While such retention had worked great for them so far, I remember pointing out to the CEO and CHRO how this would also be their biggest obstacle to transform. The leaders had thrived in a single worldview reality, in a big way, disconnected from the evolutions outside the organisation.
>
> It was appreciable that the leadership had initiated thinking on digital transformation before the need to change was forced on them. They had a good five to seven years runaway before their current business model started turning red. However, this presented another interesting reality. Except for a couple of CXOs in the current leadership, the rest would all retire by then. The leaders who would lead the tomorrow were not at the table making the important decisions on digital transformation.

This is a paradigm seen across organisations. In the same HBR article referred to earlier, the author says, "Your workforce is more adaptable than you think". The authors refer to a survey where the workers appreciate the impact of digital more strongly but are also more open and positive about the changes it can bring about.

In a conventional organisational setup, mentoring is a top-down program where senior leaders pass their wisdom to juniors. Conversely, companies as different as GE, Pepsico, AXA and many more are using reverse mentoring as a strategy to adapt to digital advancements. Younger employees handhold senior leaders in their understanding of Crypto and Blockchain. It shows one of the requirements for successful digital adoption—humility to learn and change mindset. This, in turn, helps clarify important questions around governance, leadership, mindset, brand, investments and culture.

- Would digital be a separate business or part of existing ones?
- Why would digital talent engage or want to invest their careers in a traditional behemoth?
- Who would be the leaders to invest in or own the digital future?
- What would be the success measures?

Investing in digitally savvy top teams has a significant business impact. Organisations that do well on such leadership capability tend to generate 48% higher revenue growth, higher valuations (share price to sales ratio) and 15% higher net margins.[9] They are able to foster rapid learning, empower decision making, build accountability and speed innovation. These leaders simply lead differently.

Capacity and Capability

We have outlined these two in individual chapters. However, as far as digital is concerned, capacity and capability are not two separate entities. The capacity may increase based on business numbers. However, given the dynamism of change in technology, the focus is on how well employees can enlarge their set of capabilities. The same capacity needs to deliver different

9. Peter Weill, Stephanie L. Woerner, and Aman M. Shah, "Does Your C-Suite Have Enough Digital Smarts?," *MIT Sloan Management Review*, March 3, 2021, accessed June 18, 2022, https://sloanreview.mit.edu/article/does-your-c-suite-have-enough-digital-smarts/.

capabilities at different points in time. Given their optimism about digital, employees own their ability to learn and grow, which has been explained in detail in the chapter on capability.

A key element of a digital culture is to invest in training that builds progressive maturity in digital capabilities. Various digital maturity models have been proposed to help an organisation progress. It is important to baseline where an organisation is through a planned assessment. If the organisation is at a nascent stage and the workforce has digital novices, then it is best to invest in building broad-based digital literacy. As the organisation and the workforce learn, they emerge better as digital literates. Application of such learnings to their everyday work transcends them to digital performers, and finally, through innovations and outcomes, they emerge as digital leaders. The organisation is able to embed digital in every part, and this, in turn, helps it to outperform its competition. This multi-year journey needs to be supported with the right sponsorship and finances; it cannot be a start-stop effort. It is important that every part of the organisation matures on the capability journey. We can't expect employees to provide great digital experiences to customers unless their job allows them to experience it internally.

Making the Transformation Work

A *Harvard Business Review* feature in 2019 titled "Digital Transformation Is Not About Technology" surfaced that the focus on technology only provides possibilities to drive efficiencies or customer value.[10] However, if the core, which is the mindset to change, is missing within the organisation, then digital transformation will only amplify the flawed existing processes.

Organisations realise that dedicated teams are needed for transformation and for digital transformation. Leading organisations are creating a role called Chief Digital Officer to make the transformation work.

---

10. Behnam Tabrizi et al., "Digital Transformation Is Not About Technology," *Harvard Business Review*, February 8, 2023, accessed June 18, 2022, https://hbr.org/2019/03/digital-transformation-is-not-about-technology.

Traditionally, technology was fragmented into different CXO positions on the basis of responsibilities. CIO for applications, CTO for infrastructure and even CISO for information security.

Chief Digital Officers (CDOs) are not just focused on drawing up and supporting technology roadmaps, their remit is to enable investments in technology to deliver more revenues by laser-sharp client focus. The position lies at the intersection of technology, revenue generation and employee/customer experience. To be successful, CDOs are expected to:

- Embed a data-first culture. They drive the possibility of leveraging analytics and insights to shape predictive business models.
- Multiply digital capabilities by attracting and retaining talent for impact.
- Make sense of emerging technologies and go ahead with multiple experiments.

As the CDO is a newcomer to the C-Suite, where are they being hired from? CDO profiles show a preference for hiring from a technology background compared to those from consulting, strategy and marketing.

Whether you hire a full time CDO or assign someone that responsibility, it is important to give the individual space to function, resources to invest in and commitment to stay the course. If not, digital efforts end up being fragmented and suboptimal and try to put a band-aid on existing processes and systems.

Digital HR for a Digitised Workforce

In 2021, when I joined Tesco, I experienced the digital leap the HR organisations had made due to the impact of COVID-19:

- The recruitment function was able to run the entire end-to-end process online including, assessments, document verifications, joining and onboarding.
- Learning delivery not only turned online but also built in delightful interactive experiences. Platforms like MS Teams and Zoom disrupted the need for travel. Built in

features like polls, chat, breakout rooms took connectivity and collaboration to a different level altogether. Mobile apps built in agility in working and decision making.

- Bots have been deployed to speed up processes and reduce human dependence.

What amazed me was not that HR in organisations were able to make such a transformation. I absolutely had that confidence. What stood out was the pace at which the transformation was made to shift to the work from home or hybrid work environments.

Companies embraced digitalisation swiftly during the pandemic. However, real transformation will happen when the culture to processes is changed to achieve the following:

- How would they build leaner and flatter organisations that are super agile, technology enabled and learning fast?
- How would they carve out an employee value proposition and build a brand that helps attract and retain digital talent?
- How would policies and practices be redesigned to reflect personalization and a culture of self-serve?
- How would they not just shift to, but thrive in a hybrid workplace?
- How would they differentiate and reward performance?

While on a visit to Automation Anywhere at their Bengaluru office with my HR Leadership Team in 2018, it was very interesting to see that they called out their workforce in three parts: full-time (permanent), contractual and digital. The digital workforce was accounted for through the bots they had already activated. This three-level classification was certainly ahead of its time as most organisations were still found to adapt to a growing base of contractual workforce.

To understand the digital workforce better, it is first important to focus on the digital worker. A scan through existing literature points to two broad categorisations. The first genre of definition, as that provided through 2021 research report from a study commissioned by AWS for the APAC region, considers digital workers as "individuals who have the ability to apply digital technologies on work-related tasks".[11]

The above definition of digital workers, which broadly scopes human employees with digital skills, gives way to an emerging view of digital workers consisting of robots that can be coded or trained to perform tasks or processes independently or by partnering with human colleagues. This second view of digital workers, as worded by Automation Anywhere, is "virtual employees that enhance and augment human work by combining AI, machine learning, RPA, and analytics to automate business functions from end to end". Like a human employee, digital workers can thus perform multiple tasks end-to-end in sequences. This is where digital workers differ from bots. Bots are very task-centric and are used to automate them, whereas digital workers perform complete business functions. They are able to enhance the job role itself.

The digital workforce will be the strongest enabler for successful digital transformation that an organisation decides to invest in. As organisations progress on building a human-robotic workforce, the emotional dimensions of such coexistence need to be understood better. While humans have expressed that they would be comfortable working with intelligent machines and managing them in some studies so far, they have also expressed anxiety about AI taking over jobs and driving redundancy.

The workforce of the future will be digital. What would this digital workforce comprise? The ever-increasing efforts on digital learning and training will equip current human employees with higher levels of digital proficiency. Co-existing with the human workforce would endow the digital workers with the capabilities of AI, machine learning, RPA and analytics. Human employees would be freed up from tedious, repetitive tasks that are cost-

11. Amazon Staff, "Report: Singapore Will Need 1.2 Million More Digital Workers by 2025 to Remain Competitive," *Amazon*, February 26, 2021, https://www.aboutamazon.sg/news/aws/report-singapore-will-need-1-2-million-more-digital-workers-by-2025-to-remain-competitive.

intensive. They would then, with the right skills, be able to focus more on the strategic long-term challenges. Organisations would pursue the right balance across their workforce as one of them in isolation would be ineffective.

Transitioning into this workforce of the future requires accountability both from the organisation and the individual. The investment into honing new skills has existed from the time our ancestors first invented tools. So, denial and fear cannot be relevant reasons to hold back on upskilling. Those employees who remain cocooned in their comfort zones mostly will become irrelevant.

Transformation is illustrated in Figure 8.2. HR organisations can get by with continuous improvement and reimagination when the business is on a virtuous cycle. However, there could be change brought upon either by environmental dynamism or through repeated failures to achieve the objectives.

When faced with such a situation, it is no longer enough to play with the HR toolkit. One needs to sense the root cause for change and seize opportunities for transformation. To be successful, organisations need to re-examine their purpose, values as well as culture.

Drawing upon Darwinian evolutionary theory, the future will be all about the survival of the fittest. Transformation is the process through which any organisation can change and evolve to a state of higher fitness and relevance to the future. Technology, regulatory and demographic shifts are altering the play arena at an unprecedented pace, offering organisations an opportunity to reimagine their future.

However, transformation is not easy. It involves making bold and even unpopular decisions for a future 'good', requiring a strong commitment from the very top leadership and alignment across the organisation. As we have seen in the various narrations throughout the chapter, it is both about the 'What' and the 'How'. It is about leadership. It is about capabilities and the way of working. It is about writing the story that the organisation would be proud to read a few years in the future.

In this section, we have explored the paradigm of capacity, capability, performance and transformation. How do we integrate all of them? How are companies aligning their HR to business strategy? As an HR professional, how do you prepare for the future of work? Let us move on to the concluding part.

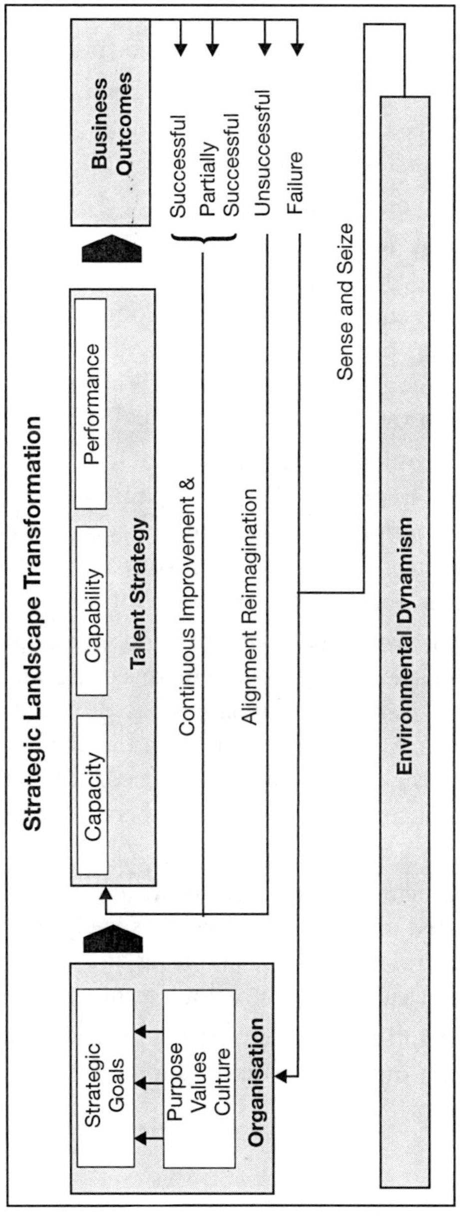

Figure 8.2: Strategic Landscape Transformation

EXECUTION: TYING IT TOGETHER

We have reviewed perspectives from practitioners on talent strategy, emerging literature and integrated frameworks.

We have also gone through the themes of workforce capacity, workforce capability, organisational performance and organisational transformation in detail.

What should you do next?

Talent strategy is not independent of business strategy. It should enable the organisation to address its big challenges. Strategic HR executives should get comfortable with the financial statements of their organisation and discern the topline, bottomline, revenue growth and so forth. When was the last time you went through the organisation's annual report?

Here, one could argue that capacity, capability and performance are important for all organisations irrespective of their business numbers. True. You also need to understand the unique challenges being faced by your organisation in the marketplace, from regulations and other forces.

This, in turn, would help you to choose the right actions, prioritise and sequence them. How to do this using our approach? We illustrate this using real companies based on their financial statements. Our analysis is illustrative and is not based on any discussion with the organisations analysed. The focus is on interpreting the business model and numbers for framing talent strategy.

The environment for businesses is always evolving. Staying on top would need us to create a context specific approach, use a toolkit for centralising and customising and be aware of the competencies that enable us in the long term.

These topics and more are covered in the last chapter, giving you clarity on not only what you need to do but also what you need to grow into.

9

Impact Delivered: Aligning with Business Strategy

There is an existing gap between HR priorities and what the business really wants, which even be jokingly referred to as "CEOs are from Mars and CHROs are from Venus". The table below is representative of the differences in perspectives.

CEO PERSPECTIVES	CHRO FOCUS AREAS
How to increase revenues?	How to incorporate social media in messaging?
How to improve profitability?	How to reduce the recruitment cost?
How to improve market share?	Should we move away from a normal distribution?
How to integrate acquisitions?	How to engage with millennials?
How to improve customer satisfaction?	How to leverage e-learning adaption?

As you may observe here, the CEO has very measurable and tangible expectations, which come from the investors represented by the board of directors. On the other hand, HR seeks primarily to act as a bridge between the employees and the organisation. On interpreting, these lead to a set of programs that are no doubt important for the organisation and for the workforce. Often, however, these are the best practices that seem to have worked elsewhere.

Middleware is a term commonly used in software engineering. There is the kernel of the computer where the processes are run and then there are the applications that provide the functionality to the users. Software that connects the two is called middleware. Let us use this analogy in an organisation. What the CEO has to deliver is the external-facing part. What HR does is the internal part. We need a middleware to connect and align the internal-facing activity to the external-facing deliverables. An effective HR strategy acts as that middleware.

FOUR ESSENTIALS

The two most important financial measures of any organisation are the revenues and the net profit. There are variants of profits, like EBITDA and EBIT, that provide a context to profits. Independent of the form, an organisation's success or failure is broadly decided by whether the revenues are growing, stagnating or shrinking and whether they are profitable or not. Based on the market environment, an organisation might choose to invest in growth or play safe to protect margins.

There are no absolute numbers as far as an organisation's revenues are concerned from which we decide whether they are doing well or not. To get a perspective, we need to look at their competitive positioning. The stock market may have the requirement to look across industries, but executives typically compare themselves with their competitors.

Let us take the example of the Indian IT services industry. In the initial stages, growth was slow and steady. Subsequently, in the late 90s, growth skyrocketed and a 100% revenue growth year on year was not unusual. This phase ended in 2001. As the organisations grew larger, it was not quite possible to grow at the same rate. In the 2000s, the growth rate was around 20%. Larger organisations crossed a billion dollars and more in revenue in this decade. The growth rates have hovered in the high single digits or low double digits now.

So, the industry has remained the same and the organisations have survived. However, any organisation that grew at 25% when the industry was growing at 100% would have been looked at as an underperformer. However, if they had shown the same growth rate when the industry was growing at 10%, they would have been looked at as world-beaters. The growth rate and performance of an organisation are often relative to the industry, which is what helps classify someone as a leader or a laggard. So, the first question one needs to clarify when crafting an HR strategy is:

- What is the industry growth rate?
- What is the growth rate of your organisation?
- Is the organisation growing faster than the industry or slower?
- Does it want to achieve higher than industry growth rates?
- What is the strategy for catching up?

The fundamental sign of organisational health lies in being profitable. Profitability is also determined by the market segment in which the organisation is present. Let us look at typical industry profitability:

- Software products: More than 20%
- Offshore IT Services: Around 20%
- FMCG Products: 10% to 20%
- Manufacturing: 5% to 10%
- Retail: 1% to 5%

The numbers shared are indicative and there would be many organisations within a range of plus or minus 5% of the industry. Assuming an organisation would like to increase its profitability, HR again needs answers to the following questions:

- What is the benchmark profitability of your industry?
- Is the profitability of your organisation comparable to that of the industry? Is it higher or is it lower?
- What would the organisation like to do with profits? Grow or protect at the same level?

Responses to these questions would help clarify the HR strategies one needs to adapt.

How does one relate organisation revenues and profits to what HR is responsible for? This is where the third important measure comes into play. This relates to the kind of assets an organisation has, the raw material for the business as well as people expenses.

Let us take a manufacturing organisation like Tata Motors. Tata Motors manufactures and markets automotive vehicles, from trucks to passenger cars. The organisation has physical assets in terms of manufacturing plants with equipment and machinery. These are used on materials procured for manufacturing vehicles, like sheet metal, castings, frames and so forth. On the one hand, people use the equipment and materials to produce cars and trucks. The process is highly disciplined, and the outcomes are standardised. Employees are expected to follow a tightly scripted process, and in general, the value added by employees is by delivering consistent quality. On the other hand, people also design and sell vehicles, which calls for innovation and ingenuity. Most of their cost structure deals with running the plants and procuring material. The 'people' cost is around 10%.

Let us look at TCS, another organisation from the Tata stable. Now, TCS delivers consulting and IT-enabled solutions to people across the globe. Their assets would be the software export offices and computers of all denominations and people. However, they aid people in doing the work. Laptops and servers depreciate fast, given Moore's law. It is people and their knowledge and skills that make the organisation deliver. As Bill Gates was supposed to have said, "The market capitalization of Microsoft goes to zero when all employees leave the office. It does not come back up till the next morning when they are back at work". While employees in TCS also work with standardised tools, their outputs are customised to individual customers and situations. There is a huge variety in programming environments, languages and domains. It is the human ability that deliver reliable outcomes across multiple scenarios, using multiple tools. So, the biggest capital for new-age organisations is human capital. Given that there is no raw material, unlike Tata Motors, TCS spends a lot more on people. More than 50% of their operating cost is spent on employee salaries and benefits. This, of course, includes the cost of having people stationed across the world.

Are there only two kinds of organisations? One where the employee costs are high as a proportion of revenues and one where it is low? Can we go ahead with the HR strategy on this basis?

While these measures are critical, they would also help us to track the business productivity in terms of employees. Essentially, the crucial indicators of the leeway available to the organisation in terms of investment into employees are:

- Revenues per employee
- Profits per employee

The four broad themes that act as middleware between business needs and HR strategy are:

- Organisation revenues and revenue growth rate.
- Organisation profitability and comparison with industry.
- People costs as a percentage of revenues.
- Revenue and profits per employee.

Let us run some organisations through this and explore strategies.[1] Let us start with Microsoft. In 2020, Microsoft reported revenues of 125.8 billion dollars. They grew topline at 14% year on year. They earned 39 billion dollars in net income. Their net profit percentage stood at 31%. From the financial statements it is difficult to directly extrapolate a single number for their payroll cost. However, it can be safely estimated to be between 25% to 35%. They employed approximately 1,44,000 employees across the world.

So, what is their revenue per employee? Again, typically, annual reports state end-of-year numbers and average numbers. However, since we are doing a rough and ready analysis, let us go ahead with the approximate numbers and also assume the people cost to be 30%.

Revenue per employee = 125.8/144,000 = 0.87 million dollars

Profits per employee = 39/144 = 0.27 million dollars

Microsoft is among the global leaders in terms of market capitalisation, comparable to Amazon, Alphabet and Apple. So, their performance puts them in the very best category of

1. Details taken from Annual Reports of Microsoft, Tata Motors, Infosys and Future Retail for FY 2019–20 from respective websites

performance. Their growth rate, profitability and so forth are all best in class.

Let us do another ratio. Often headlines talk about employee layoffs because of a need to increase operating profits. While Microsoft is very profitable, what if it wants to boost its margins? Will it be required to rationalise the workforce? Let us create a simple ratio of 'people' cost to net profit. Assuming 30% people cost, the ratio is 31/30 which is approximately 1.

Now, let us return to Tata Motors and focus on some of their financials. For fiscal 2018, their consolidated revenues were Rs 2,92,340 crores. From this, they had a net profit of Rs 6813 crores. They employed approximately 80,000 full-time employees. The 'people' costs were 10.7% of their overall costs. Let us calculate the ratios:

- Profitability: 2.3%
- Revenues per employee: Rs 3.65 crores / 0.5 million dollars (At Rs 70 to a dollar)
- Profits per employee: Rs 8 lakhs / 0.01 million dollars
- People cost to net profit = 10.7/ 2.9 = 3.7. People costs of the organisation were 3.7 times the profitability.

Given how mature the auto industry is, there are a number of ratios like contribution per unit sold, revenues per full-time employee and so on. Interested readers can examine the same in depth.

Let us pick a retail organisation now. Let us choose Future Retail, the largest listed Indian retail entity. For fiscal 2018, they had revenues of Rs 18,489 crores. They earned a net profit of Rs 615 crores on this. They employed close to 38,636 people across their stores, incurring a cost of Rs 930 crores. Let us derive the ratios:

- Profitability: 3.3%
- Revenues per employee: Rs 47 lakhs / 0.07 million dollars
- Profits per employee: Rs 15 lakhs / 0.02 million dollars
- People cost to net profit: 1.51

The numbers and ratios do not seem comparable to the ratios given earlier. However, it generally represents the retail industry, where a significant portion of money passes from the end customer to the organisation that manufactures the products, and the retailer makes money on the pass-through.

Let us round it up with one more organisation from Indian IT Services. We have talked about TCS earlier, let us focus on Infosys this time.

For the year 2018, Infosys had revenues of 10.9 billion dollars, on which it earned 2.5 billion dollars as net profits. They employed 2,04,000 people with a total people cost of Rs 34,670 crores, which equates to 49.2% of the revenues. The ratios then are:

- Profitability: 23%
- Revenues per employee: Rs 34 lakhs / 0.05 million dollars
- Profits per employee: Rs 7.8 lakhs / 0.01 million dollars
- People cost to profits: 2.16

Before we go forward with a consolidation, let us also look at the economic situation of these firms.

Microsoft is an organisation spanning personal productivity to cloud computing. The organisation has been growing revenues, and its mission is to "Empower every person and every organisation to achieve more".

Tata Motors' mission is "We innovate mobility solutions with passion to enhance the quality of life", and the organisation has a vision statement to become the most aspirational Indian auto brand by 2024 using strategies including creating a highly engaged workforce. The organisation has grown revenues and has gone to profits from making losses the previous year.

Future Retail has this as part of their mission, "We will be the trendsetters in evolving consumer brands and delivery formats and by making consumption affordable for all customer segments. We shall infuse Indian brands with confidence and renewed ambition. We shall be efficient, cost-conscious and committed to quality in whatever we do." The organisation is profitable and has been growing revenues year on year.

Infosys tagline says they help their customers navigate to the next. The organisation has been successfully growing topline and bottom-line.

So, all four organisations are profitable and growing, having enunciated a mission statement (albeit with different levels of clarity). Let us return to the key ratios we derived.

Company	Headcount	Revenues/ Person	Profits/ Person	% People Cost	People Cost/ Profit
Microsoft	144,000	6.4 crores	2.1 crores	30	1
Tata Motors	80,000	3.65 crores	8 lakhs	10.7	3.7
Future Retail	38,636	47 lakhs	15 lakhs	5%	1.51
Infosys	2,04,000	34 lakhs	7.8 lakhs	49.2%	2.16

For ease of comparison, let us look at these numbers using charts.

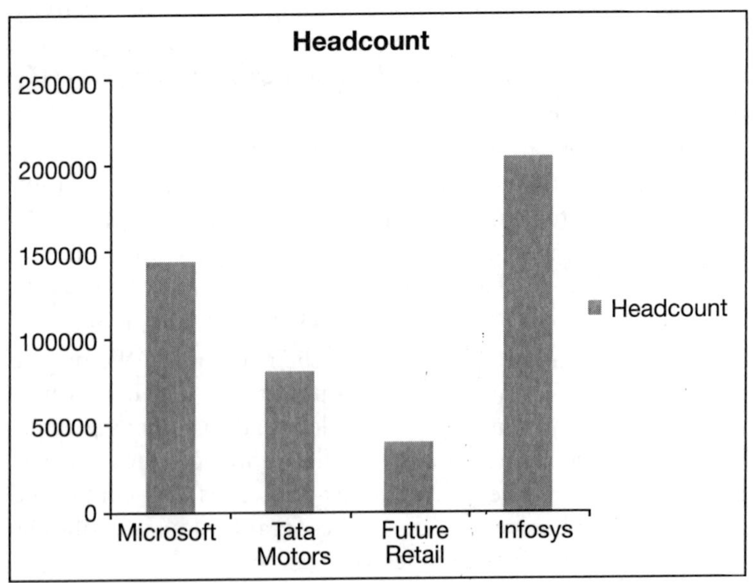

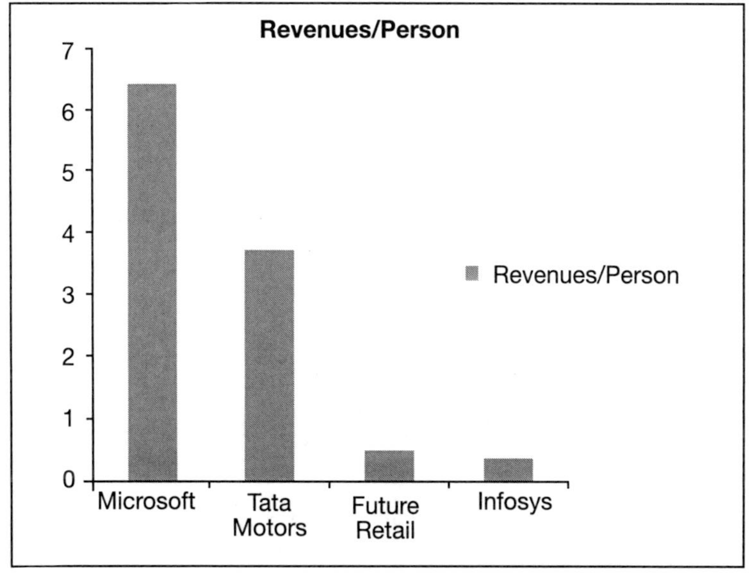
Revenues/Person
7
6
5
4
3
2
1
0
Revenues/Person
Microsoft
Tata Motors
Future Retail
Infosys

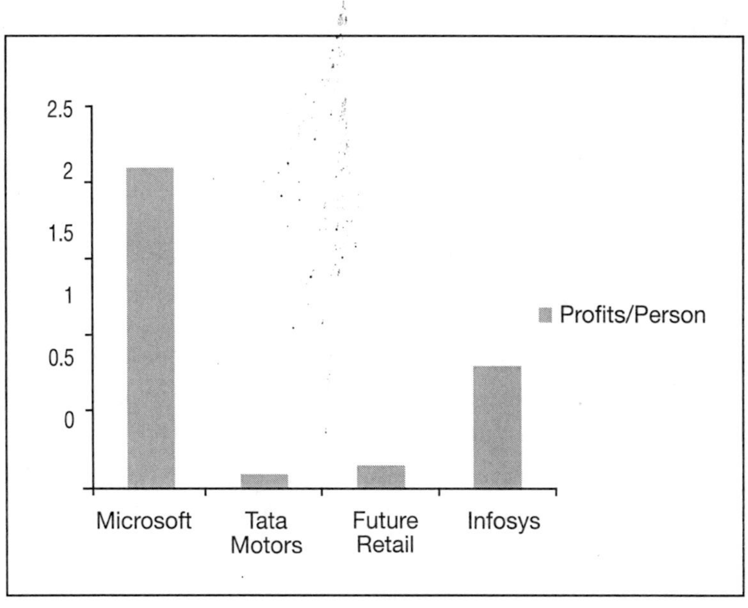
2.5
2
1.5
1
0.5
0
Profits/Person
Microsoft
Tata Motors
Future Retail
Infosys

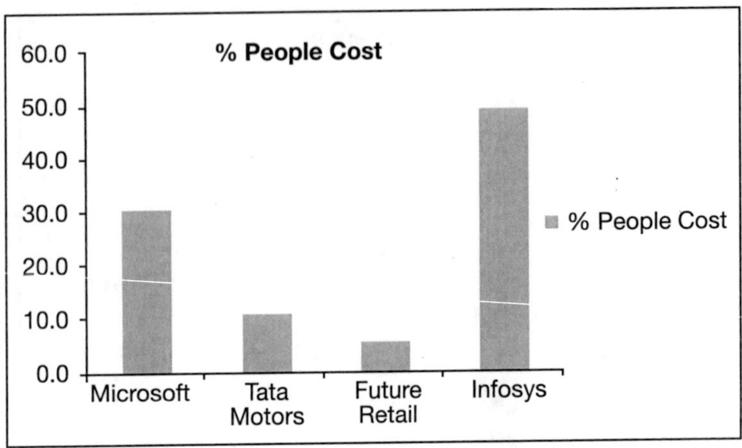

Figure 9.1: Visual Comparison of Key Ratios

These numbers set the context. We can do an in-depth analysis by going through the financial statement and comparing their assets, etc. However, let us do a preliminary evaluation using the metrics that we have so far. Let us look at growing the business first.

DERIVING SPECIFIC HR STRATEGIES

Microsoft operates a near monopoly on their operating systems side. They are also a leading cloud organisation. They are facing competition in their core areas from organisations like Google and also go head-to-head against organisations like Amazon in their expansion.

What does an organisation in this situation typically do?

1. The organisation is operating in a domain where technology continues to evolve. So, it needs to have very high technological capabilities, which are dependent on the quality of employees they have. Employees may be hired or brought on board through acquisitions.
2. Microsoft has been a leading industry player for a long time. Over a period of time, the culture would have acquired deep strengths as well as blind spots. To thrive continuously, they need to focus on the culture and take

conscious steps to keep pace with where the industry is headed. In the words of their CEO Satya Nadella:

> "One of the things that I've come to realise is that in companies that have been successful, one of the things that happens is the original idea or the concept that became a hit, the capability you built around it, and the culture that implicitly grew as you were growing the business all get into this beautiful, virtuous cycle. But there's no such thing as a perpetual-motion machine. At some point, the concept or the idea that made you successful is going to run out of gas. So, you need new capability to go after new concepts. The only thing that's going to enable you to keep building new capabilities and trying out new concepts long before they are conventional wisdom is culture.
>
> I would argue that for a successful organisation, you will have to overemphasise [creating] the right culture so that you can continue to cultivate new capabilities and new concepts. When I became CEO, we were already a 40-year-old organisation, and I felt that it was very important for us to make culture a first-class, explicit conversation so that we could then reinvent ourselves and invent new things."[2]

The organisation then needs to articulate culture and integrate it with different elements of talent management.

Marketing and enterprise sales capabilities help the organisation thrive against competition. For that, there needs to be a strong performance management framework and a fair way of incentivizing business development.

The organisation's talent strategy essentially needs to focus on:

---

2. McKinsey & Company, "Microsoft's next Act," *McKinsey Quarterly*, April 3, 2018, accessed June 17, 2022, https://www.mckinsey.com/industries/technology-media-and-telecommunications/our-insights/microsofts-next-act.

Organisational capacity and capability

- Attracting and retaining high quality talent in chosen areas of capability.
- Investing in enhancing capabilities needed for the future.

Organisational performance

Compensation and incentive structures especially for business development and sales.

Organisational transformation

Renewal of the culture.

As an organisation operating across the planet, they are required to be able to attract and retain high-quality talent globally. This, in turn, needs the organisation to be inclusive and a champion of diversity. This can be a separate theme for the talent strategy or an important subset of organisation culture. Same way, they need to be good at retaining and leveraging talent from organisations that they have acquired.

The organisation is highly profitable and enjoys very high revenue productivity per employee and a strong cash position. As such, they may be using analytics to enhance the employee experience, but cost control or raised productivity are not necessarily primary strategies for them.

Now, let us look at revenue growth strategies for Infosys, as their workforce is similar to that of Microsoft, primarily programming staff.

While that is true, the strategic challenges are very different.

Infosys offers enterprise business services. They work with a wide variety of clients across the world. The clients are in different domains like BFSI, Retail, Utilities and so forth. Unlike Microsoft, width is of importance here. While Microsoft creates technology, Infosys utilises different technologies.

While the organisation is highly profitable, they employ a lot more people. Infosys revenues per person are a little more than 5% of that of Microsoft. The organisation employs a large number of teams across the world to earn their revenues. What would their drivers be?

Organisational Capacity

Workforce planning and staffing: The ability to predict skill demands and match them with skills availability is the engine on which the organisation runs. In a technology services organisation, people move continuously from one project to another project. The matrix of technology/ domain/ location is quite complex and is akin to the supply chain of large manufacturing companies. So, in Infosys, the efficiency of allocating people at the right time to the right project and minimising bench time is very important.

Organisational Capability

- Capability building: The company's business model requires expertise across analytics, IT applications, web development and digital. As technology trends keep evolving, Infosys needs to ensure that they have the right set of technical skills at any given point in time. Hence, technical capability building at scale is critical. This includes the skilling of newcomers as well as the reskilling of employees in digital technologies.
- Talent management: Talent management is critical for all companies. However, an organisation like Infosys has many moving parts: many accounts, service lines, etc. So, it is important to identify the key roles accurately and then go on with matching suitable talent. Since there are many people, people management ability becomes important, hence investing in it.

Organisational Performance

Performance management and compensation: When you have 200,000 employees and 50% of your costs in employee compensation, it becomes critical for you to ensure the money spent rewards the right performers and creates the right incentives. You need to give the right reinforcement to both top performers and mediocre performers.

In addition to these points, the organisation should also focus on developing the right culture—customer-oriented and responsive to changes.

So, we find some similarities but differences as well between the two companies depending on their business model. Let us move on to Tata Motors. In this list, Tata Motors has the second highest revenues per person. So, does it allow them to follow a talent strategy similar to that of Microsoft, with a little dilution?

We need to look at the other ratio, too. It is true that Tata Motors has revenues per person of 36.5 million rupees. However, Microsoft does not have to invest much in plant and machinery or even inventory management. Being in the automotive business, Tata Motors has big plants and a large inventory consisting of all parts that go into the vehicles. Their people costs are 3.7 times their profits. This, in turn, indicates that they need to manage 'people' costs with diligence as it matters to the profitability. Tata makes both commercial (competitive) and passenger (very competitive) vehicles, among others. What would be their strategies?

Organisational Capacity

Productivity: Unlike software-oriented companies, Tata Motors' challenge is less about attracting and retaining talent. The Company needs to run its operations with high productivity and manage its resources frugally. Shop floor productivity is of paramount importance, but other processes like supply chain and inventory control also need to be highly productive. Flexible staffing is another dimension.

Organisational Capability

Talent Management: The critical roles of the organisation lie in product design, production and supply chain. The organisation needs to have a clear talent management strategy to have best-in-class people handling these roles.

Organisational Performance

- Compensation management: The Company needs to have the right mix of variable and fixed compensation and align it to the achievement of business goals.
- Performance should leverage a culture that blends engineering and design culture to the demands of a competitive marketplace. The culture should also enable high quality and safety.

Organisational Transformation

Tata Motors already has Jaguar Land Rover as a separate division. This arguably allows them to segment and focus across customer and geographic differences while at the same time blending design capabilities from JLL into Tata Motors.

Now, we have the megatrend of Electric Vehicles. Electric mobility is similar and, in some ways, still very different from traditional fossil fuel-based mobility. While Tata Motors is the leading Indian EV maker right now, the future may require them to migrate from primarily petrol or diesel-fueled vehicles to battery-powered vehicles. How does an organisation develop capacity and capability for it? What happens to the workforce on traditional lines of business? What about influencing the ecosystem?

The shift to EVs is a transformation that will have an impact on all components of their HR strategy.

Now, let us look at the fourth organisation on the list, Future Retail. The organisation reports higher revenues per person than Infosys. How is it possible? It could be because the total sales of the organisation include products that are made elsewhere. Tata Motors, for instance, produces all their products. Future retail hardly produces anything they sell. The organisation is a place to sell products of different companies, some of which could be their own brand. Increasing revenues per employee comes more from the unit value of products sold. That is why most brick-and-mortar retailers have their profitability in single digits. Their 'people' cost is often 1.5 times their profit, which means not only has the organisation optimised their employee base to a great extent, but the cost of employment would still be a focus.

Retailing is also faced with disruption due to e-commerce. In India, people continue to patronise brick-and-mortar stores while also relying on e-commerce. So, what should Future Retail talent strategy focus on?

Organisational Capacity

- Optimising payroll and compensation costs: The company needs to continuously look at their payroll costs and look at using technology to minimise them. They already use an outsourced staffing model. In future warehouse robots, video technologies all need to be used to reduce the total cost of operations.
- Future retail already has an e-commerce component. Their business strategy would have to include that, as well as exploring different formats. This, in turn, demands capabilities of technology, change management and commercial acumen. The organisation should focus on capability building in these areas.

Organisational Capability

Talent Management: A retail organisation has critical roles in merchandising, supply chain and inventory management. They need to ensure that best-in-class employees occupy these roles and are retained.

Organisational Performance

Employee engagement: The Sears Roebuck study in 1998 clearly established the impact of employee engagement on store performance.[3] Higher employee engagement leads to better customer satisfaction and sales. Given the high degree of competition, Future Retail can use employee engagement as a differentiator.

---

3. Anthony J. Rucci, Steven P. Kirn, and Richard T. Quinn, "The Employee-Customer-Profit Chain at Sears," *Harvard Business Review*, August 1, 2014, accessed June 17, 2022, https://hbr.org/1998/01/the-employee-customer-profit-chain-at-sears.

So, based on a reading of the financials, we have been able to outline the likely talent impact areas for four organisations when they are in growth mode. What happens in a crisis?

When there is a slowdown, companies obviously need to cut down on their operating costs. How much it will impact people depends on people cost percentage and people cost to profitability ratio. So, both Tata Motors and Future, with their relatively lower profitability, will have to rationalise people count. Infosys, even though it is more profitable, still needs to rationalise people costs as their people costs form nearly half of total expenses. Microsoft has so far not seen a crisis of that magnitude in its core business. However, their acquisition of Nokia did not go too well. So, there could be businesses inside Microsoft which are less profitable and there, rationalisation could be a strategy.

The principles of capacity, capability, performance and transformation cut across industries. What actions they lead to depends upon the industry.

SUMMARY

Many organisations seem to have generic talent strategies focused on being 'a best employer' and treat other functions like L&D or Talent Acquisition as processes. Here, we have seen how looking at the financial statement would give us a better understanding of the position of the organisation and help us fine-tune our strategies. The following questions are relevant for anyone trying to craft their talent strategy:

- What is the market position of my organisation?
- If we are the market leaders, do we see disruption? What are going to be the sources of disruption? What capabilities will help defend against the disruption?
- If not the market leader, what are we trying to catch up? Better branding? New product introduction?
- What is our primary goal? Revenue growth?
- How do we compare against competition on productivity measures like revenues per person and profits per person?
- What areas are we trying to grow revenue from? How does that convert into a staffing plan?

- What are our key roles? What capabilities should they have?
- How attractive is our brand to potential employees in the skills we are trying to attract?
- What does our investment in development look like? How much is it focused on strategic areas of importance?
- What is our time to compete? How fast are we able to get new hires to full performance?
- Is our compensation aligned to the capabilities and positions that are critical to business growth?
- What are the costs and benefits of alternative staffing models? Are we doing enough pilots?
- What are we trying to become? (Irrespective of the business model, all the companies mentioned above are trying to become something else in addition to what they are). In what timeframe? Do we have the roadmap? What is the talent strategy for enabling it?

Asking such questions and going through your data, would help in prioritising your HR strategy. These principles apply to small companies as much as they apply to large-listed corporations.

We have used specific illustrations here. Per HR literature, what we have used here is a contextual or Best Fit HR Model. It would benefit the readers to look up different HR Management frameworks. A well-known paper is "Linking Competitive Strategies with Human Resource Management Practices" by Randall S. Schuler and Susan E. Jackson.

Additionally, since the writing of this chapter, there have been some notable changes. Most noticeably, Future Retail got embroiled in an M&A situation, resulting in a decline in their market capitalisation. However, this analysis is based on reported financial numbers and Future's numbers are representative of their industry.

10

Into the Future: Talent is The New Oil

The Age of Imagination

In 1996, the most valuable organisations in the world were:[1]

1. General Electric
2. Royal Dutch Shell
3. The Coca-Cola Company
4. Nippon Telephone and Telegraph
5. ExxonMobil

Allowing for a variation of an organisation or two, extending into the mid-90s, one can potentially infer a higher valuation to the existence of high-quality tangible assets like manufacturing plants (GE), pipelines and refineries (Royal Dutch Shell, ExxonMobil) or a widespread network (NT&T). Coca-Cola aligned the power of intangible brands to bottling operations. Organisations like Microsoft were gaining value and were headed to the top, but not just yet.

Let us now look at the most valuable organisations in the world in 2021 (25 years' time). For the fourth quarter, the organisations with the highest market capitalisation were:

1. "List of Public Corporations by Market Capitalization," *Wikipedia*, November 9, 2023, accessed June 17, 2022, https://en.wikipedia.org/wiki/List_of_public_corporations_by_market_capitalization#1996.

1. Apple
2. Microsoft
3. Alphabet
4. Amazon
5. Tesla

Microsoft and Alphabet are mostly software product and platform organisations. Microsoft does have its successful Surface line of devices, and Alphabet does have its Pixel line of phones. However, these are designed in-house but manufactured by someone else. Apple designs and sells highly sought-after devices like computers, phones and wearables. However, they don't own factories. Amazon is, again, mostly an e-commerce platform that has warehouses, except, of course, they also own Whole Foods, an organic retailer, but very few physical stores. Tesla manufactures and sells Electric Vehicles. However, their physical assets are far less when compared to traditional auto companies like Toyota or GM.

You could say that market capitalisation is also an indication of investor sentiment. However, four of these five companies gained their market cap in the last 20 years. Amazon was founded in 1994, Alphabet in 1998 and Tesla in 2003. Apple went through a near-death experience before rebounding with the return of Steve Jobs in the late 1990s.

Unlike GE, ExxonMobil and Royal Dutch Shell of the 90s had been in business for close to a century. They had established asset-heavy mainstream businesses.

In the twenty-first century, value has been created through disruptive entrepreneurship using internet technologies. Valuation is not on the basis of accumulated experience or assets but the power of imagination. Amazon and Google, for instance, have their server farms and warehouses. These are, by no means, unique (unlike a custom factory, for instance). It is how Amazon or Google have used the internet and leveraged these server farms and warehouses that have been a differentiator.

Let us look at the Indian stock market. As of 2021, the most valuable organisation is Reliance.[2] Reliance has petrochemical refineries, telecom networks and retail stores. They do have significant physical assets. The second most valuable organisation is TCS, which has offices and servers, but in 2021, their market capitalisation remained high even with more than 90% of employees working out of their homes.

The market capitalisation stems from their ability to deliver services using their workforce. Reliance combines talent with assets, while for TCS, it is mostly talent. As the old TCS tagline went, "Indian ingenuity, global impact".

This is not to say that the future will be full of internet-enabled businesses and that other organisations will be sidelined. However, being a large, established monolith with a long history does not guarantee success in the future. Any organisation that is built on the talent of its employees will be able to achieve rapid scaling and disruptive success as long as they are able to retain them and continuously innovate.

We have grown used to the phrase, "Data is the new oil". We definitely have made progress in building businesses exploiting data. Conversely, concerns are being raised about the exploitative nature of businesses that are built on collecting and disseminating individual data.

While every age may look unique, in India, we are in the middle of:

- Transition to a digital economy going all the way from payments to commerce to education. As the number of people accessing the internet continue to grow, this trend is likely to accelerate even further. Product and services organisations are growing, and start-ups are in the race to become unicorns.

2. "Reliance Industries Tops '2021 Burgundy Private Hurun India' List of 500 Most Valuable Companies," *Money Control*, December 9, 2021, accessed June 17, 2022, https://www.moneycontrol.com/news/business/reliance-industries-tops-2021-burgundy-private-hurun-india-list-of-500-most-valuable-companies-7809361.html.

- Transition from fossil fuel to EVs and sustainable energy. This has the ability to transform the power, utility and automotive industries.
- Production Linked Incentives (PLIs) by the Government of India to encourage inclusion of India in global supply chains across different industries.

These trends have resulted in unprecedented demand for engineering and programming talent. Although millions graduate with an engineering degree, most are not employment-ready. In fact, some industry studies estimate that the employable talent on campus is less than 20%.[3]

Our ability to achieve is really limited far more by the quality of talent we have. Being a finite resource, talent is not just the new oil but is far more important.

HR has always been tasked with the attraction, development and retention of talent. In a situation of 10% to 15% attrition rate, it was a functional responsibility. When it is more than 25%, it becomes a business responsibility. In the talent economy, people are everyone's responsibility, from the CEO all the way down to the first-line manager.

Is HR ready to handle the challenge of ensuring the organisation leverages this scarce resource effectively? The past decade holds the clue. There have been many seminars starting in 2011 on "HR 2020" or on "VUCA". But when 2020 did arrive, it came with a unique and unprecedented problem. The world did become Volatile, Uncertain, Complex and Ambiguous. Organisations had to ensure the safety of employees, protect their mental health, and, where possible, enable them to work from home. HR was right in the middle of this change, and the function responded to this sudden challenge extremely well. Organisations were able to carry forward regular HR processes like recruiting, training, performance management and compensation reviews in the middle of a pandemic.

---

3. "80% of Indian Engineers Not Fit for Jobs, Says Survey," *Business Today*, March 25, 2019, accessed June 17, 2022, https://www.businesstoday.in/latest/corporate/story/indian-engineers-tech-jobs-survey-80-per-cent-of-indian-engineers-not-fit-for-jobs-says-survey-181442-2019-03-25.

A lot was thrown at HR, and the function has emerged with enhanced credibility. How does this tired but revitalised HR take up the challenge of talent being the new oil? It is one thing to react well using fast responses, but another to embrace the slow and steady of being strategic.

What should HR be doing to embrace the future? We had discussions with renowned academics, seasoned professionals and HR entrepreneurs who work extensively with the "talent as oil" organisations. The perspectives shared in the viewpoint section will answer many of the questions that you may have.

VIEWPOINT: HR in the Startup World (Anurag Srivastava, CEO, HR Next)

We have been discussing the emerging challenges for the HR function. As of February 2022, India has 88 unicorns; 44 achieved this status in 2021 and 8 in 2022. More than 90% of these startups are in the information technology space.

Hypergrowth, agility and people-based businesses all characterise these start-ups. What roles does HR play there?

Criticality of Core Talent to Business

You start with a core team of seven to eight engineers and a product manager. In the services world, success is still correlated to the number of people an organisation has. The success of the startup does not depend upon the number of engineers you have. Products like Snapchat and WhatsApp became successful with a core team of less than 50 engineers. Success comes from your ability to build a great core team. It is possible to build a successful product with a high-quality core team. Then comes the challenge of what you want to do with the product. Do you want it to be niche? Or ride the growth curve?

Delhivery was a courier services organisation that was operational only in Delhi in the pre-internet era. When the digital comes into play, you start looking at the relative size of the pie. Do you want to own 80% of 10 crores or 10% of 1000 crores? Growing the pie needs investment, and so, the start-ups go through Series A, B and C funding.

Scaling up means having to handle millions more transactions in a day and strengthening the DevOps and cloud technology.

The Venture Capitalists may be influenced by the potential they see in the founders, whose success, in turn, depends on the first 20 people they are able to hire and retain. In the olden days, founders used to be more task-oriented. It is not universal yet, but many of the new-age founders do realise the value of keeping their core team intact and this, in turn, makes them appreciate the softer aspects of people management early on.

Great techies are not doing their job, biding their time for the next promotion. While India has millions of software engineers, the ones who can make a difference lie between 10,000 to 15,000. The country also saw VC investments of 77 billion dollars in 2021. Essentially, the 15000 engineers influence which part of the 77 billion dollars deliver RoI. This explains the demand for such talent. So, what does HR do?

Traditional HR is about appraisal cycles, annual reviews and stock options with a five-year vesting cycle. The employee value proposition is for different segments of employees. It is a set of processes reviewed by committees and implemented by managers. Since the processes need to provide for exceptions, there need to be manuals. Internal parity is a key expectation.

Developing a core team is about individualised value propositions. It is about being agile with wealth generation opportunities for employees in synchronisation with the organisation becoming more valuable. Flexibility and simplicity are the norm. So, we have:

- New employees who are being offered salaries that violate the principles of external equity and internal parity. A candidate getting Rs 3 million, for instance, in the normal course would have an offer of Rs 4 million. But the present demand means that he can get Rs 6 million, too. The assumption is that you should pay on what value the person can create.

- A new employee getting Rs 6 million while an existing employee getting Rs 4 million for the same job affects internal parity, which becomes a concern if you conduct salary corrections annually. Agile responses allow you to adjust internal salaries when there is a perception of unfairness, even on a quarterly basis.
- Traditionally, stock options were tied to the organisation going IPO. Prior to that, the options had value but unless the organisation proceeded with an IPO, you could not monetise them. Google first conducted a private placement before an IPO to generate wealth for employees. It is more mainstream now in start-ups, wherein the options vest in more frequent windows than a year (monthly or quarterly), but the organisation uses funding rounds to buy back options from the employees, thereby generating wealth.

Given the huge scope for digitisation and digital businesses in India, this demand for core talent will not go away anytime soon. The base numbers will improve annually with fresh graduates, but that will not be enough. Moreover, this is not something that can be achieved by training above-average engineers over a period of time. Even now, organisations like Google or Facebook ensure that their core product team is high quality and do not compromise with their standards.

Such exceptional practices, especially from a hiring perspective, predominantly apply to engineering talent. Other functions are generally handled in a manner similar to that in normal organisations.

A successful product grows and reaches a stage of maturity. This is when the start-up also brings in more seasoned talent for corporate functions, like the CHRO. What does a successful CHRO do?

- Become a valued member of the leadership team, with the ability to understand the founder's perspective and translate it into people's actions. Relate to the founders at a human level.
- Shape the culture in a way that creates a positive value proposition. Many organisations are getting people back to their offices after the pandemic. Meesho has gone ahead and announced a permanent hybrid work mode, creating the capacity for doing the same. It is not necessary that all start-ups need to be employee-oriented. There have been very successful start-ups with a task orientation as well. Even there, HR has to shape the culture in a way that rewards execution.
- Develop a flexible and simple to understand way of doing things. Have policy guidelines but not thick dossiers.
- Treat talent acquisition as a strategic function. In mature companies, recruitment is looked at more operationally. The processes are strong, and so the impact of individual performance is limited. On the other hand, in a rapidly growing organisation with tight deadlines, the quality of talent makes all the difference. Hence, the CHRO has to put in place a bulletproof process to ensure the quality of talent stays high.
- Hire leadership from a long-term perspective. This also means that you don't just go with brand names. A professional with a top product organisation need not be a star in a start-up, where a very different mindset is needed in terms of responsibility, empowerment and risk-taking.
- Ensure that if dramatic salaries are being paid, the impact should also measured. Performance assessment should be based on contributions and direct rewards to where they are most deserved.

- Improvise on the battlefield. Competitive advantages last barely for months before you need to devise the next differentiator.
- Provide growth options and career choices in the medium term that could be technical or tech+domain (retail, food, fintech and so forth).

In short, given that many of the founders are interested in their teams, aligning with them to create value would need robust HR combined with agility and flexibility.

Takeaways for HR Professionals

We find that what is leading edge today becomes mainstream soon enough. By 2030, many organisations would either be wholly inheriting some of the start-up ethos or, as is already visible, have different portions of their organisation march to faster beats. How does a professional adapt to these changes?

We think the first should be a shift into looking at themselves as business people who happen to work in HR. This has been advocated by gurus for a long time. However, the operating system for HR is a lot different from what is articulated.

In India, for instance, the most influential source for HR professionals is from top MBA colleges offering an HR specialisation. Subjects like organisational behaviour, industrial psychology and HR processes like training and compensation characterise these courses. Early on, the person identifies herself more with the specialisation and less with business. This is similar to how the finance profession certifies people through Chartered Accounting, Cost accounting and so forth. However, those are harder skills, while HR courses are more about concepts. HR folks, in general, tend to operate as a closer-ended community. They read similar things and attend similar conferences. Once, in an 'HR All Hands', I asked, "How many of you actually go for lunch with people from other functions?" and it was greeted with silence!

This is not to say that the HR community has a fluffy role as often caricatured in memes. I have also seen senior HR professionals exude ratios like ROCE, usually to justify lowering costs and laying off employees.

These are important, no doubt. However, it is more important for HR professionals to understand the business framework well. They should be able to answer questions on:

- What is the business model of my organisation? Where do our profits come from? What's our expenditure?
- Who are our customers?
- Who are our main competitors?
- What is happening in the marketplace? Where do we stand against competition? What are our products or services? What are the differentiators?
- What are the internal programs that are aimed at improving our competitiveness?

Asking these questions requires curiosity, not an MBA. Moreover, if you happen to work for an organisation listed in the stock market, it is not difficult to get caught up in the talk about market capitalisation. It pays to look at:

- Quarterly and annual numbers and their direction
- Market share, innovation, etc.
- How do these numbers compare with the competition?
- How is it being interpreted by the analysts?

Again, it is quite safe to remain in the HR space in the early years and focus on employee attrition, engagement surveys and so forth. However, to be impactful, one has to expand as one grows. Successful CHROs are differentiated by their ability to synchronise the HR delivery to business strategy.

Business awareness should supplement deep functional awareness. When talent becomes mainstream, it becomes the leadership agenda. I have seen more business leaders make the additional effort to understand HR paradigms. Of course, there are others who are happier sharing newspaper articles on salary increases. They also have a better hands-on understanding of people management. Senior leaders preside over teams in hundreds or occasionally in thousands. The biggest HR span is usually in the hundreds. The reflected awareness of people management issues will always be greater for business leaders. HR professionals need a deeper functional depth to relate to and provide solutions from a position of expertise. There has been a tendency to focus narrowly on program management and buy such expertise from consulting organisations.

What should be the building blocks for the HR leader of the future? What challenges are they going to face because of the advancement of the knowledge economy?

VIEWPOINT: Future Trends and Competencies (Prof. Vasanthi Srinivasan, IIM Bangalore)

In general, we are living through complex times, especially from a business perspective. We have been through three slowdowns in the last 20 years, two funding booms, outsourcing, offshoring, digital and now a pandemic. The phrase VUCA (Volatile, Uncertain, Complex and Ambiguity) does not mean that when the change subsides, we go to a steady state. We would rather stay on a punctuated equilibrium model; the pace of change is up.

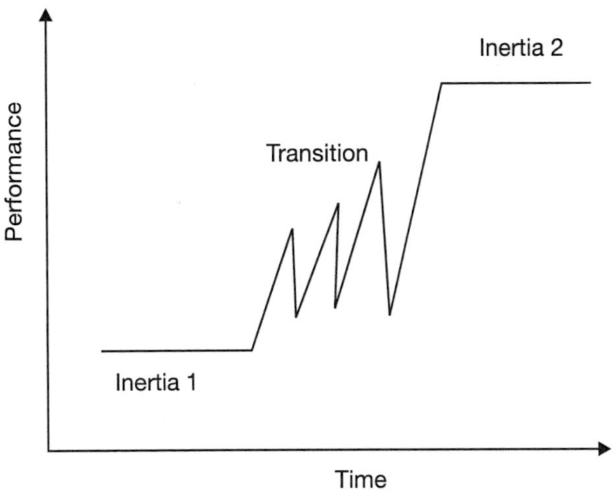

Figure 10.1: Punctuated Equilibrium Model

When the pace of change is higher, change can often come as a shock. When reacting to a shock, there isn't time to think through the consequences. Unprecedented actions are taken, and HR often tends to handle the tail of unintended consequences. Let us look at the performance ratings over the past couple of years. Given the mental stress, organisations have been more lenient with ratings. In five years' time, this could show up as flab. Then, HR has to take actions that undo what happened in the last couple of years.

Given these, let us look at four trends for the future and four competencies required to navigate these trends. The trends for the future will be C3R: Contracts, Capital, Culture and Roles.

Contracts

Traditionally, employment contracts have tended to be homogenous and include legalese to primarily establish the employer's prerogative. The employment contracts often come with 10-page attachments that provide a cover for almost all foreseeable situations. For example, some contracts include clauses for new campus recruits where the organisation says that in case the employee is to be held in custody by police, it is not the employer's liability. Nice starting point for a relationship, especially those just starting out!

There are two contracts—one about the working conditions and the other, a psychological contract, which is far more crucial than the normal one. Organisations need to change and reflect the employee's interests, which brings us to the point of who the employee is going to be. Previously, it used to be a person who would work within a specified time (at the least) on specific days at a specific location, with a predefined salary structure. For more than 95% of the workforce, there was no scope for preferences. Typically, employees worked five or six days a week, from nine to six at the office.

Now, at least in some sectors, each of these variables may be decided by employee preferences. The work contract has become flexible, accommodating different models. Presently, each organisation may have different versions for employees, contractors and consultants. It may be worth looking at the number of unique contracts within. However, in time, the employee contracts themselves will have to accommodate the flavours of consultants, part-time, flex-time, remote, hybrid and so on.

It would be good for organisations to start by consolidating all the contracts they are presently using and building from there. The employees of the future would also like to negotiate and ensure clauses that protect them as much as the present clauses protect the organisation.

Another challenge for organisations would be ensuring all contributors are fairly treated irrespective of their nature of engagement. How would you ensure some sort of parity for similar quality of work between a contractor, consultant, part-timer and full-timer? Presently, the great differentiation seems to be in the benefit packages for which full-time employees are eligible. However, courts are ruling in favour of gig workers, saying they should also be eligible for benefits. What happens then? Would we reach a stage where the job market really becomes a marketplace with schedule and rate negotiable?

How do you ensure legal defensibility across multiple contracts? Employment contracts may look like a simple and operational output, but they are at the intersection of several workplace trends.

Roles

Role descriptions may be the starting point, but the conduct of a role is in fulfilling a series of expectations from significant others at work. We have looked at roles and careers from the dry prism of policies and documents. We miss the fact that learning is not only an emotional process but also a social process. Work is not pneumatically sealed, it is embedded in social context.

Morgenson, Humphrey and Nahrgang, in their "Meta-Analysis of Work Design", looked at the following constructs of job design and their impact on performance and retention outcomes:[4]

Motivational characteristics as defined by job autonomy, skill variety, task identity, task significance, feedback from the job as well as complexity and information processing.

1. Social characteristics as defined by dealing with others, feedback from others, social support and interaction outside the organisation.
2. Work context characteristics as defined by physical ease, work conditions and ergonomics.

By cherry-picking from the extensive research, we find that:

- Motivational characteristics explain a lot of attitude variables, like not just job satisfaction and growth but also organisational commitment.
- Social characteristics also have a strong impact on turnover intentions, job satisfaction and organisational commitment. Social characteristics explain the intention to leave more than motivational characteristics.
- Social characteristics and motivational characteristics explain 64% of organisational commitment.
- Role ambiguity is not restricted to motivational characteristics alone. 25% of role ambiguity is explained by social characteristics as well. Essentially, the stress of role ambiguity is also social.
- Work context characteristics explain stress. However, they have no impact on commitment or intention to quit.

---

4. Stephen E. Humphrey, Jennifer D. Nahrgang, and Frederick P. Morgeson, "Integrating Motivational, Social, and Contextual Work Design Features: A Meta-Analytic Summary and Theoretical Extension of the Work Design Literature," *Journal of Applied Psychology* 92, no. 5 (January 1, 2007): 1332–56.

Let us take the example of TCS, where, at the highest level, the business model is similar to other IT services organisations, but their ability to retain people is higher. Among other things, this is also due to the relative richness of the projects they are working on. Employees grow by handling different types of responsibilities. Rotation leads to retention.

This is not implemented through a centralised HR policy. It is embedded in the managerial ethos. Business leaders who are responsible for growth also own the need to retain employees, which, in turn, leads to formal and informal approaches to proactively providing job variety, leading to retention. Business leaders of the future own their people and ensure the motivational characteristics of job autonomy and skill variety, as well as the social characteristics of feedback and social support. The social and contextual elements of work are only going to grow with remote work, changing the nature of contracts and human-machine interface. It is inevitable that a complementary role for line managers has to be explicated. They are not agents of HR as translators of policy or implementers but are legitimate contributors to effective HRM.

Job design is intangible, while flashy buildings with foosball are not. So, most organisations start with creating great offices but focus far less on enabling motivational and social characteristics at a team and unit level. This still happens but there is a wide variation on the basis of individual leaders. The challenge for HR is to take a peer-level approach to enabling these more widely than through the top-down policy.

Culture

When it comes to culture, often there is this metaphor of an organisation being a plane which has to be transformed mid-flight, which seems practically impossible and no wonder so many so-called cultural transformations struggle!

Often, organisations are forced to transform due to shifts or shocks. Such transformations need a lot of emotional energy.

You need stability to replenish the reserves. Let us again take TCS. The organisation is transforming its business end to reflect digital. However, the positives of their work culture provide stability.

A more accessible metaphor is one of the trains and the track. Trains may change and may be driven by coal, diesel or electrical; the tracks remain constant. In volatile times, the culture should offer stability unless things are really broken, and that exact culture needs to be transformed.

It is a challenge to preserve culture in a normal work environment. How do you align a hybrid workforce to a common culture? How do you do it in an environment where people, bots and AI work together? Can you train AI to reflect culture?

On the other dimension, what happens to the work culture when the gender balance reflects the general populace? Does it become kinder and fairer? What other dynamics do we need to be aware of?

Capital

We have seen the Resource Based View Model earlier. The model has caught on, and even in annual reports, the focus is not just on financial capital. Even accounting standards talk about the following capitals:[5]

- Financial
- Manufactured
- Intellectual
- Human
- Social
- Natural

5. Andrea Coulson et al., "Capitals Background Paper for IR," *Integrated Reporting*, March 2003, accessed June 17, 2022, https://www.integratedreporting.org/wp-content/uploads/2013/03/IR-Background-Paper-Capitals.pdf.

They provide status on each of these (mostly financial still) in the annual reports of organisations. Sustainability is no longer a buzzword. Demand for sustainable fashion, for instance, is on the rise, and it even includes buying pre-owned garments. Sustainability is reshaping the automotive industry itself, enhancing the value of Natural capital. Tiny digital native companies can disrupt legacy businesses and command multi-billion evaluations using intellectual capital.

The opportunity for HR is to champion human capital in a tangible manner, enable the development of intellectual capital and leverage social capital.

This is a huge canvas when compared to the traditional HR role of supporting the successful management of financial capital. Of course, that is not to say that the traditional role will somehow vanish. If anything, with more companies relying on human capital and intellectual capital, just managing through attrition would be a big challenge!

What are the social dynamics of a networked organisation where leadership is the custodian of human and intellectual capital with its emphasis on inversion of the power equation?

Each of these four themes has brought up questions that are not so common today. For us to leverage these trends, we need competencies different from what we have been used to in a largely hierarchical organisation. What competencies would help us thrive?

1. Sensing the environment and managing paradoxes

With increasing complexity, leaders are required to engage with "and" paradigms because of conflicting views from different stakeholders as against one true "either/or": freedom and rigour, freedom and discipline, participation and centralisation, etc. There is a need to understand the environment and make decisions that influence the environment.

Editor's Comments

I was once working in an organisation that was growing at 100%. Learned HR colleagues wondered what impact it would have on the culture and whether we should grow slowly. In a year, there was a downturn, and growth plateaued out. Then we realised the paradox of growth and culture and not one at the expense of another. Often, senior leaders talk to HR about their need to be more empowered as if someone will tap their shoulder and say you are empowered! This is another good "and" example. A process of empowerment solves many problems. Process by nature is control. Even empowerment and process go together. You could always review their relative balance.

2. Agility in response

A traditional mindset is about collecting facts, analysing and sharing with committees to arrive at the one right decision. A dynamic world does not afford such liberties. The manager needs to get comfortable doing quick and even parallel pilots, get insights and go ahead with fine-tuning the approach. The decision-making needs to be guided by data and not opinions. These require agility, resilience and a quest for objectivity, as mentioned in the earlier viewpoint by Anurag, too.

3. Collaboration mindset

There is no top or bottom in a networked organisation. Leaders are not omniscient people who can make the right decisions. To be successful, they need to acknowledge their vulnerabilities, seek support and empower the right level of organisation most capable of addressing different challenges. Complex technology and regulations have the capacity to create barriers that can be offset only by the interconnectedness of a network. A collaboration mindset creates psychological safety in experiments.

4. Being conscious of one's own biases

Managing paradoxes and being agile in response and collaboration needs an individual to be self-aware. It is easy to identify obvious areas of improvement in skills. Biases need honest feedback, humility to accept and an interest in working through the negative impact of such biases.

The schematic below frames these requirements well:[6]

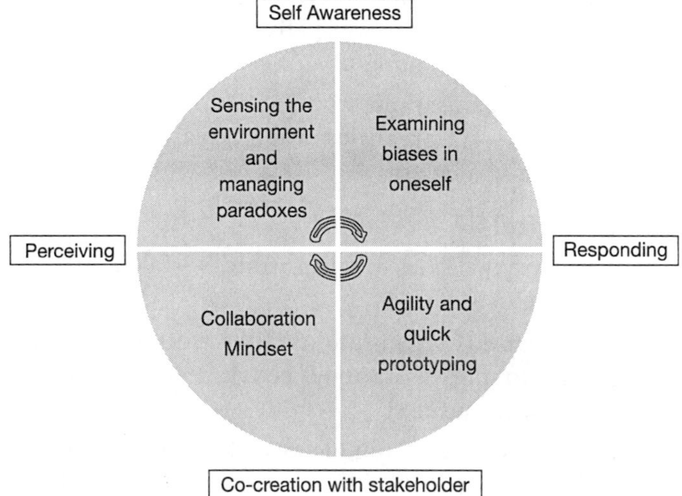

Figure 10.2: Future Ready Competencies

There may be a perception that to develop a strategy. One needs to be either at the top of the pyramid or outside the fray as a consultant. These four competencies would enable an HR leader to develop strategy by being comfortable in a networked organisation, being agile and sensing and reacting to what is required.

We had discussions with nearly 50 senior professionals, and the collective wisdom is incorporated in the chapters. Let us call out some specific observations.

6. V. Srinivasan, Raj Srinivasan, and Ankur Jain, "Future-Ready Leadership Competencies," *NHRD Network Journal* 10, no. 4 (October 1, 2017): 21–29.

Organisation Size

- Smaller organisations may not feel the need for talent strategy. They are more focused on the here and now and being competitive. The HR person is chosen to be more all-purpose.
- Organisations need to think about the future when they have to scale up or adapt to face business challenges. Then, too, they look for spot solutions.
- Businesses may not demand HR strategy. However, business does not prevent HR from working on an HR strategy and detailing it.
- In large organisations with a focus on different industry segments—the realities vary greatly, necessitating different strategies.

Business Vertical

- There are two sides to talent strategy—talent market and internal.
- Talent-based organisations (like software products) seemed to think more about people because of an integral tie-up with business.
- HR is less valued in industries where people spend very little (less than 10%, like manufacturing). It really, then, does not matter. Similarly, in MSMEs, the maturity of HR is not high, and thus, the HR leader may not be directly involved in the Strategic Planning process.

Positive Enablers

- HR now has a seat at the table and thus has the responsibility to be deeply involved in the strategic planning process. Trust in the HR leader is a significant factor in how organisations invest in people. Strong HR leaders are able to drive changes and build their credibility.
- High expectations for HR to have strong business acumen. Only then are they able to focus on the right issues.

- The sweet spot is a progressive leader—a growing or changing organisation and a progressive HR head is ideal.

Business Dynamics

- More and more companies are driven by short-term pressures. Here, HR ends up being the executor. However, even in such industries, using a long-term HR approach delivers results.
- Business is being impacted by big titanic shifts at a much faster pace. Complexity is much higher. It is a global environment. What happens in one part of the world affects the others.
- Organisations now have to be agile and fluid. They need to learn in real-time and change continuously. Post facto big bang transformations will not work.

Strategic Planning

- Frameworks are not widely adapted except as starting points. Homegrown business frameworks are also used. Organisations go with what works best for them. Metrics often are not sharp and reviews tend to assess progress on key initiatives.
- There is a structured approach to framing Business Strategy. CXO leadership is involved. Time allocated for strategic planning with a governance framework. In less mature organisations, it is Revenue (CFO), Sales, Supply Chain and Production driven.
- Business strategy helps lead into four pieces—business plan, functional plans, finance plan and talent plan. The fourth piece is what is missed out often.
- Narrowing down the priorities has to be based on certain key agreed-upon principles. Trade-offs are involved. A successful HR leader has the ability to articulate the top pillars with clear linkage to business strategy.

- HR strategy should align strongly with the Culture and Values that the organisation believes in. These should show up in the various Talent Processes.

Obviously, one faces many of these challenges during a long career. So, we had a chat with a seasoned HR executive who has worked with one of the global leaders across different roles, geographies and over a long time frame and got him to respond on what one sees hands-on.

VIEWPOINT: HR's Role in Strategic Planning (Pavan Bhatia, Former SVP & CHRO, Asia & MENA, PepsiCo.)

There is a misplaced view that HR is composed of processes, policies and programs. In this view, HR is not explicitly responsible for organisational strategy. HR responsibility starts when they start implementing programs that align with the goal.

That is a sub-optimal way of looking at HR's role. Often, HR leaders hold back, thinking they don't have the competence for organisation strategy. To negate this, HR leaders should be knowledgeable about the market, competition and disruptions.

Strategic planning in large organisations is typically done by a group dedicated to coming out with the plan. That is the planning process. For instance, in Pepsi, the revenue numbers used to come from top-down based on annual planning exercises. They might say the Middle East should grow at 7%, India at 10%, China at 12%, etc. The plan stops there and it is for the leaders to detail it out as to how exactly they are going to achieve it.

The plan has to segue into the leadership system to be successful. Leaders need to have open discussions before arriving at:

- Where are we going to play, and how are we going to win?
- What goals are we going to take in the areas chosen?
- Do we have the resources, finances and talent to achieve these goals? What should we plan for?
- What trade-offs are we having to make?
- How do we sort out different priorities? Turf issues?

The challenge with business strategy is not that the different leaders do not know about it. The critical part is getting them to discuss, sort out their priorities and align on where the organisation is going to play and how they are going to win. This is how HR can leverage its seat at the table—not as an expert in sales or production, but as a facilitator in getting the leadership team to work together. This may not be a defined responsibility but a moral accountability.

Unless the business strategy is arrived at as an outcome of leadership alignment, the HR strategy derived will go down the drain.

While HR's strengths play to how the strategy is arrived at, it should not stop from having input on what the organisation should be doing; this is where a well-prepared HR head would be able to contribute as a business leader on par with others. Be it in cost take-outs or trade-offs like improving the bottom line vs investing in the future.

Let us take the hypothetical example of an automotive battery firm getting into making batteries for Electrical Vehicles. It is important to create an organisational structure to enable this:

- Should it be a separate division or aligned to an existing division?
- Should it have a product structure or regional structure?
- Should we have a dedicated sales team or bolt the goals onto the existing sales team?

All these questions need to be answered before HR gets into the act of creating a structure for the business. For that, they need to have been involved in the discussions of "Where to play and how to win". Otherwise, the function would not be operating below potential as a business partner and would be looked at more as a specialist.

Developing an HR Strategy

The majority of HR organisations do not follow a standard framework like 7S or "where to play, how to win" for articulating their strategy.

In the following scenarios, you end up having to catch up:

- When you are not involved in influencing organisational strategy.
- When you do not use a methodology for developing an HR strategy.

Often the catch-up strategy involves looking at what are trending topics and trying to implement them. When not grounded in the business needs, these programs look good on paper, but their impact is questionable. When the impact is vague, we seek to mitigate it by multiplying activities. Being busy gets noticed, but being noticed only for being busy is not a good place to be in. This also leads to many stand-alone themes connected neither to each other nor to business outcomes. HR becomes good in many things but excellent in nothing.

In a large organisation, doing a unique program is, unfortunately, one way of getting recognised. Australia would be doing a management development program, and Sweden would be focusing on program on career development. Both are important, but in the absence of last-mile connections to business end up being used more for personal differentiation than business impact.

It would be great if we could pay in the highest quartile work in modern offices and offer great career development. Unfortunately, we typically have neither the resources nor the bandwidth to do all that. Hence, we need to be able to make educated trade-offs so that the two to three programs that we do focus on have the greatest impact. These should be chosen on the basis of impact on strategy as well as offer moments that matter to talent.

DEVELOPING CAPABILITIES

Capabilities are a great way of aligning HR to business.

> For instance, at Pepsi, we have 750 leaders with functional capabilities in traditional trade and 25 in modern trade. Modern is growing, so can we move people from traditional to modern? If so, what capabilities do we need to develop?
>
> We assess leadership capabilities through performance management, 360 reviews, etc. One of the focus areas is global acumen. We found that 70% of leaders were scoring three-fourths or below on this. How does one build this? Programs are launched for this.
>
> Being digital savvy is another competence. We have decided that the entire leadership team will have a mentor who is a digital native and every mentor will have a performance goal for the mentorship.

This is how we can bring programs and initiatives together to achieve an outcome that has an impact on business. When properly aligned and based on collaboration, we can manage with more informally documented strategies.

STRATEGY PLANNING PROCESS

Pepsico has a mature process. By March, the business strategic plan will be defined and signed off. By May, the functional strategic plans will be presented and signed off. From August, we start doing programs for the next year linked to the key strategic themes.

The organisation comprises a global business division and a geographical market. At the market level, there should be initiatives and not a full-blown strategy. These should factor in local nuances. There are one or two priorities for each market. Obviously, the market will have more than one or two priorities. These are then categorised into two. First, where the need is acknowledged but not acted upon in the immediate future. This is documented unmet demand. The second category is identified as choosing not to go after.

It is incumbent upon the regional HR leader to explain to the business why some needs were dropped. Occasionally, these can even be a favourite of the business leader. HR needs to find a way to logically assess the demands and objectively decide and communicate to the market teams. This needs a lot of skills.

With time, the process has evolved from stopping with a presentation to taking it deeper and linking it to the operating plan. The plans are reviewed using a scorecard of measures. Reviews happen on the scorecard as well as program implementation rather than on-end measures.

Business leaders need to understand the direct impact of what HR is doing. One way is by having strong metrics that are aligned with business. Another is to invite them to co-create programs and hold them accountable for the success of programs, making them play a larger, more visible role.

ALIGNING WITH BUSINESS ON HR STRATEGY

Before documenting the HR strategy, ask for perspectives from business stakeholders. It is advisable to take perspectives based on specific insights emanating from both internal and external happenings, such as:

- Employee climate survey.
- Changes in the talent market and their impact.
- Change programs being pursued in the organisation.

Collating their perspectives and insights and sharing them with them formally (using a presentation) co-opts them into the solution. The absence of such a consultative process could easily end in disconnects and diversion of energy into problem identification instead of problem-solving. After this, we get into the pillars.

All strategies should lead to tangible actions. For that, we need to get the high-level intent into specific outcomes that can be reviewed. The sequence of the flow will be as follows:

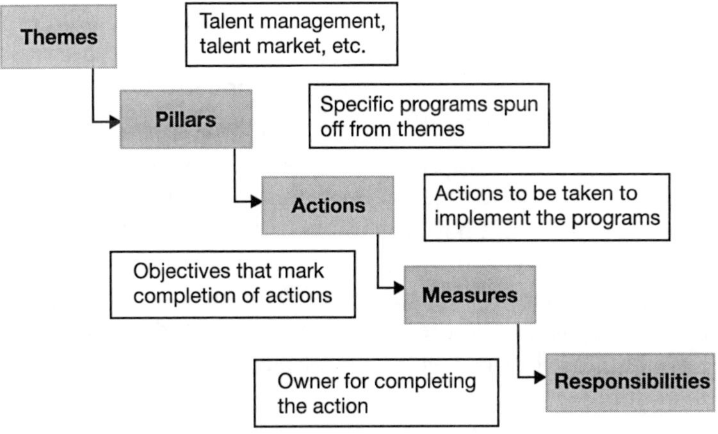

Figure 10.3: Strategy Flow

For instance, the market dynamics and business needs will require an organisation to shift from a fixed staffing model to an anytime model. This, in turn, leads to an impact on how talent acquisition is structured and may need new investments. If these are the pillars, then there are specific actions such as identifying partners, reviewing the process and so on. These actions have a complete date and an owner assigned.

The strategy will be successful when detailed out like this, and it also becomes a working document for discussions with the leadership team. Otherwise, the exercise could end up as a theoretical one.

It is important for the themes to be large enough to cover a long span of time, preferably years. One should review them annually, but in a well-made strategy, only the actions need to change year on year.

MAKING IT WORK

In most organisations, the broad themes won't be very different. It is usually talent, culture, etc.; only specific outcomes and priorities would vary.

Around 10 to 15 years ago, there used to be one to two major shifts in a decade, like the internet or mobility. However, in recent times, we have witnessed one to two major changes in a single year. Demonetisation, GST, Digital India and COVID-19 all happened within a five-year timeframe.

Such complex challenges happen in a globally connected environment. What happens in one country has an impact on others. Given the velocity, there isn't enough time for classic change management. We need to build agile organisations that can respond fast. For that, they need to have choices. In the psychology of change, choices enable flexibility.

SILVER BULLETS VS SYSTEMIC SOLUTIONS

When making a change, we often tend to look at what is most visible and then add a program to fix it.

Let's take the example of a talent acquisition process. There may not be enough transparency in the flow of resumes. The reporting may be sub-par. The most obvious solution is to automate the process. It is quite stimulating to look at different technology options, choose a product and get it implemented. It looks good on the function and also on the individual in charge of TA. But does it fix the problem?

What if in the organisation:

- Is the culture not process-oriented? Then, we will have the technology, but we would still be having offers being run through a manual route.

- Are the power equations strong? Rank and file may follow the process, but the CEO may have the propensity to come up with three candidates for whom appointment orders need to be sent without following any process. The requisitions may not have been opened, and even the job descriptions for the candidates may not be there.

This is not an unusual scenario. The system might be fully implemented and yet not very successful. It is true that implementing new systems or processes is part of change management. However, it is important for us to look at the challenge in its entirety and design the approach. This will help us identify parallel threads. Action has to be taken simultaneously on the parallel threads to be effective. We can also do it sequentially, but then it takes away the energy from getting something solved, and users end up counting the number of changes. There would always be something that we have not foreseen so it is better to factor for that and ensure we get to action on threads we have identified in parallel. When we surface the true scope of change, we also plan for the right resources.

Editor's Comments

In the chapter on Capacity, we wrote about the Internal Talent Market, an idea that seems to be a solution for many problems. However, we have also seen the earlier version of the talent market, Internal Job Postings, up close in organisations. Getting an IJP policy formulated and an IT application enabled is very easy. However, what is critical is how the typical manager looks at talent. Do they look at it as an organisational resource or their own? If this is not clear, the organisation would put in place an IJP policy and even announce jobs on that. But the people desirous of moving may not be encouraged to apply for fear of incurring the wrath of the manager. In which case, either the scope for IJP needs to be limited, or the IJP needs to be truly open by addressing the cultural issues in parallel.

HOW CAN HR LEADERS BE STRATEGIC?

Many upcoming HR managers are differentiated by their ability to do something quickly. However, to evolve, they also need to develop curiosity. As an old saying goes, "When the CEO says jump, don't ask how high but why".

It is alright to be a good order taker and executor in the initial stages of the career. However, that should not be at the expense of suppressing innate curiosity.

To be truly successful HR leaders, one has to have the ability to ask "why". Even when having the right questions, HR leaders hold back from asking because they may be wished away or ignored. After all, handling employees calls for HR professionals to be thick-skinned. Not every interaction is going to be present. Similarly, some CXOs may not take kindly to HR, asking pointed questions on why they want a certain outcome. Sharpness aligned with a thick skin helps navigate such conversations.

To be taken seriously when asking "why", HR leaders need to educate themselves on the business beyond the numbers, what the competition is doing, where things are evolving and the transformational possibilities. This builds credibility. When faced with the choice of learning more about business or more about the latest in HR, many choose to do the latter. That, unfortunately, leads to many silver bullets that don't kill the problems.

HANDLING POWER EQUATIONS

Strategy does not get executed in a vacuum. There are leaders who like to throw their weight around and see how they can get exceptions through. When they get their way, it sends a wrong message that stays within the organisation. After all, before eating strategy, culture eats the process! The HR role as custodian of process and consistency is inherently designed for conflict.

Some might opt to become the CEO's shadow and wield power from the background, subsuming one's own voice. Real credibility comes from ensuring consistency visibly. It is also important to convert the boundary issues and share them on a scorecard. Assume that you have a policy that people will not be moved from one role to another for 18 months. In reality, it may be violated 5% of the time. Then, you need to track:

- Number and percentage of cases where people were moved before 18 months.
- What were the reasons? It could easily be due to personal reasons (health emergency, dual careers), business growth or employees being consciously moved out of temporary roles. Reasons remove the randomness from exceptions.
- Even after accounting for these, there could be some which were discretionary. Sharing the numbers function-wise provides visibility into where it is happening and acts as a check against whimsical leadership actions.

In many companies, there are internal audit mechanisms. Rely on them to reveal the inconsistencies and take necessary actions. Consultative design of processes, consistent execution and surfacing and addressing discrepancies ensure that power equations lean in favour of HR.

Still, HR is seen more as art and less as science. To be effective, one needs to move the needle to become more scientific.

SHOULD ONLY LARGE COMPANIES BE STRATEGIC?

It is possible that in smaller companies, the HR person is a catch-all, hired at a relatively junior level. Some make the mistake of taking that assigned role as the eventual role and do not develop any insights about the basis, or if they do, hold back from sharing it. The organisation chart is the starting point. How one plays outside the boundaries of the individual box is what determines success.

Demonstration of capability means sharing thoughts. Regardless of the size of the organisation, one has a big role to play in sharing insights and pushing back if required.

These conversations have detailed:

- The challenges that will be faced by HR in the coming decade.
- What a successful operating model would be.
- Processes and practices to build a talent strategy in different scenarios.
- Capabilities needed for the future.

We trust these conversations to have addressed not just the queries that you may have had about delivering strategy, but also the shape of things to come and being prepared for it.

Conclusion

> In my lifetime, we have seen India go from a poor quality-high cost country to being a high quality-low cost country exporting across the world.[1]
>
> —Venu Srinivasan,
> Chairman TVS Motor Company

Across the book, there have been multiple references to cricket. Let us revisit it one last time.

In the late 1970s, I was presented with a book called *All About Cricket,* written by a popular commentator. The book was an excellent primer to the game for a schoolboy. It had the antecedents of the game, the rules, umpiring signs and even some stories. About the game itself, the book detailed five great test matches and chose one player every year (from 1947, I think, to 1975).

For an Indian, it was deeply disappointing not to see any Indian test match or a single Indian player feature as player of the year. It would not have been unusual in 1975 to have most lore dedicated to countries like England, West Indies, Australia, South Africa and so forth.

Even then, the seeds were being sown for success, with emerging batting and bowling stars. When Wisden ran a survey of experts to pick the five players of the twentieth century, three Indians featured in the top 20 based on how well they did in the 1970–2000 timeframe.

1. AutoCar India (@autocarindiamag), "In my lifetime we have seen India go from a poor quality-high cost", *Twitter*, March 16, 2022, https://twitter.com/autocarindiamag/status/1504102046508589061.

If the same author were to write the book in 2022, he would be hard-pressed not to write about Indian successes.

This holds good for business, too. In 1975, a book on global business practices might have mentioned the Tata Group and not much else. Let us look at comparative GDP numbers since then:

YEAR	INDIA GDP (Rs crores)	US GDP (Rs crores)	US/INDIA
1975	9,847	1,68,000	17.6
1990	32,097	5,96,000	18.5
2000	46,839	10,25,000	22
2020	2,62,000	20,94,000	8

What this illustrates is that after being only around 5% of the American economy at the turn of the decade, India is now just around 12%.[2] This has been achieved because the GDP grew more than five times between 2000 and 2020, whereas that for the US doubled.

A lower base means a greater percentage of growth. However, even today, most management literature in India focuses on case studies, illustrations and discussions about what happened in the US. This is because the US has a more mature business ecosystem with collaboration between businesses, researchers, authors and academic institutions.

How many books or research papers have emerged in India based on the outstanding GDP growth in the last 20 years? This book, based primarily on our experiences in the past 25 years in India in engineering and technology, is a sincere attempt to bridge this gap. While the principles elucidated are universal, and we do refer to global companies, the context of fast growth and change is more at home in India. Why is it important now?

By many estimates, Indian GDP is expected to double in the next ten years and cross 5 trillion dollars or 5 lakh crore dollars. The country is already:

2. "Place Explorer," *Data Commons*, accessed June 17, 2022, https://datacommons.org/place.

- The biggest user of digital financial transactions in the world.[3]
- Host to the third-highest number of unicorns in the world.[4]
- A global power in vaccine manufacturing that has been self-sufficient in vaccinating most of its populace.

India is also keeping up with the evolving themes of digital, clean energy and sustainability. At the same time, the country also has challenges of:

- Providing quality jobs to the highest population below 30 years in the world.
- Ensuring more women enter the workforce.
- Enabling the pipeline of employment through investment in primary and secondary education.
- Addressing inequality in wealth.

This journey to a 5 trillion dollar economy will not happen because the country suddenly unlocked a magical well of oil or rare minerals. As we have seen in the last 25 years, India's biggest advantage is the availability of people. The country shall grow by designing, developing and delivering for itself and for the world using its people. It will involve a great deal of employment generation, skill building and inclusivity. Dedication and imagination of the workforce will be the oil that powers this journey and HR professionals need to have strategies to deliver this.

---

3. "Indian Digital Payments Landscape Is Projected to Be at US$10 Trillion by 2026: PhonePe Pulse & BCG Report on Digital Payments," *Money Control*, June 7, 2022, accessed June 17, 2022, https://www.moneycontrol.com/news/trends/features/indian-digital-payments-landscape-is-projected-to-be-at-us10-trillion-by-2026-phonepe-pulse-bcg-report-on-digital-payments-8654371.html.
4. Nikhil Patwardhan, "India Overtakes UK to Come Third in Unicorn Race: Hurun Report," *Mint*, December 22, 2021, accessed June 30, 2022, https://www.livemint.com/companies/start-ups/india-overtakes-uk-to-come-third-in-unicorn-race-hurun-report-11640169766405.html.

In the course of our conversations, more than one HR executive working for a global corporation said that they find the quality of discussions around people and the importance given to HR to be greater in India than they find in their home location. Another expert went to an HR Tech show and felt that the products showcased would not have been out of place in the US.

Already being on a strong wicket, Indian HR professionals need to develop strategies for their organisational success—be it a start-up or a mature organisation turning around.

We hope this book and its resources will enable you to begin your journey or assist you in accelerating it, wherever you are. It is our hopeful wish that as the country continues to grow and evolve, more such books will be written, much like what has transpired in the world of cricket!

Annexure: Survey Questions & Responses

Survey Period Jul-Aug 2020
No of Respondents 109

Question 1

The Role I presently play in my organisation

(a) Business Leader	38	35%
(b) HR Leader	56	51%
(c) Experienced Practitioner in a different domain	15	14%
(d) A Consultant	0	0%

Question 2

My organisation is

(a) Large-cap listed	33	30%
(b) Mid / Small-cap listed	17	16%
(c) Privately owned	33	30%
(d) Privately owned MSME	9	8%
(e) Start-up	11	10%

Question 3

My organisation is

(a) Market Leader	46	42%
(b) Challenger	21	19%
(c) Mature and stable	23	21%
(d) Mature but declining	3	3%
(e) Early-stage start-up	13	12%
(f) Other	3	3%

Question 4

My organisation is

(a) American headquartered MNC	31	28%
(b) Europe headquartered MNC	10	9%
(c) India headquartered	56	51%
(d) Other	12	11%

Question 5

My organisation operates in

(a) Software products	25	23%
(b) Technology services	27	25%
(c) FMCG	5	5%
(d) Financial services	7	6%
(e) Pharma	6	6%
(f) Telecom	4	4%
(g) Other	35	32%

Question 6

The top challenges facing my organisation are (Please select upto Top 3)

(a) Revenue growth	55	50%
(b) Profit growth	35	32%
(c) Market share improvement	41	38%
(d) Customer delight	20	18%
(e) Internationalisation	17	16%
(f) Quality	9	8%
(g) Transformation of business model	58	53%
(h) Rapid product development	33	30%

Question 7

My involvement in the strategic planning process in my organisation has been .....

(a) Anchored the process	35	32%
(b) Participated in the process	20	18%
(c) Been updated on the process	50	46%
(d) What Strategic Planning?	4	4%

Question 8

The frequency of strategic planning in my organisation

(a) Broad long-term Strategy (eg 3 years) with Annual Reviews	70	64%
(b) No broad strategy but Annual Planning	39	36%

Question 9

In my organisation strategic business plan is accompanied by a detailed HR strategy

a. Yes	64	59%
b. No	32	29%
c. Not Sure	13	12%

Question 10

HR strategy is developed because

a. We need to show something strategic	7	6%
b. It is required to comply with our organisational quality framework	4	4%
c. It is imperative given the business demands	83	76%

Question 11

The Frameworks used by my organisation to devise strategy include

a. HR Scorecard	11	10%
b. SWOT analysis	11	10%
c. People CMM	3	3%
d. 7S framework	3	3%
e. Design thinking	18	17%
f. OKRs	24	22%
g. Valuing Talent	6	6%
h. Others	33	30%

Question 12

The processes governed by the strategic HR Plan are

a. Workforce planning	33	30%
b. Talent attraction and value proposition	28	26%
c. Organisation structure	13	12%
d. Employee cost management	9	8%
e. Performance management	10	9%
f. Learning and development	8	7%
g. Compensation and benefits	2	2%
h. Inclusivity and diversity	6	6%

Question 13

The following phrases are often used in my organisation (You can select multiple phrases)

a. "We are an employer of choice. A great place to work"	46	42%
b. "We have a high-performance work culture."	53	49%
c. "We are employees first."	27	25%
d. "We are an inclusive employer."	37	34%
e. "We recruit and retain the best."	22	20%
f. "We have a very balanced and attractive C&B."	1	1%
g. "Our talent helps us win."	61	56%

Question 14

My organisation actively involves HR in strategic planning

1 (Hardly)	10	9%
2	7	6%
3	25	23%
4	41	38%
5 (Always)	26	24%

Question 15

The HR Strategic Plan is

a. Documented and reviewed regularly at the CEO/Board level	53	49%
b. Documented and reviewed regularly at HR Head level	24	22%
c. Not documented, but elements are known	19	17%
d. Documented but forgotten	3	3%
e. Neither documented nor known	10	9%

Question 16

The progress on the HR Strategic Plan is

a. Reviewed and measured at a defined cadence	44	40%
b. Reviewed but measures are not clearly defined	29	27%
c. Reviewed in an ad-hoc manner	25	23%
d. Not reviewed at all	9	8%

Question 17

The presence of a formal strategic planning process

a. Enables us to perform better	82	75%
b. Comes in the way of us performing well	8	7%
c. Neither enables nor prevents our functioning	19	17%

Bibliography

"6 Tactics Schneider Electric Used to Amp Up Internal Mobility," May 26, 2020. Accessed June 18, 2022. https://www.linkedin.com/business/talent/blog/talent-management/schneider-electric-internal-mobility.

Amazon Staff. "Report: Singapore Will Need 1.2 Million More Digital Workers by 2025 to Remain Competitive." Amazon, February 26, 2021. https://www.aboutamazon.sg/news/aws/report-singapore-will-need-1-2-million-more-digital-workers-by-2025-to-remain-competitive.

Apascaritei, Paula, and Marta M. Elvira. "Dynamizing Human Resources: An Integrative Review of SHRM and Dynamic Capabilities Research." *Human Resource Management Review* 32, no. 4 (December 1, 2022): 100878.

AutoCar India (@autocarindiamag). "In my lifetime we have seen India go from a poor quality-high cost", Twitter, March 16, 2022, https://twitter.com/autocarindiamag/status/1504102046508589061.

Baeza, Ramón, Lars Fæste, Christoph Lay, Tuukka Seppä, Simon Bartletta, Amit Ganeriwalla, Ralf Moldenhauer, and David Webb. "The Comeback Kids: Lessons from Successful Turnarouds." *BCG Turn*, November 2017.

Barney, Jay B. "Firm Resources and Sustained Competitive Advantage." *Journal of Management* 17, no. 1 (March 1, 1991): 99–120.

BBC News. "Robots 'to Replace up to 20 Million Factory Jobs' by 2030," June 26, 2019. Accessed June 18, 2022. https://www.bbc.com/news/business-48760799.

Becker, Brian E., and Mark A. Huselid. "High Performance Work Systems and Firm Performance: A Synthesis of Research and Managerial Implications." In *Research in Personnel and Human Resources Management*, edited by Gerald R. Ferris, 16:53–101. JAI Press Incorporated, 1998.

Becker, Brian E., Mark A. Huselid, and Dave Ulrich. *The HR Scorecard: Linking People, Strategy, and Performance.* Boston: Harvard Business Press, 2001. http://ci.nii.ac.jp/ncid/BA5142836X.

Bidwell, Matthew. "Paying More to Get Less: The Effects of External Hiring versus Internal Mobility." *Administrative Science Quarterly* 56, no. 3 (September 1, 2011): 369–407.

Booth, Barbara. "A Year Later, What Uber Has Done to Revamp Its Troubled Image." *CNBC*, June 20, 2018. Accessed June 18, 2022. https://www.cnbc.com/2018/06/20/a-year-later-what-uber-has-done-to-revamp-its-troubled-image.html.

BusinessLine. "Flat Response: Tata Motors Brings Back Designations," January 11, 2018. Accessed June 18, 2022. https://www.thehindubusinessline.com/companies/flat-response-tata-motors-brings-back-designations/article64269831.ece.

Business Today. "80% of Indian Engineers Not Fit for Jobs, Says Survey," March 25, 2019. Accessed June 17, 2022. https://www.businesstoday.in/latest/corporate/story/indian-engineers-tech-jobs-survey-80-per-cent-of-indian-engineers-not-fit-for-jobs-says-survey-181442-2019-03-25.

Cascio, Wayne F. *Employment Downsizing and Its Alternatives.* SHRM Foundation, 2009. https://www.shrm.org/hr-today/trends-and-forecasting/special-reports-and-expert-views/documents/employment-downsizing.pdf.

CFI Team. "McKinsey 7S Model." Corporate Finance Institute, October 15, 2023. Accessed June 21, 2022. https://corporatefinanceinstitute.com/resources/management/mckinsey-7s-model/.

Confederation of Indian Industry. "CII National HR Excellence Award." Accessed June 21, 2022. http://ciihrexcellenceaward.com/.

Coulson, Andrea, C. Adams, T. Emmelkampt, R. Greveling, G. Kluth, and M. Nugen. "Capitals Background Paper for IR." Integrated Reporting, March 2003. Accessed June 17, 2022. https://www.integratedreporting.org/wp-content/uploads/2013/03/IR-Background-Paper-Capitals.pdf.

"Country Rankings," Universum, April 29, 2022. Accessed June 18, 2022. https://universumglobal.com/rankings/india/.

Curtis, Bruce, William E. Hefley, and Sally A. Miller. "People Capability Maturity Model (P-CMM) Version 2.0." *Carnegie Mellon University*, June 1, 2001. https://apps.dtic.mil/sti/pdfs/ADA395316.pdf.

Data Commons. "Place Explorer." Accessed June 17, 2022. https://datacommons.org/place.

Deloitte Insights. "Are You Overlooking Your Greatest Source of Talent?" Accessed June 18, 2022. https://www2.deloitte.com/us/en/insights/deloitte-review/issue-23/unlocking-hidden-talent-internal-mobility.html.

Del Rey, Jason. "Amazon's Warehouse Robots and Their Complicated Impact on Workers." *Vox*, December 11, 2019. Accessed June 18, 2022. https://www.vox.com/recode/2019/12/11/20982652/robots-amazon-warehouse-jobs-automation.

"Digital Culture: The Driving Force of Digital Transformation," World Economic Forum, June 2021. Accessed June 18, 2022. https://www.weforum.org/publications/digital-culture-the-driving-force-of-digital-transformation/.

Digital Transformation Institute. "The Digital Culture Challenge: Closing the Employee-Leadership Gap." *Capgemini*, 2017. Accessed June 18, 2022. https://www.capgemini.com/wp-content/uploads/2017/12/dti_digitalculture_report.pdf.

D'Monte, Leslie. "Robots Are Coming for India's Shop Floors." *Mint*, September 10, 2019. Accessed June 18, 2022. https://www.livemint.com/technology/tech-news/robots-are-coming-for-india-s-shop-floors-1568135022807.html.

Doz, Yves L. "The Strategic Decisions That Caused Nokia's Failure." INSEAD Knowledge, November 23, 2017. Accessed June 18, 2022. https://knowledge.insead.edu/strategy/strategic-decisions-caused-nokias-failure.

Drucker, Peter. *The Practice of Management*. 1954. Reprint, New York: Harper Collins, 2010.

ET Bureau. "Car Sales Fall 13% in December as Chip Shortage Hurts Production." *The Economic Times*, January 15, 2022. https://economictimes.indiatimes.com/industry/auto/auto-news/car-sales-fall-13-in-december-as-chip-shortage-hurts-production/articleshow/88908171.cms.

European Foundation for Quality Management. "The EFQM Model." EFQM. Accessed June 21, 2022. https://efqm.org/efqm-model.

Fortune Editors. "The Greatest Business Decisions of All Time." *Fortune*, June 10, 2014. Accessed June 18, 2022. https://fortune.com/2012/10/01/the-greatest-business-decisions-of-all-time/.

Francis, Sonam Choudhary. "Design Thinking @ Infosys." LinkedIn, March 8, 2018. https://www.linkedin.com/pulse/design-thinking-infosys-sonam-choudhary/.

Friedman, Thomas L. "Opinion | How to Get a Job at Google." *The New York Times*, February 22, 2014. Accessed June 18, 2022. https://www.nytimes.com/2014/02/23/opinion/sunday/friedman-how-to-get-a-job-at-google.html.

Fuller, Joseph. "Your Workforce Is More Adaptable than You Think." Harvard Business Review, November 24, 2020. Accessed June 18, 2022. https://hbr.org/2019/05/your-workforce-is-more-adaptable-than-you-think.

Financial Times. "Prospering in the Pandemic: The Top 100 Companies," June 19, 2020. Accessed June 21, 2022.

https://www.ft.com/content/844ed28c-8074-4856-bde0-20f3bf4cd8f0.

Fortune. "Great Place to Work Rankings." Accessed June 18, 2022. https://fortune.com/great-place-to-work-rankings/.

Green, David. "How Unilever Has Created a Culture of Internal Talent Mobility," March 7, 2021. https://www.linkedin.com/pulse/how-unilever-has-created-culture-internal-talent-mobility-david-green/.

Groysberg, Boris, Linda-Eling Lee, and Ashish Nanda. "Can They Take It with Them? The Portability of Star Knowledge Workers' Performance." *Management Science* 54, no. 7 (July 1, 2008): 1213–30.

Heck, Patrick R., Daniel J. Simons, and Christopher F. Chabris. "65% of Americans Believe They Are above Average in Intelligence: Results of Two Nationally Representative Surveys." *PLOS ONE* 13, no. 7 (July 3, 2018).

Helfat, Constance E., and Ron Adner. "Corporate Effects and Dynamic Managerial Capabilities." *Strategic Management Journal* 24, no. 10 (2003): 1011–25.

Helfat, Constance E., Sydney Finkelstein, Will Mitchell, and Harbir Singh. *Dynamic Capabilities: Understanding Strategic Change in Organizations*. Hoboken: John Wiley & Sons, 2007.

Helfat, Constance E., and Margaret A. Peteraf. "Managerial Cognitive Capabilities and the Microfoundations of Dynamic Capabilities." *Strategic Management Journal* 36, no. 6 (April 1, 2014): 831–50.

Homer, Jennifer. "Tech Leader Focuses on Future-Proofing Employees." Association for Talent Development, July 20, 2020. Accessed June 18, 2022. https://www.td.org/magazines/td-magazine/tech-leader-focuses-on-future-proofing-employees.

Humphrey, Stephen E., Jennifer D. Nahrgang, and Frederick P. Morgeson. "Integrating Motivational, Social, and Contextual Work Design Features: A Meta-Analytic Summary and Theoretical Extension of the Work Design

Literature." *Journal of Applied Psychology* 92, no. 5 (January 1, 2007): 1332–56.

Janjigian, Lori. "These Are the 10 Best Countries for Computer Programming - and the US Didn't Make the List." *Business Insider*, August 31, 2016. Accessed June 18, 2022. https://www.businessinsider.in/enterprise/mobile/these-are-the-10-best-countries-for-computer-programming-and-the-us-didnt-make-the-list/articleshow/53953309.cms.

John, Nevin. "75% TCS Staff to Work from Home by 2025, R&D to Occupy Vacant Office Space." *Business Today*, November 20, 2020. Accessed June 18, 2022. https://www.businesstoday.in/latest/corporate/story/75-tcs-staff-to-work-from-home-by-2025-r-d-to-occupy-vacant-office-space-279170-2020-11-20.

Johnson, O'Ryan. "IBM Plans Massive European Layoffs Ahead Of 'NewCo' Spin-off: Report | CRN." *CRN*, November 30, 2020. Accessed June 18, 2022. https://www.crn.com/news/channel-programs/ibm-plans-massive-european-layoffs-ahead-of-newco-spin-off-report.

Lawrence, Paul, and Jeffrey Pfeffer. "The Human Equation: Building Profits by Putting People First." *Administrative Science Quarterly* 43, no. 4 (December 1, 1998): 956.

Leary, Brent. "Raju Vegesna of Zoho: High School Grads Get Tuition Free Training through Zoho University – and 1800 Get Jobs with the Company." Small Business Trends, July 28, 2020. https://smallbiztrends.com/2019/01/zoho-university.html.

Lemann, Nicholas. "The Kids in the Conference Room." *The New Yorker*, October 11, 1999. Accessed June 18, 2022. https://www.newyorker.com/magazine/1999/10/18/the-kids-in-the-conference-room.

Lester, Donald L., John A. Parnell, and Shawn M. Carraher. "Organizational Lifecycle: A Five-Stage Stage Empirical Scale." *International Journal of Organizational Analysis* 11, no. 4 (April 1, 2003): 339–54.

Livemint. "BharatPe Starts Giving BMW Bikes to IT Professionals as Joining Bonus, Extends Offer." *Mint*, July 29, 2021. Accessed June 18, 2022. https://www.livemint.com/companies/news/bharatpe-starts-giving-bmw-bikes-other-perks-to-it-professionals-extends-offer-11627559450874.html.

McKinsey & Company. "Microsoft's next Act." *McKinsey Quarterly*, April 3, 2018. Accessed June 17, 2022. https://www.mckinsey.com/industries/technology-media-and-telecommunications/our-insights/microsofts-next-act.

———. "Reborn in the Cloud," July 1, 2015. Accessed June 18, 2022. https://www.mckinsey.com/capabilities/mckinsey-digital/our-insights/reborn-in-the-cloud.

Microsoft. "The Next Great Disruption Is Hybrid Work—Are We Ready?," March 22, 2021. Accessed June 18, 2022. https://www.microsoft.com/en-us/worklab/work-trend-index/hybrid-work.

Moore, Alex. "2020 Excellence in Practice Award Winner: SAP." Association for Talent Development, July 20, 2020. Accessed June 18, 2022. https://www.td.org/magazines/td-magazine/2020-excellence-in-practice-award-winner-sap.

Moore, Geoffrey. "Core, Context, and the Future of Work." LinkedIn, August 6, 2021. Accessed June 18, 2022. https://www.linkedin.com/pulse/core-context-future-work-geoffrey-moore.

Moorthy, Swathi. "Cognizant's '2020 Fit For Growth' Plan: 7,000 Mid, Senior Level Employees Laid Off." Moneycontrol, November 1, 2020. Accessed June 18, 2022. https://www.moneycontrol.com/news/business/cognizants-2020-fit-for-growth-plan-7000-mid-senior-level-employees-laid-off-6044001.html.

Money Control. "Indian Digital Payments Landscape Is Projected to Be at US$10 Trillion by 2026: PhonePe Pulse & BCG Report on Digital Payments," June 7, 2022. Accessed June 17, 2022. https://www.moneycontrol.com/news/trends/features/indian-digital-payments-landscape-is-projected-to-be-at-us10-trillion-by-2026-phonepe-pulse-bcg-report-on-digital-payments-8654371.html.

———. “Reliance Industries Tops ‘2021 Burgundy Private Hurun India’ List of 500 Most Valuable Companies,” December 9, 2021. Accessed June 17, 2022. https://www.moneycontrol.com/news/business/reliance-industries-tops-2021-burgundy-private-hurun-india-list-of-500-most-valuable-companies-7809361.html.

Netflix. “Netflix Culture—Seeking Excellence.” Accessed June 18, 2022. https://jobs.netflix.com/culture.

Nokia. “Nokia’s Strategy.” Accessed June 21, 2022. https://www.nokia.com/about-us/company/nokias-strategy-2021/.

Ogg, Sandy. “Connecting Talent to Value.” *SHRM*. Accessed June 18, 2022. https://www.shrm.org/executive/executive-events/strategic-hr-forum/Documents/Sandy%20Ogg.pdf.

Patwardhan, Nikhil. “India Overtakes UK to Come Third in Unicorn Race: Hurun Report.” *Mint*, December 22, 2021. Accessed June 30, 2022. https://www.livemint.com/companies/start-ups/india-overtakes-uk-to-come-third-in-unicorn-race-hurun-report-11640169766405.html.

Phadnis, Shilpa, and Sujit John. “Simpler Structure, Transforming Employees: A Frenchman Sitting in Paris Turns Wipro Around.” *The Times of India*, October 18, 2021. Accessed June 18, 2022. https://timesofindia.indiatimes.com/business/india-business/a-frenchman-sitting-in-paris-turns-wipro-around/articleshow/87091176.cms.

Pink, Daniel H. “Free Agent Nation.” *Fast Company*, December 31, 1997. Accessed June 18, 2022. https://www.fastcompany.com/33851/free-agent-nation.

Platner, Hasso. “An Introduction to Design Thinking PROCESS GUIDE.” *Institute of Design at Stanford*, n.d. https://web.stanford.edu/~mshanks/MichaelShanks/files/509554.pdf.

Rozovsky, Julia. “The Five Keys to a Successful Google Team.” *Google*, November 17, 2015. Accessed June 17, 2022.

https://rework.withgoogle.com/blog/five-keys-to-a-successful-google-team/.

Rucci, Anthony J., Steven P. Kirn, and Richard T. Quinn. "The Employee-Customer-Profit Chain at Sears." Harvard Business Review, August 1, 2014. Accessed June 17, 2022. https://hbr.org/1998/01/the-employee-customer-profit-chain-at-sears.

Schmidt, Frank L., and John E. Hunter. "The Validity and Utility of Selection Methods in Personnel Psychology: Practical and Theoretical Implications of 85 Years of Research Findings." *Psychological Bulletin* 124, no. 2 (September 1, 1998): 262–74.

Smallwood, Norm. "Capitalizing on Capabilities." Harvard Business Review, August 1, 2014. Accessed June 18, 2022. https://hbr.org/2004/06/capitalizing-on-capabilities.

Srinivasan, V., Raj Srinivasan, and Ankur Jain. "Future-Ready Leadership Competencies." *NHRD Network Journal* 10, no. 4 (October 1, 2017): 21–29.

Sutton, Bob. "A Compilation of Euphemisms for Layoffs." *Work Matters*, November 16, 2018. Accessed June 18, 2022. https://bobsutton.typepad.com/my_weblog/2008/11/a-compilation-of-euphemisms-for-layoffs.html.

Tabrizi, Behnam, Ed Lam, Kirk Girard, and Vernon Irvin. "Digital Transformation Is Not about Technology." Harvard Business Review, February 8, 2023. Accessed June 18, 2022. https://hbr.org/2019/03/digital-transformation-is-not-about-technology.

Tata. "Redefining The Future Of Steelmaking," November 2020. Accessed June 18, 2022. https://www.tata.com/newsroom/business/tata-steel-plants-redefining-future-steelmaking.

Teece, David J. "Business Models and Dynamic Capabilities." *Long Range Planning* 51, no. 1 (February 1, 2018): 40–49.

———. "Explicating Dynamic Capabilities: The Nature and Microfoundations of (Sustainable) Enterprise

Performance." *Strategic Management Journal* 28, no. 13 (January 1, 2007): 1319–50.

Teece, David J., Gary P. Pisano, and Amy Shuen. "Dynamic Capabilities and Strategic Management." *Strategic Management Journal* 18, no. 7 (August 1, 1997): 509–33.

Thakker, Nilesh, Amita Goyal, Ankit Mishra, Aditya Raj, and Ranodeep Shome. "COE Hotspots of the World 2023." Zinnov, April 11, 2023. Accessed June 18, 2022. https://zinnov.com/global-capability-center-setup-location-analysis-2023-report/.

The Textile Magazine. "KPR Mill's Education Initiative for Women Employees Yields Excellent Results," June 3, 2021. Accessed June 18, 2022. https://www.indiantextilemagazine.in/kpr-mills-education-initiative-for-women-employees-yields-excellent-results/.

Unilever. "Our Leadership," September 18, 2023. Accessed June 18, 2022. https://www.hul.co.in/our-company/our-leadership/.

Van Vulpen, Erik. "15 HR Analytics Case Studies with Business Impact." AIHR, September 27, 2023. Accessed June 17, 2022. https://www.aihr.com/blog/hr-analytics-case-studies/.

Wattles, Jackie. "GE CEO Jeff Immelt Says All New Hires Will Learn to Code." CNNMoney, August 4, 2016. Accessed June 18, 2022. https://money.cnn.com/2016/08/04/technology/general-electric-coding-jeff-immelt/index.html.

Weill, Peter, Stephanie L. Woerner, and Aman M. Shah. "Does Your C-Suite Have Enough Digital Smarts?" MIT Sloan Management Review, March 3, 2021. Accessed June 18, 2022. https://sloanreview.mit.edu/article/does-your-c-suite-have-enough-digital-smarts/.

Wikipedia. "List of Public Corporations by Market Capitalization," November 9, 2023. Accessed June 17, 2022. https://en.wikipedia.org/wiki/List_of_public_corporations_by_market_capitalization#1996.

World Economic Forum. "The Future of Jobs Report 2020," October 20, 2022. Accessed June 18, 2022. https://www.weforum.org/publications/the-future-of-jobs-report-2020.

Yoshimoto, Catherine, and Ed Frauenheim. "The Best Companies to Work For Are Beating the Market." *Fortune*, February 27, 2018. Accessed June 18, 2022. https://fortune.com/2018/02/27/the-best-companies-to-work-for-are-beating-the-market/.

Zahra, Shaker A., Harry J. Sapienza, and Per Davidsson. "Entrepreneurship and Dynamic Capabilities: A Review, Model and Research Agenda*." *Journal of Management Studies* 43, no. 4 (May 26, 2006): 917–55.

About the Authors

Ramesh Soundararajan brings three decades of rich experience in the field of human resources, having held key leadership roles at renowned organisations such as Whirlpool, Infosys and Sasken. His expertise spans diverse organisational contexts, including periods of turnaround, stagnation, rapid growth and transformative change. Notably, Ramesh has been a driving force behind influential talent strategy initiatives that underwent rigorous review at the board level.

In his most recent ventures as a partner at Culstran Consulting LLP, a firm specialising in strategic HR and People Analytics, Ramesh has been instrumental in spearheading collaborations with organisations to craft compelling vision, values, strategy, KPIs and HR roadmaps, alongside partnering impactful rejuvenation endeavours. His adeptness as an assessor utilising the PCMM and CII Model of HR Excellence has enabled a systems-driven approach to organisational analysis.

Ramesh has actively partnered with XLRI Delhi, Upgrad, Jigsaw Academy and SHRM in delivering transformative programs in Strategic HRM and People Analytics. Numerous working executives in India and abroad have benefited from these programs. Thriving on Talent is his second book, having co-authored the fairly successful Winning on HR Analytics.

Somnath Baishya is a Global HR Executive with proven expertise in driving business successes through talent. With extensive leadership experiences at Tesco, Intuit, Adobe, Nokia, Infosys and Tata Motors, he has championed the people agenda through various organisational life-cycle stages of high growth, transformation and renewal. He has successfully shaped and nurtured organisational cultures prioritising high employee engagement and inclusion. His acclaimed contributions include Tesco being recognised as the 'World's Best GBS' and Intuit being ranked #1 'Best Company to Work For in India' and #4 in Asia. An alumnus of IIT and XLRI, Somnath has significantly influenced academia, industry and startups through his mentoring, thought leadership, consulting engagements and exclusive memberships by invitation. Embodying the principle of 'Learn, Teach & Learn', he continuously strives to expand the ecosystem's knowledge through his publications.